What This Book Will Do for You

We know you don't want to read a dry reference book about Mac OS 8, and we didn't want to write one. We've tried to put together an easy, step-by-step way for you to learn not only the fundamentals of Mac OS 8, but all the other facets of the computing experience. Operating systems like Mac OS 8 don't work without a computer and other peripherals, so we've encapsulated much of the knowledge we've garnered over the last ten years testing and writing about computer products.

Who Should Read This Book

This book is both for new users of Mac OS 8 and users who are upgrading from a previous version of the Macintosh operating system. Mac OS 8 represents some significant changes for the operating system, especially with a completely new interface. Thus, we believe all users will benefit from reading it. (We'll refer to earlier versions of the Macintosh operating system as System 7.X.)

Conventions Used in This Book

Each hour contains a section called "term review" to explain the new concepts that we introduced. There is a question-and-answer section at the end of each hour that anticipates questions or problems you may encounter along the way.

In addition to typographical conventions, the following special elements are included to set off different types of information to make them easily recognizable.

JUST A MINUTE

Special notes augment the material you are reading in each hour. They clarify concepts and procedures.

TIME SAVER

You'll find numerous tips that offer shortcuts common problems.

CAUTION

The caution sections warn you about pitfalls. ....ng them will save you time and trouble.

Teach
Yourself
MACINTOSH
in 24 Hours

Teach Yourself

MACINTOSH

in 24 Hours

Howard Baldwin
Anita Epler

Hayden
Books

201 West 103rd Street
Indianapolis, Indiana 46290

Teach Yourself Macintosh in 24 Hours
©1997 Hayden Books

Library of Congress Catalog Number: 96-72159
ISBN: 1-56830-408-0

Copyright © 1997 Hayden Books

Printed in the United States of America 1 2 3 4 5 6 7 8 9 0

Warning and Disclaimer

Trademark Acknowledgments

President   Richard Swadley
Associate Publisher   John Pierce
Publishing Manager   Laurie Petrycki
Managing Editor   Lisa Wilson
Director of Marketing   Kim Margolius

Acquisitions Editor
Patty Guyer

Development Editor
Brian-Kent Proffitt

Production Editor
Michael Brumitt

Copy Editor
Meshell Dinn

Technical Editor
Bill Vernon

Publishing Coordinator
Karen Flowers

Cover Designer
Aren Howell

Book Designer
Gary Adair

Manufacturing Coordinator
Brook Farling

Production Team Supervisors
Laurie Casey
Joe Millay

Production Team
Aleata Howard
Kristin Nash
Laure Robinson
Elizabeth San Miguel
Pamela Woolf

Indexer
Chris Barrick

About the Authors

As *Macworld* Features editor, **Howard Baldwin** oversees the evolution from idea to print of the magazine's in-depth technology previews and product round-ups. His previous technology publishing experience includes covering PCs for *PC Computing*, Unix systems for *UnixWorld* and *Open Systems Today*, and everything from palmtops to mainframes at *Corporate Computing*. He received a degree in English from Stanford University the year after Apple was founded.

Anita Epler serves as *Macworld*'s reviews editor and speaks on numerous expert panels at tradeshows around the country, including Macworld Expo. Before joining *Macworld* in 1995, she covered operating systems and PC hardware for *InfoWorld*. Prior to her career as a magazine editor, she was a quality assurance engineer at Apple Computer, and a project leader at ZD Labs where she tested hardware and software for *MacUser* magazine. Anita studied print journalism at the University in Southern California, and has more than 10 years experience with the Mac OS.

Acknowledgments

Our collective thanks to our executive editors at *Macworld*, Galen Gruman and Carol Person, who agreed that if we were going to cover Mac OS 8 in the magazine, it was probably it was a good idea that we write a book about it. Our thanks also to *Macworld* lab's director, Lauren Black, without whose support we could not have written this book.

Our gratitude also goes to Patty Guyer, Jim Chalex, and Brian-Kent Proffitt of Hayden Books, who guided us carefully through uncharted territory. Thanks too to Peter Lowe and Staci Sheppard at Apple who were always ready to answer any question or request. We're also indebted to friend and attorney Mike Healy and *Macworld* contributing editors Tom Negrino and Deke McClelland for steering us safely through the pitfalls of book contracts.

Howard thanks his wife Monica for her infinite patience, not only during the creation of this book, but also whenever the conversation turns to technology (one of her least favorite topics). He also thanks Tuxedo and Fluffy, who always made sure that he didn't get so engrossed in his work that he couldn't take time out to pet them.

Anita could never have survived her first book without the help of Cameron Crotty. As a published book author, his experience helped keep things in perspective, and more practically, his services as chief cook and moral supporter were invaluable. She also owes an unfathomable debt to her supportive family, and to her friend and mentor Dominick Corradino, who helped her learn to think critically, and to write well.

Hayden Books

The staff of Hayden Books is committed to bringing you the best computer books. What our readers think of Hayden is important to our ability to serve our customers. If you have any comments, no matter how great or how small, we'd appreciate your taking the time to send us a note.

You can reach Hayden Books at the following:

Hayden Books
201 West 103rd Street
Indianapolis, IN 46290
317-581-3833

Email addresses:

| America Online: | Hayden Bks |
| Internet: | hayden@hayden.com |

Visit the Hayden Books web site at http://www.hayden.com

Overview

Introduction   xxii

Part I: Learning the Basics

Hour 1   Welcome to Mac OS 8   3

     2   The Desktop   15

     3   Menus and Dialog Boxes   27

     4   The Finder's Menu Bar   47

     5   Floppy Disks and Hard Drives   61

     6   The Apple Menu   73

     7   The System Folder   87

     8   Your Filing System   103

     9   Help   115

Part II: Improving Your Expertise

Hour 10   Fonts   135

     11   Applications   151

     12   Networking   169

     13   Printing   181

     14   File Sharing   203

     15   Setting Up Your Internet Connection   215

     16   Using Your Internet Connection   231

Part III: Customizing Your Macintosh

Hour 17   Customizing the Finder and Software   253

18   Hardware   271

19   Memory   285

20   Multimedia   301

21   Security and Safety   315

22   Compatibility with DOS and Windows   325

23   Advanced Networking   337

24   Automation   351

Appendixes

A   What's New in Mac OS 8   363

B   Contact Information   369

Index   **373**

Contents

		Introduction	xxii
Part I		**Learning the Basics**	**1**
Hour 1		**Welcome to Mac OS 8**	**3**
		Understanding System Software	4
		Learning the Basics	4
		Getting Up and Running	4
		Using the Mouse	6
		Launching Applications	10
		Shutting Down	10
		Summary	13
		Term Review	13
		Q&A	14
	2	**The Desktop**	**15**
		Icons	16
		Drive Icons	17
		Trash Icon	17
		Folder and File Icons	18
		Application Icons	18
		Windows	19
		Opening and Closing Windows	20
		Minimizing and Maximizing Windows	21
		Resizing and Scrolling Windows	22
		Pop-Up Windows	24
		Summary	25
		Term Review	25
		Q&A	25
	3	**Menus and Dialog Boxes**	**27**
		Menus	28
		Menu Dragging	28
		Keyboard Shortcuts	29
		Ellipses and Nested Menus	30
		Dimmed Items	32
		Dialog Boxes	35
		Dialog Box Components	35
		Universal Dialog Boxes	38
		Opening Files	39
		Saving Files	41
		Summary	44
		Term Review	44
		Q&A	45

4   The Finder's Menu Bar   47

Components of the Menu Bar 48
    Apple Menu 48
    File Menu 48
    Edit Menu 53
    Application Menu 56
    Other Menus 57
Summary 58
Term Review 58
Q&A 59

5   Floppy Disks and Hard Drives   61

Floppy Disks 62
    Erasing a Floppy Disk 62
    Naming a Floppy Disk 64
    Ejecting a Floppy Disk 64
    Saving to a Floppy Disk 65
    Dealing with a Zip Drive 66
Hard Drives 66
    Checking Your Hard Drive's Capacity 67
    Adding External Hard Drives 67
    Partitioning a Hard Drive 68
    Changing the Startup Disk 69
Summary 70
Term Review 70
Q&A 71

6   The Apple Menu   73

Important Stuff 74
    About This Computer 74
    Apple System Profiler 75
    Control Panels 75
    Chooser 75
Cool Tools 76
    Find File 76
    Key Caps 77
    AppleCD Audio Player 78
    Calculator 79
    Graphing Calculator 79
Shortcuts 80
    Recent Applications 80
    Desktop Printers 81
    Automated Tasks 82
    Connect To… 82
Fun Stuff 82
    Scrapbook 83
    Jigsaw Puzzle 84

Stickies 84
Note Pad 85
Summary 85
Term Review 86
Q&A 86

7   The System Folder   87

Control Panels 88
General Controls 88
Date & Time 90
Desktop Pictures 92
Control Strip 93
Extensions 95
Startup and Shutdown Items 96
Preferences 97
Summary 101
Term Review 101
Q&A 101

8   Your Filing System   103

Organizing Your Desktop 104
Setting Up Folders 104
Setting Up Hierarchies 104
Viewing Your Desktop 106
Choosing Your Viewing Options 106
Choosing More Viewing Options 108
Cleaning Up Your Desktop 109
Navigating Your Desktop 110
Viewing Pop-up Windows 110
Viewing Spring-open Folders 110
Using Aliases to Navigate and Launch 111
Using the Apple Menu as a Shortcut 112
Summary 112
Term Review 113
Q&A 113

9   Help   115

Mac OS Help 116
Index 116
Topics 118
Look For 119
Application Help 120
Balloon Help 121
Balloon Help within Mac OS 8 121
Balloon Help within Applications 122

Mac OS Info Center 123
    Show Me What I Can Do 124
    Help Me Solve a Problem 126
    Help Me Explore the Internet 127
Technical Support 127
    Apple's Web Sites 128
    (800)SOS-APPL 128
    Local User Groups 129
Summary 130
Term Review 130
Q&A 130

Part II   Improving Your Expertise   133

Hour 10   Fonts   135

Font Basics 136
    Bitmapped versus PostScript Fonts 136
    Screen Fonts versus Printer Fonts 137
    TrueType 140
Font Usage 140
    Installing Fonts 140
    Using Font Utilities 142
Font Aesthetics 144
    Serif, Sans Serif, and Others 144
    Picking the Right Font for the Job 145
    Typesetting, Not Typing 146
Summary 148
Term Review 148
Q&A 149

11   Applications   151

Choosing the Right Applications 151
    Commercial Software 152
    Freebies 159
    Installing Applications 163
Summary 166
Term Review 166
Q&A 167

12   Networking   169

LAN Basics 169
The Physical Connection 170
    Serial Connections 170
    LocalTalk Connections 170
    Ethernet Connections 173
The Software Connection 174
    Using the Mac OS Setup Assistant 174
    Setting up Manually 177

Summary 179
Term Review 179
Q&A 180

13   **Printing**   **181**

The Chooser 181
    Setting up Your Laser Printer 182
    Serial Printer Drivers 185
Page Setup 187
    PostScript Options 188
    Application-Specific Windows 189
    StyleWriter Page Setup 189
Print Dialog Boxes 191
    General Controls 191
    Background Printing 193
    Cover Page 193
    Color Matching 194
    Layout 195
    Error Handling 195
    Save as File 196
    Printer Specific Options 196
    StyleWriter Variants 197
Desktop Printing 198
Summary 200
Term Review 200
Q&A 201

14   **File Sharing**   **203**

Setting Up File Sharing 204
    Sharing Files and Folders 204
    Linking Programs 205
    Changing Passwords 206
Setting Up Users & Groups 207
    Arranging Access Privileges 208
    Designating Groups 208
    Giving Groups Access 210
    Monitoring Access 211
Connecting to Shared Disks 212
    Getting to Your Mac From Elsewhere 212
Summary 213
Term Review 213
Q&A 214

15   **Setting Up Your Internet Connection**   **215**

Installing Your Modem 216
Using the Internet Setup Assistant 216
    Registering as a New User 216

Updating Your Settings 222
Automating Log-on and Log-off... 227
Summary 229
Term Review 229
Q&A 230

16 Using Your Internet Connection   231

Understanding the Internet 232
    The World Wide Web 232
    Electronic Mail 232
    Usenet News 232
    Other Uses of the Internet 233
    Netiquette, FAQs, and Other Net.Miscellany 233
Logging on to the Internet... 234
Using Your Internet Software 235
    Web Browsers 235
    Email Clients 242
    News Readers 243
    Mac OS Shortcuts 247
Logging Off... 248
Summary 249
Term Review 249
Q&A 250

Part III   Customizing Your Macintosh   251

Hour 17   Customizing the Finder and Software   253

Customizing the Finder's Interface 254
    Appearance Control Panel 254
    Desktop Pictures Control Panel 257
    Other Control Panels... 259
    Finder Preferences.. 261
    The View... Menu 262
    Other Finder Tricks 263
International Customization 266
Summary 268
Term Review 268
Q&A 268

18   Hardware   271

Monitoring Monitors 272
    Types and Sizes... 272
    Connecting Your Monitor 273
    Adjusting Your Monitor 273
Investigating Input Devices 274
    Keyboard 274
    Mouse... 275

Trackpad 275
Tablets 276
Scanners 277
Digital Cameras 277
Surveying CD-ROM Drives 278
What Speed Rating Means 278
New Speeds Available 279
Mastering Modems 279
How To Set Up a Modem 280
What Speed Rating Means 281
New Speeds Available 281
Adding Accessories 282
What Internal Cards Do 282
When To Add Cards 283
Summary 283
Term Review 283
Q&A 284

19   Memory   285

Memory Essentials 286
The Memory Control Panel 288
Disk Cache: An Easy Speed Boost 289
Virtual Memory: Double for Nothing? 290
RAM Disk: A Virtual Hard Drive 291
Applications Use RAM, Too 293
Adding More Memory 297
Summary 299
Term Review 299
Q&A 300

20   Multimedia   301

Audio Actions 302
Monitors & Sound Control Panel 302
Speech Control Panel 304
Playing Speech-to-Text 306
Setting Up a Shut-Down Sound 307
Adjusting the Apple CD Audio Player 307
Video Ventures 311
Playing with QuickTime 311
Using Cameras 312
Videophone and Videoconferencing 313
Summary 313
Term Review 314
Q&A 314

21   Security and Safety — **315**

Physical Security 316
  Backing Up Your Files 316
  Storing Backup Files 317
  Protecting Your Mac from Theft 318
  Protecting Your Mac from Disaster 319
Digital Security 319
  Folder Locking 319
  File Locking 320
  Utilities 321
Summary 322
Term Review 323
Q&A 323

22   Compatibility with DOS and Windows — **325**

Moving Files Back and Forth 326
  Using PC Exchange 326
  Using Rich Text Format 328
  Understanding File Formats 328
  Exchanging Files Between Macs and PCs 329
Investing in Other Hardware and Software 331
  DOS Mounting Utilities 331
  Windows 95 File-Transfer Utilities 332
  Other Third-Party Products 333
Summary 335
Term Review 336
Q&A 336

23   Advanced Networking — **337**

Accessing Files on Servers 338
  Encountering Restricted Access 341
  Changing Your Server Password 343
  Automating Your Log-on Process 344
Using Personal Web Sharing 345
Accessing Files Via Modem: ARA 346
Summary 349
Term Review 349
Q&A 350

24   Automation — **351**

Shortcuts 352
  Icon Shortcuts 352
  Windows Shortcuts 352
  List Shortcuts 353
  Dialog Box Shortcuts 353
  Restarting Shortcuts 354
  Reviewing Other Shortcuts 354

Learning About AppleScript 354
  What It Is 355
  Who Uses It, and Where 355
Using AppleScript Automated Tasks 356
  Where to Find Automated Tasks 356
  How to Take Advantage of Automated Tasks 357
Other Automation Tools and Tips 358
  QuicKeys 358
  Other Tips 359
Summary 360
Term Review 360
Q&A 360

Appendixes

A   **What's New in Mac OS 8**   **363**

B   **Contact Information**   **369**
     Macintosh Web Sites 372

Index   **373**

Introduction

So you're sitting there thinking, "The Macintosh is supposed to be the easiest computer of all. Why the heck do I need a book to teach myself Mac OS 8?" Of course, you're right—the Macintosh is an easy computer to learn. But it's also a very powerful computer, and it only takes a little bit of knowledge to unleash that power. That's what this book is for.

Even better, the Macintosh embodies the *personal* in personal computer. There is much you can do to personalize your Macintosh with your own touches, so that it's as comfortable to use as a favorite chair is to sit in. That's also what this book is for.

JUST A MINUTE

> The information in this book is based on information on Mac OS 8 given to the authors in the spring of 1997. Because this information was delivered prior to the final release of the operating system software, there may be some differences between the information in this book and the final version of Mac OS 8. We encourage you to visit Apple's web site (www.apple.com) for updated information once you're up and running with Mac OS 8.

Who Should Read This Book

If you're never used a Macintosh before, this is the place to start. If you already know how to use a Macintosh, and want to learn more about Apple's latest operating system, this is also the place to start. We'll teach you the basics of the Macintosh, how to improve your expertise, and then how to customize your Macintosh.

For those readers who already use a Macintosh, you might want to read Appendix A, "What's New In Mac OS 8." It looks at what's new and improved in Mac OS 8 if you're familiar with System 7.X.

Can This Book Really Teach Mac OS 8 in 24 Hours?

Friends of ours suggested we bundle a coupon for a six-pack of Jolt Cola in with this book, so we had to explain to them that it wasn't necessarily 24 *consecutive* hours. We've tried our best to keep the chapters consistent in the time you'll spend reading them. Some of them have more pages than others simply because sometimes we could explain what we needed in text, and other times we needed pictures to explain concepts best. But yes, if you set aside an hour a day for a month (or a couple of hours each weekend), you'll have the basics of Mac OS 8 down pat.

By the way, we put a lot of thought into the order of these hours, so everything would be explained in a logical path. Ideally, you'll be able to use what you learn in one hour in a succeeding hour. That said, feel free to jump around. We've made every effort to refer you both backwards and forwards so you can find what you want to learn when you want to learn it.

What You Need

We assume that you have a Macintosh computer equipped with a Motorola 68040 or PowerPC CPU, keyboard, and monitor, or at least have access to one. We don't assume that you have installed any other applications, though we do make some recommendations for software that we use ourselves.

Typographical Conventions

Here is a summary of the typographical conventions:

- ☐ The first time a new term appears, the term is italicized.
- ☐ Web addresses appear in a special monospaced computer font.
- ☐ If a task requires you to select from a menu, the book separates menu commands with a vertical bar. Therefore this book uses File➡Save As to select the Save As command from the File menu.

PART

I

Learning the Basics

Hour

1 Welcome to Mac OS 8

2 The Desktop

3 Menus and Dialog Boxes

4 The Finder's Menu Bar

5 Floppy Disks and Hard Drives

6 The Apple Menu

7 The System Folder

8 Your Filing System

9 Help

Hour 1

Welcome to Mac OS 8

This hour introduces you to the basics of using your Macintosh and its operating system, Mac OS 8.

If you're already among the millions of people using a Macintosh computer, Mac OS 8's new features and improved user interface enable you take better advantage of your hardware and software. If you're new to the Macintosh platform, Mac OS 8 builds on Apple's legendary ease of use to offer you powerful computing capabilities without making you delve into the details of how your computer works. Novices and experts alike, Macintosh users enjoy the benefits of using a computer platform that's ranked number one for customer loyalty, reliability, and ease of use.

The highlights of this hour include:

- ☐ How Mac OS 8 functions
- ☐ How to turn on your Macintosh, and get started using it
- ☐ How to use your mouse
- ☐ How to launch applications
- ☐ How to shut down your Macintosh safely

Understanding System Software

All computers—Macs, PCs, and even large computers used by factories and large corporations—rely on an *operating system,* software the computer uses to perform basic tasks and to let applications (programs like your word processor or your email software) talk to the hardware (the computer itself). If you or someone you know uses a PC, you're already familiar with an operating system, probably Windows or Windows 95. On the Macintosh platform, we also refer to the operating system generically as *system software.*

The Macintosh platform's current operating system is known as Mac OS 8, and it performs basic tasks such as memory management and file handling. Mac OS 8 also controls the look and feel—the *interface*—of the computer, including the files and menus you'll use to operate the computer. Mac OS 8 is responsible for enabling application programs to communicate with one another and with the computer's hardware, and for giving each application a similar appearance.

Learning the Basics

In this section, we'll teach you the minimum skills you'll need to use your Macintosh: turning it on, using the mouse, launching applications, and shutting down your computer.

Getting Up and Running

After you've taken your Macintosh out of the box and assembled, you'll need to locate its power switch. In the upper-right corner of your keyboard, you'll see a key with a triangle, as seen in Figure 1.1.

Figure 1.1

This key—located in the upper-right corner of your keyboard—is the power switch for your Macintosh.

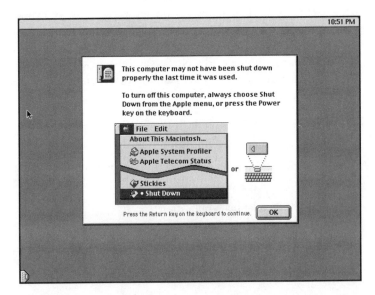

To turn on your Macintosh, perform the following steps:

1. Locate the power key in the upper-right corner of your keyboard.

2. Press the power key.

3. Your Macintosh will play a musical sound to indicate that it has powered on.

TIME SAVER

On some Macintosh systems—especially low-cost models—you'll also need to find a second hardware power switch. Typically, it's a rocker switch like those found on household appliances. On some older Power Macintosh and Centris models, the power switch is a round push button on the front of the system.

After you've successfully located the power key and turned on your Macintosh, it performs its system checks and displays a series of images to let you know all is well.

Briefly, you'll see an image known as the "Happy Macintosh" icon. This image—which goes back to the very first days of the Macintosh, as evidenced by its depiction of a *very* old Macintosh—tells you that the various components of the computer's main logic board have passed their internal checks.

The next image you'll see is the Mac OS logo: two blue stylized faces and the words "Mac OS" beneath them. The logo first appears with the words "Welcome to Macintosh" beneath it, which then changes to "Starting up…". At this point, you'll see a status bar appear, which shows how far along your Macintosh is in the software portion of its startup process.

CAUTION

If you don't see the "Happy Macintosh" or the Mac OS logo when you first turn on your Mac, you'll want to refer to the documentation that came with your computer for assistance.

As the status bar fills to indicate progress, a row of tiny images will appear at the bottom of your screen. These small images—known as *icons*—represent the various portions of the Mac OS becoming active. We'll talk more about the Mac OS pieces that these icons represent in Hour 7, "The System Folder."

After these startup icons have finished their march across the bottom of your monitor, you'll see a basic gray screen with a few icons on it, as seen in Figure 1.2. This basic view is the core interface to the Mac OS. It's known as the *desktop*, because—just like on your real desk—you'll start most of your work here.

Figure 1.2

The Mac OS 8 desktop.

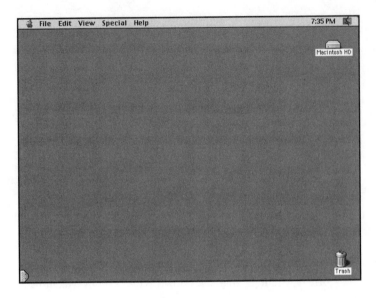

On the desktop, you'll see the icons for your hard drive (called "Macintosh HD")—the storage place where your Macintosh keeps your files and programs. You'll also see a trash can, a light gray bar at the top of the screen, and a small tab at the lower right corner that lets you access the Control Strip (we'll discuss the Control Strip in Hour 7, and the Trash in the next chapter, Hour 2, "The Desktop").

The light gray bar at the top of your screen is known as the *menu bar* (see Figure 1.3)—the place where you'll find many of the menus that you'll use to access of many of Mac OS 8's basic features. We'll discuss the menu bar's functions in depth in Hour 4, "The Finder's Menu Bar."

Using the Mouse

Mastering the mouse is relatively simple, but it takes a bit of practice to develop the necessary hand/eye coordination to use the mouse with ease. Luckily, all of the terms related to using a mouse are simple and straightforward. The two most basic mouse maneuvers are *pointing* and *clicking*.

To practice pointing and clicking, perform the following steps:

1. Put your hand on the mouse, and move it around until you locate the arrow cursor (see Figure 1.4).

1

Figure 1.3

The menu bar is at the top of the window.

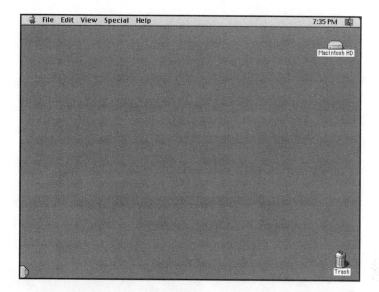

Figure 1.4

The arrow cursor points to the Trash.

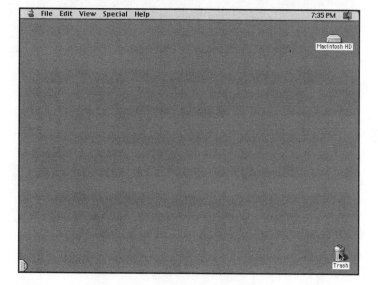

2. Move the mouse so that the arrow cursor points to the Trash icon in the lower-right corner of the screen.

3. Press the mouse button and hold it down using your index finger. The Trash icon will change color to indicate that it is selected.

4. Release the mouse button—notice that the Trash icon changes back to its original colors. It is now deselected.

Congratulations. You've learned your first mousing basics: pointing and clicking. Now we'll move on to more advanced mouse tasks: *dragging* and *dropping*.

To practice dragging and dropping, perform the following steps:

1. Click on the Trash icon. It will change color to indicate that it is selected. Don't release the mouse button.

2. While holding down the button, move (drag) the mouse to move the icon around the desktop. As you drag the Trash icon, you'll see a shadow version of the icon following the cursor, to indicate its new location (see Figure 1.5).

3. Release the mouse button to drop the icon in its new location.

Figure 1.5

A shadow version of the Trash icon indicates its new tentative position before dropping.

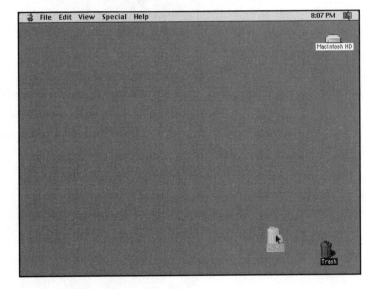

You'll need to learn one last mouse technique before we move on: *double-clicking*. As the name implies, double-clicking is much like clicking, except that you depress the mouse button twice in rapid succession.

To practice double-clicking, perform the following steps:

1. Point to the Hard Drive icon.

2. Push down on the mouse button twice in rapid succession.

3. The Hard Drive icon will open, showing the folders inside it (see Figure 1.6).

Figure 1.6

After double-clicking, the hard drive icon opens to reveal its contents.

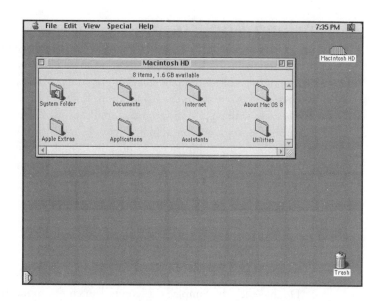

You've now learned how to double-click. Practice it again by opening the Applications folder on your hard drive; instead of moving over the hard drive, place the arrow over the Applications folder. It makes no difference whether you're opening a hard drive or a folder—you need to double-click both types of containers to open them. Your opened Applications folder will look something like Figure 1.7.

Figure 1.7

The opened Applications folder.

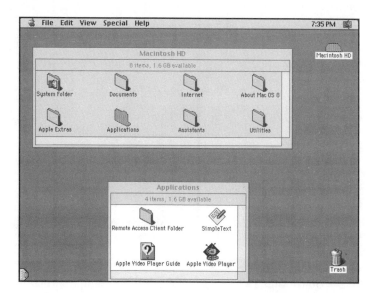

Launching Applications

When an icon represents a container—such as the hard drive or a folder—double-clicking opens the icon to display its contents. But what about icons that represent other types of files? Software programs like word processors or graphics programs—known as *applications*—are also represented by icons. In the Applications folder in Figure 1.7, you see one folder and three other icons, all representing various applications. The icons often give some clue as to the nature of the program's function. In Figure 1.7, the Apple Video Player icon, for example, shows a graphic of a TV, hinting at its purpose. SimpleText is a basic text editor, much like a word processor without all of the fancy features. (We'll talk more about SimpleText in Hour 11, "Applications.")

To use applications like Apple Video Player and SimpleText, you need to *launch*, or open, them.

To launch SimpleText, perform the following steps:

1. Point to the SimpleText icon in the Applications folder.
2. Double-click the SimpleText icon to launch the application.
3. SimpleText will launch, showing an empty (untitled) document, as seen in Figure 1.8.

Figure 1.8

After double-clicking on its icon, SimpleText launches, opening an untitled, empty document.

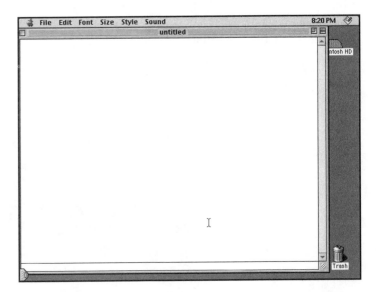

Shutting Down

Unlike your TV or your toaster, you can't simply switch off your Macintosh when you're done using it without risking damage to your hardware or your files. One of Mac OS 8's prime duties is keeping track of files and their status and contents; without a proper shut down procedure, the Mac OS has no way of making sure that everything has been properly accounted for.

To safely shut down your computer, perform the following steps:

1. Click on the word Special in the menu bar and hold the mouse button down. A list of actions will appear (see Figure 1.9).

Figure 1.9

Clicking on the Special item in the menu bar.

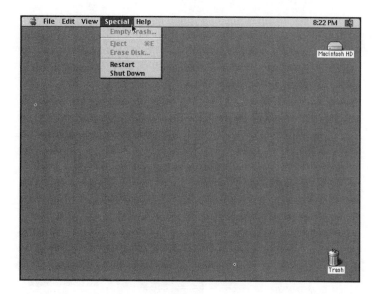

2. Drag down through the menu until the words Shut Down are highlighted (see Figure 1.10).

3. Release the mouse. The Macintosh will turn off.

Figure 1.10

To safely turn off your Macintosh, drag down the Special menu until Shut Down is high-lighted, and then release the mouse.

JUST A MINUTE

On Macintosh models with a hardware power switch, you'll see a
message that it is now safe to turn off your Macintosh.

You've now safely shut down your Macintosh. (You've also just learned the most basic step
of menu navigation, dragging down a menu. We'll cover more menuing basics in Hour 3,
"Menus and Dialog Boxes.")

TIME SAVER

Aside from Special➡Shut Down, there's another way to safely turn off
your Macintosh: pressing the power key (the key in the upper-right corner
of your keyboard) while the computer is turned on will bring up a dialog
box asking whether you want to shut down.

CAUTION

Because not shutting down properly can be detrimental to your computer's
well-being, doing so will produce the warning shown in Figure 1.11 upon
your next startup.

Figure 1.11

*Your Macintosh will
warn you if you haven't
properly shut down.*

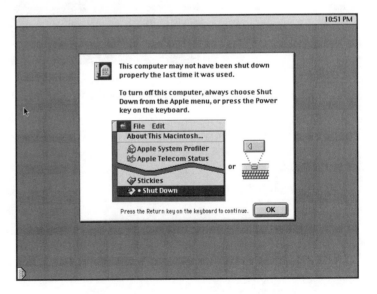

Summary

This hour taught you the basics of using your Macintosh.

The Macintosh operating system—known as Mac OS 8—performs memory and file management, controls the interface, and enables application programs to communicate with one another and with the computer itself.

To turn on your computer, locate the power key in the upper-right corner of your keyboard. Some systems may also have a hardware switch, which varies among models.

Basic navigation requires the use of the mouse, specifically: *pointing* (moving the cursor over an icon), *clicking* (pointing to an icon and pressing the mouse button), *dragging* (clicking on an icon and moving the mouse) and *dropping* (releasing an icon to a new location).

To use applications, you need to *launch*, or open, them. To launch an application, double-click its icon.

To prevent damage to your Macintosh and its files, you must properly shut down your Macintosh when you're done using it. To turn off your Macintosh safely, drag down the Special menu until Shut Down is highlighted, then release the mouse button.

Term Review

Click   Pointing to an icon with the cursor, and pressing the mouse button.

Desktop   Mac OS 8's main working view, visible when no applications are running, where you find the Trash and your hard disk's icon.

Drag   Clicking on an icon and moving the mouse to change the icon's location.

Drop   Releasing an icon to a new location after dragging.

Icons   Small graphics that represent files, folders, applications, and other items on your Macintosh.

Interface   The look and feel of a computer and its applications.

Launch   Opening an application to run.

Menu bar   The light gray band at the top of the desktop.

Mac OS 8   The current operating system of the Macintosh.

Operating system   The program used by a computer to perform file management, inter-application communications, and application-to-hardware connections.

System software   A generic term for the combined component parts of the Macintosh operating system.

Q&A

Q My Macintosh is all set up, but I can't figure out how to turn it on. What do I do?

A You'll need to locate its power switch. In the upper-right corner of your keyboard, you'll see a key with a triangle. On some Macintosh models—especially low-cost models—you'll also need to find a second hardware power switch.

Q I have a word processor on my Macintosh, and I don't know how to start using it. What should I do?

A Locate the application's icon, and double-click on it. For more information on using various programs, see Hour 11, "Applications."

Q I'm finished using my Macintosh. Can I simply unplug it?

A No. To turn off your Macintosh safely, drag down the Special menu in the Menu Bar until Shut Down is highlighted, then release.

Hour 2

The Desktop

In this hour, you will learn about the desktop—what you see on your screen after you turn on your Macintosh. It's called a desktop simply because it represents a real desktop. It's both where you do your work and where you'll find what you need to do your work. This hour encompasses everything except the strip of light gray at the top of the screen (that strip is called the menu bar, which was mentioned in Hour 1, but you'll learn more about in Hour 3, "Menus and Dialog Boxes").

Right now there are probably just three items on your desktop—an icon representing your hard drive, one representing a trash can, and an oddly-shaped icon that belongs to a tool called the Control Strip (see Figure 2.1), which we'll talk about in Hour 6, "The Apple Menu" (see Figure 2.1). By the end of the first section of this book, you'll have many more items on your desktop, and you'll know exactly what they represent and how they got there. Later, you'll even be able to change the background of your desktop so that you can look at something that you've chosen rather than a plain gray background.

Figure 2.1

Your desktop will look like this when you start up.

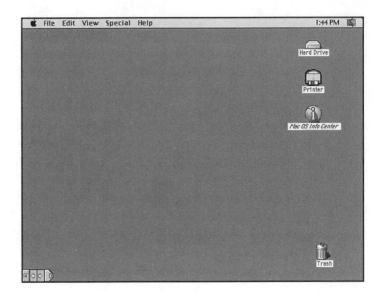

The highlights of this hour include:

☐ How to identify what the icons on your desktop represent

☐ How to create folders to organize your documents

☐ How to rename folders and icons so that you can more easily recognize what they represent

☐ How to open, close, and resize windows for easy control over what you see

Icons

In the previous hour, you learned all about the basics of operating your Macintosh. You probably even clicked and dragged some of the icons that we're going to talk about in this hour. If anyone asks you what makes the Macintosh a great computer, just say one word: *icons*. Simply put, these are the graphical representations of objects, designed to be easily recognized.

The Macintosh was the first personal computer to represent information with icons rather than characters or symbols. Why? Because people learn and remember graphics more easily than words. If you put what looks like a yellow M in front of most Americans, they'll identify it as McDonald's golden arches. Think of how easy it is to recognize that logo, and hopefully every icon you see on the desktop will be just as easy to recognize.

We're going to look at all the icons that can appear on your desktop: ones that represent your hard drive and floppy disks, the trash, folders, files, and your applications.

2

If you've used older versions of the operating system, you'll notice that Mac OS 8's icons now look three-dimensional, whereas before they were two-dimensional and flat. Now they're much more pleasing to the eye.

Drive Icons

Notice the icon on your desktop labeled Macintosh HD. If you have a floppy disk handy, slip it into the floppy drive. It will appear on the desktop with its own icon (see Figure 2.2). Click on the hard drive icon—just once. See how it's highlighted? That means it's *active*, and if you click on the icon and hold down the mouse button, you can drag it anywhere you want on the desktop. (We'll talk specifically about hard drives and floppy drives in Hour 4, "The Finder's Menu Bar," but right now we're just interested in their icons.)

Figure 2.2

The hard drive and floppy disk icons.

Trash Icon

At the bottom of the screen is the Trash icon. Appropriately, it looks like a garbage can with the lid on. If you drag a file to the Trash, it will disappear and the top will appear to be leaning up against the side of the trash can (see Figure 2.3). There will also appear to be papers inside. This graphically lets you know that there's something in the Trash. In earlier versions of the Macintosh operating system, the Trash Can would bulge when something was in it.

Figure 2.3

The Trash icon after you've dragged something into it.

Folder and File Icons

You'll need to know about two other basic icons that will appear on your desktop. One looks like a manila folder; appropriately, it's called a *folder*. The other looks like a dog-eared sheet of paper, and it's called a *file* (see Figure 2.4). Both of these icons work the same way; if you click on any part of the icon, you make it active. Once it's active, click and hold it to drag it on the desktop.

Figure 2.4

Appropriately, a folder looks like a manila folder and a file looks like a sheet of paper.

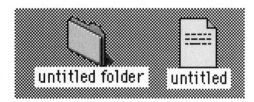

Now that you know about folders and the trash can, let's throw something away to see how these two icons work together. Just follow these steps:

1. Press the ⌘-key and the letter *N* simultaneously. A new untitled folder will appear on your desktop.

2. Click on the untitled folder and drag it over the Trash (the Trash icon will be highlighted, because it's now active).

3. Let go of the mouse button. The untitled folder will disappear and the Trash icon will indicate that something is in it.

4. To empty the Trash, select Special➟Empty Trash.

JUST A MINUTE

> Until you specifically tell the Macintosh to empty the Trash, you can still retrieve what you've put there. This is perfect for those who throw anything away (or delete important information) just minutes before they realize they really need it.

Application Icons

Any application that you run on your Macintosh will also have an icon, whether it's a word processing application for writing letters or a personal finance application for balancing your checkbook. Whenever it's represented on your desktop, it will appear as an icon.

One of the great things about the desktop is the way it lets you easily rename items on it. That way, if the graphic doesn't help you recognize a file, the name you give it will. For instance, you may install an application whose icon is named something unspeakable like *MegaMerged Inc. Spreadsheet Application Version 9.7*. That long title doesn't have to take up all that room on your desktop.

2

To change an icon's name, perform the following steps:

1. Click on the hard drive icon's name. After a moment, the border of the title will turn white.
2. Type "My New Macintosh."
3. Click outside the title area again to make the icon inactive.

JUST A MINUTE

You can rename any icon on the desktop, except the Trash icon. It's always called Trash.

TIME SAVER

If you're impatient when you rename an icon on the Macintosh, just click on the title and then move the cursor off the name. That will eliminate the traditional delay you get and the icon can now be immediately renamed. If you don't want to change the name, but just want to add a notation at the beginning or end of the name, hit the up or down arrow key, respectively.

JUST A MINUTE

You don't have to use icons at all to view your files and folders. If you prefer to see things in alphabetical lists, simply click on View➧by Name. New to Mac OS 8 is another feature called Buttons. When you click on View➧as Buttons, the icons are surrounded by squares that you can easily click on. For more on viewing options, see Hour 3.

Windows

Now let's talk about windows. Yes, we know that other operating system is named Windows (with a capital W), but the Mac OS had windows long before the other guys did; the Macintosh windows are lowercase *w*. They will always have the same look and act the same, whether you're in a folder or a file (see Figure 2.5).

Figure 2.5

Your basic Mac OS 8 window.

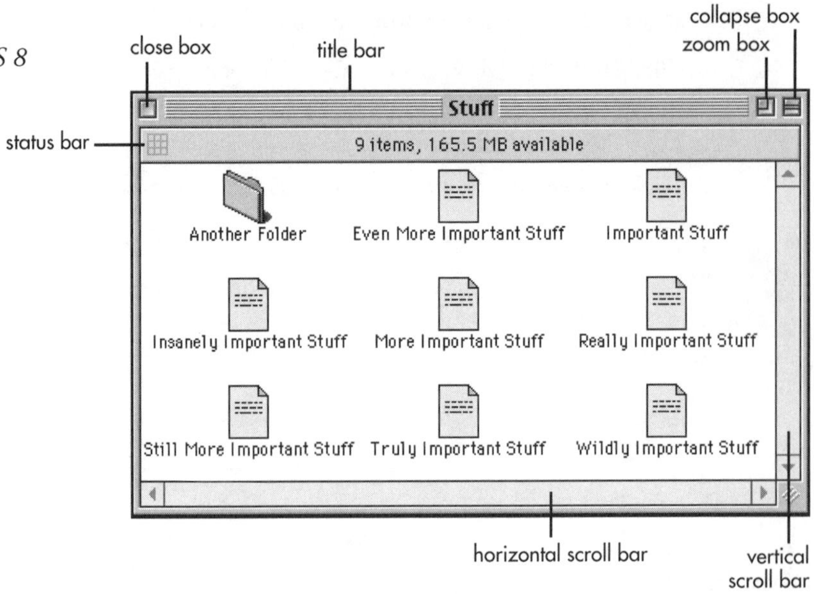

close box   title bar   collapse box / zoom box

status bar

Stuff

9 items, 165.5 MB available

Another Folder   Even More Important Stuff   Important Stuff

Insanely Important Stuff   More Important Stuff   Really Important Stuff

Still More Important Stuff   Truly Important Stuff   Wildly Important Stuff

horizontal scroll bar   vertical scroll bar

In this instance, we're looking at a folder we've named Stuff. At the top is the *title bar.* There are three boxes within the title bar at the top. From left to right, they are the *close* box, the *zoom* box, and the *collapse* box. The *status bar* is just below the title, and it indicates how many items are in the window and how much space is on your hard drive.

On the right side and the bottom of the window are the *horizontal scroll bar* and the *vertical scroll bar.* Each of these have triangles in them to indicate the direction you want to move. They work just like arrows. The triangles aren't highlighted because there are not other items in the Stuff folder (see, it says *nine items* in the status bar). If the window contained more items, the triangles, and the scrolling boxes would be lit up—just another example of the way Mac OS 8 helps you with visual clues.

JUST A MINUTE

> The triangles point like arrows, because in previous versions of the operating system—they were arrows.

Opening and Closing Windows

It's easy to open a window. Any time you double-click on a folder icon, up will pop a window. Let's try it now with an untitled folder by following these steps:

1. Click on the ⌘-key and the letter *N* to create an untitled folder.
2. Double-click on the folder to open it. Notice that its icon has become dimmed, indicating that it's open (see Figure 2.6).

Figure 2.6

Your newly created, newly opened window looks like this.

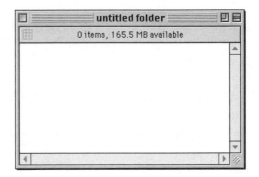

3. To close the window, click on the Close box in the upper-left corner. It's back to the folder icon.

Minimizing and Maximizing Windows

The Macintosh enables you to open, close, and resize windows so you can get them out of the way when you don't need them. To resize the window, perform the following steps:

1. Double-click on the untitled folder again.
2. Click inside the smaller box within the zoom box (see Figure 2.7). Presto, this makes the window larger.
3. Now click outside the smaller box within the zoom box. This minimizes the window to its original dimension.

Figure 2.7

The zoom and collapse boxes enable you to resize your windows.

You can even make the entire window disappear by using the *collapse box* (see Figure 2.8). This is the button to click if you're working on something private and someone walks into the room. One click and it disappears. The title bar stays, so you'd better hope you haven't named it something incriminating like, say, "Embezzlement Plans." Try this now:

Figure 2.8
The Stuff folder has now been collapsed.

1. Click on the collapse box in the top-right corner to close everything but the title bar.
2. Click on the collapse box again to maximize the window.

JUST A MINUTE

Before Mac OS 8, you could double-click on the title bar and the window would disappear, leaving only the title bar. It was like rolling up a windowshade, which is what the command was called. The collapse box replaces this capability.

Resizing and Scrolling Windows

There are other ways to arrange the way you look at windows on the desktop. You can resize the window by clicking on the *grow box*, those diagonal lines (Size Lines in the lower-right corner of the window) and dragging it in any direction. Let's see how small we can make it. You can make the window almost any size you prefer, making it big enough to cover the entire desktop, or as small as a Saltine cracker. The problem with this size is that you can't read anything, including the name of the folder. For all you know, it relates to a guy named Stu (see Figure 2.9).

Figure 2.9
A completely minimized window.

2

Now let's get some experience with the horizontal and the vertical scroll bars. By adjusting these, you can see all the items in any given window without having to maximize the window every time. Perform the following steps:

1. Create a new folder.
2. Within that folder, create at least a half-dozen new folders (the triangles and the scroll bars won't appear unless some material is hidden).
3. Resize the window so that some of the files are hidden (see Figure 2.10).

Figure 2.10

With the vertical scroll bar at the top and the horizontal scroll bar at the left, you get one view of your files.

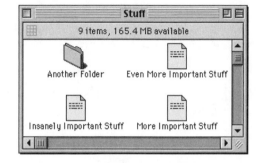

4. Click on the box in the vertical scroll bar and drag it down.
5. Click on the box in the horizontal scroll bar and slide it to the right. You should be able to see the hidden files (see Figure 2.11).

Figure 2.11

With the vertical scroll bar at the bottom and the horizontal scroll bar at the right, you get a different view of your files.

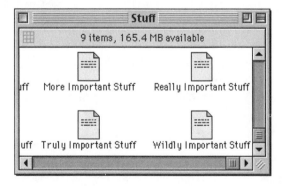

Now's the perfect time to let you know that if you want to move from one highlighted folder or file to another, just press the Tab key. To go in the opposite direction, press the Tab and Shift keys simultaneously. You can also use the arrow keys on your keyboard.

Pop-up Windows

Apple has added still another way of playing with folders. This isn't superfluous, either—it's actually something very helpful if you don't have a large monitor. This new feature is called *pop-up windows*, and it will help you save what we call screen *real estate*. Perform the following steps to learn how to use this feature:

1. Open a previously created folder on your desktop.

2. In the menu bar, click View➡as Pop-up Window.

3. The folder will sprout a rectangular tab that will probably remind you of a manila folder. Click on that tab.

4. The folder minimizes itself at the bottom of the desktop, with only the tab remaining (see Figure 2.12). That way, it's easily accessible.

Figure 2.12

How a minimized pop-up window appears on your desktop.

5. To open it, click on the tab.

6. To return it to a window, you can either go back to the menu bar and click View➡as Window, or you can simply drag the tab on the desktop. It'll revert to a window instantly.

You cannot transform a folder into a pop-up window unless it is open. Highlighting it will not enable you to select the pop-up window option.

Summary

During this hour, you learned the basics about the icons and windows on your desktop and how they behave.

Icons can represent any number of items, from your hard drive to a file folder, from an application to the Trash. By clicking on an icon's title, you can easily rename it so that you can more easily identify it.

You'll almost always be working with the windows that appear on the Macintosh desktop, and now you know the many ways that you can resize and rearrange windows so that they're handy when you need them and out of the way when you don't. This reflects just one of the many ways in which the Macintosh lets you set up your desktop so that it's most comfortable for you.

2

Term Review

Pop-up window   Mac OS 8's feature for minimizing folders along the bottom of the desktop.

Scroll bar   A navigational tool for showing items that may not be immediately visible in a window.

Window   The basic container in which the Macintosh shows the contents of files, folders, and other components of the operating system.

Q&A

Q. What happens if I accidentally drag my hard drive icon into the Trash?

A. This is the digital equivalent of accidentally putting a brick on your car's accelerator and aiming for a cliff. But while your car won't know to stop, your Macintosh will. It will give you an error message saying that such a maneuver is impossible.

Q. Do I have to rename an untitled folder as soon as I create it?

A. No. If you press ⌘-N 12 times in a row, you'll get 12 untitled folders; the first will be named "untitled folder," and the rest will be named "untitled folder 1" through "untitled folder 11."

Q. Is there a way to get through a window containing many items without continually sliding the box in the vertical scroll bar?

A. Just click on the track of the scroll box. The box will jump to that point, and the cursor's place in the document will as well.

Hour **3**

Menus and Dialog Boxes

In this hour, you'll learn how to navigate the Finder using menus, how to copy and paste information from one location to another, and how to open and save files within applications. It sounds ambitious, but like much of Mac OS 8, once you've learned how one menu or dialog box works, you'll have a great foundation for using the others.

The highlights of this hour include:

☐ How to navigate the Finder and applications using menus and dialog boxes

☐ How to interpret the various items you'll see in menus

☐ What to expect when you see a menu bar inside an application

☐ How to use the Clipboard to move text (and graphics) from one place to another

☐ How to interpret the basic elements of a dialog box

Menus

All applications have a menu bar and many of the Finder's menus are similar to those within applications. In order to navigate Mac OS 8's menus, you'll need to master a few basic skills.

Like most Macintosh tasks, learning to use menus is a simple matter of learning a few basic techniques and then applying them to other, similar purposes. This section will teach you the skills you'll need to use menus in the Finder, and within applications.

Menu Dragging

You might have heard the term *pull-down menu*. When you click on a menu's title in the menu bar, it drops down to reveal the features of the Mac OS (or the application) that you can access using it. By dragging (or pulling) your way down the menu, you can select the feature you want to use.

You may remember that we pulled down the Special menu back in Hour 1 "Welcome to Mac OS 8," in order to turn off the computer safely. Let's practice another task using menu dragging: creating a new document. To create a new folder on the desktop by pulling down a menu, perform the following steps:

1. Click on the word File in the menu bar, without letting go. A list of actions will appear (see Figure 3.1).

Figure 3.1

Clicking on the File menu in the menu bar displays a list of its actions.

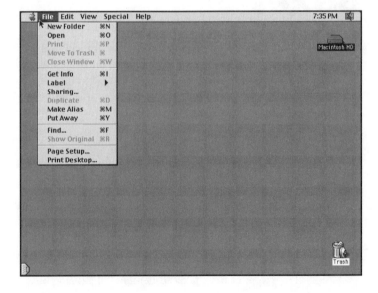

2. Drag down through the menu until the words "New Folder" are highlighted (see Figure 3.2).

3. Release the mouse. A new untitled folder will appear on the desktop.

3

Figure 3.2

*To create a new folder on
the desktop, drag down
the File menu until
"New Folder" is high-
lighted, then release.*

That's it. Dragging a menu to select one of its functions is really quite simple. Activating any of the other features of the File menu—or any other menu—is just as easy.

Keyboard Shortcuts

When you dragged down the File menu, you may have noticed that many of the menu items were followed by a cloverleaf symbol and a letter. You'll notice the same symbol on the keys to the right and left of the space bar on your keyboard. When you hold down this key—known as the *Command key*—in combination with the letter shown to the right of the menu task, you're invoking a *keyboard shortcut.* Keyboard shortcuts are handy for tasks you use frequently because you don't have to remove your hands from the keyboard to use the mouse.

If you click on the File menu, you'll see that many of its tasks have shortcuts (see Figure 3.3).

Mac OS 8 makes it easy for you to remember keyboard shortcuts; they're often (but not always) the first letter of the command or feature you want to use: Command-P for Print, Command-N for New, and so on.

JUST A MINUTE

We've spelled out "Command" here just to get you started with the concept of keyboard shortcuts. From now on, you'll see the symbol ⌘ when we want you to press the Command key.

To create a new folder using a keyboard shortcut, perform the following steps:

1. Click on the File menu to view the keyboard shortcut for New Folder. You'll see that ⌘-N is the appropriate key combination.

Figure 3.3

The File menu, showing keyboard shortcuts for its tasks.

2. Press the ⌘ key, and hold it down. (Remember, most Macintosh keyboards have command keys at either side of the space bar.)

3. While holding down the ⌘ key, press the N key. A new untitled folder appears.

Figure 3.4

⌘-N is the keyboard shortcut for New Folder.

Ellipses and Nested Menus

You probably also noticed that some of the entries in the File menu didn't have shortcuts but did have other symbols to the right side of the menu items. Some entries have ellipses (three consecutive dots, like this: ...) or a triangle facing off the right edge of the menu itself (see Figure 3.5).

3

Figure 3.5

Some entries in the File menu have ellipses or triangles to the right of them.

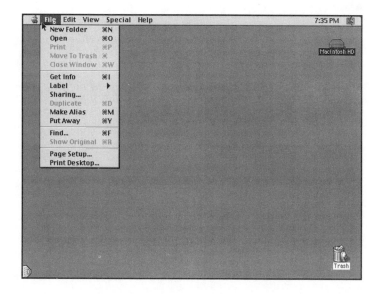

Within a menu, ellipses and triangles mean that there's more to a command than the Mac OS has room to display in the small space of a menu. Ellipses and triangles serve slightly different purposes, though.

The right-facing arrow indicates that the menu is *nested*—that is, that if you drag down to an entry with a right-arrow indicator, another menu will appear (see Figure 3.6).

Figure 3.6

A nested menu appears when you select a menu item with a right-triangle on the right side.

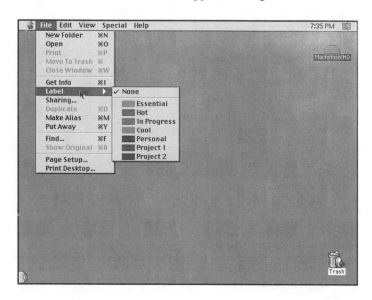

Ellipses indicate a different sort of "to be continued" scenario. When you select a menu with an ellipsis on the right side, a dialog box appears.

To see what we mean, perform the following steps:

1. Click on the File menu.

2. Drag down to Find…

3. With Find… selected, release the mouse button. A new dialog box will appear (see Figure 3.7).

Figure 3.7

A dialog box appears when you select a menu item with ellipsis on the right side.

Dimmed Items

You've no doubt noticed by now that some items in the File menu are dark gray, not black, and don't become highlighted when you drag past them. These items are known as *dimmed* selections, and they're Mac OS 8's way of letting you know when a menu item isn't available for your use (see Figure 3.8).

Figure 3.8

If you drag past a dimmed item (such as Move To Trash here) it won't become highlighted. Dimmed items are Mac OS 8's way of telling you which menu items aren't applicable for your current use.

3

Some menu items (including most of the tasks in the File menu) become dimmed or active depending on what type of items you have open or selected in the Finder.

To investigate situation-dependent menu items, perform the following steps:

1. Click on the open gray area of the desktop to deselect any items you may have selected.

2. Click on the File menu. You'll notice that most of it's options are dimmed (see Figure 3.9).

Figure 3.9

With no desktop items selected, most items in the File menu are dimmed.

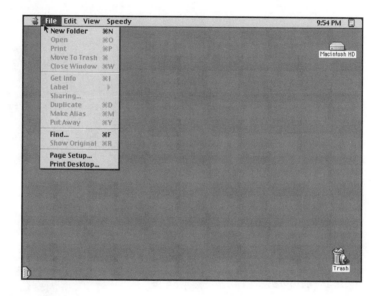

3. Release the menu.

4. On the desktop, click your hard drive's icon.

5. Click the File menu again. Now you'll see that many more of the menu's options are active (see Figure 3.10).

So, what about the items that remain dimmed even when the hard drive is selected? They'll become active when an item they relate to becomes active. Duplicate, for example, works when files and folders are selected and makes an exact duplicate of the selected item.

Some items even change their function when different types of icons are selected. Look back at Figure 3.10, above. Notice that the last menu item is "Print Desktop...".

To check out how changing your selection can change a menu, perform the following steps:

1. Double-click the hard drive icon to open it. The hard drive window opens on the desktop and its title text is black (not dimmed) to show that it's active (you learned about this in Hour 2, "The Desktop").

Figure 3.10

With the hard drive icon selected, most items in the File menu are active.

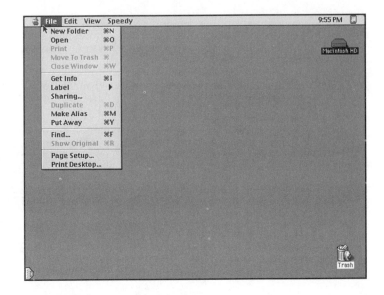

2. With the hard drive window open and active, click again on the File menu. You'll notice that the last item has changed to "Print Window..." (see Figure 3.11). The Close Window command has also become active.

Figure 3.11

With the hard drive window open and active, the File menu's options change.

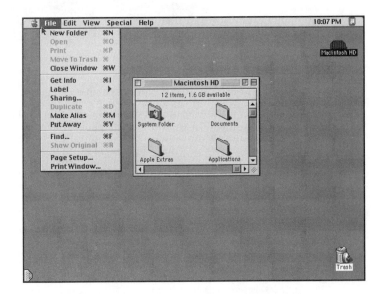

3

Dialog Boxes

Any message box that the Mac OS or any application puts up on the screen to let you define information is a *dialog box*.

To see one example of a very simple Mac OS dialog box, go into the Apple menu and drag down to Connect to…. This brings up the dialog box shown in Figure 3.12.

Figure 3.12

The Connect to… dialog box presents a very simple interface.

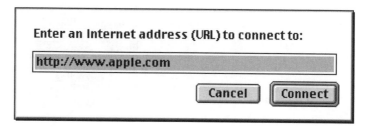

Enter an Internet address (URL) to connect to:

http://www.apple.com

Cancel   Connect

The field where you currently see the address for Apple's main World Wide Web page is a *text entry* field; that is, an area of a dialog box where the Mac OS or an application expects you to type in information.

This dialog box also has two other areas you can use to tell the Mac OS what you want it to do. Both of them are buttons, but you'll notice that the one marked "Connect" appears slightly different from the one marked "Cancel." A *default button*—indicated by a shaded double outline around the button itself—is the action that the dialog box expects most users will take. In this case, it assumes you'll want to connect to the address shown. For now, though, click the Cancel button instead (the dialog box will disappear).

TIME SAVER

> As a time-saver, any default button can be selected by simply hitting return or enter. You don't actually have to click on it if you don't want to.

Dialog Box Components

The Connect to… dialog is dramatically less complicated than most dialog boxes. The Finder's Preferences dialog shows many of the other types of items you can expect to encounter in dialog boxes (see Figure 3.13). To view it, select Edit➡Preferences from the Finder.

The area next to "Font for views:" is actually a *pop-up menu*. Like a drop-down menu, a pop-up menu offers you a series of choices from which to select, but it pops up from the current selection, rather than dropping down from a menu bar. Click the area that says "Geneva" to activate the pop-up menu (see Figure 3.14).

Figure 3.13

The Finder's Preferences dialog shows most of the types of fields you're likely to encounter in dialog boxes.

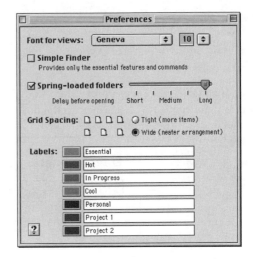

The font size field in this dialog box is a combination of two different types of dialog features. You can select the font size in two ways: selecting from a list of preset options in a pop-up menu (activated by the arrow button to the right of the number 10) or by typing a number in the *numeric entry* field if none of the presets meets your needs. If you try to type non-numeric characters into this box, a warning will appear (see Figure 3.15).

Figure 3.14

A pop-up menu in action.

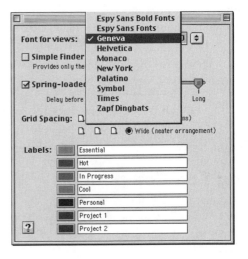

The fields for selecting or deselecting Simple Finder and Spring-loaded folders are known as *check boxes*. When a check box is activated, a check mark will appear; when it's deactivated, it will be empty. (In Figure 3.13 above, Simple Finder is turned off, while spring-loaded folders are turned on.) Generally, you can select as many check boxes as you want or need.

3

Figure 3.15

Typing letters into a numeric entry box will result in a warning like this one.

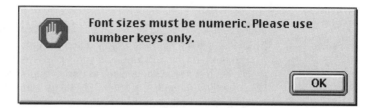

Figure 3.16

Select among a range by ragging a slider's thumb to a new location.

The Spring-loaded folders selector also features a **slider**. By dragging the ridged indicator (known as a *thumb*, just like in scroll bars), you can select among a range of choices (see Figure 3.16).

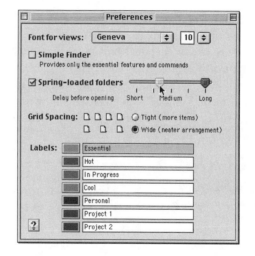

In this example, you're specifying how long the Mac OS will wait before springing a folder open, but other sliders can control percentages, time, volume, or any other criteria that can be represented as a range.

The Grid Spacing preference is set using *radio buttons*. Unlike check boxes, radio buttons always come in sets of two or more, and represent mutually-exclusive choices. In this case, you're choosing between wide spacing of documents (the currently selected choice) and tight spacing. If you click the Tight button, the Wide button becomes deactivated. (The same principle holds true if you've got three or more buttons, too, by the way.)

The Labels categories are another example of text entry fields. Pretty simple, isn't it? Of course, there are other types of fields you'll find in dialog boxes, but these are the most common. Nearly all of the elements you'll find in dialog boxes are just as intuitive as these are.

TIME SAVER

If you need to navigate around text entry boxes quickly, you don't need to click into each field separately before typing. When you finish typing in one field, hit the Tab key, and you'll pop over to the next field in series. Hit the Tab key multiple times to step through the fields. You can also hold down the Option key (Option-Tab) while performing the same task to reverse your tabbing direction.

Universal Dialog Boxes

Some universal dialog boxes perform similar functions within nearly all applications.

Alerts and *Warnings* are really just dialog boxes with limited choices that enable you to proceed with your work (sometimes "OK" is the only option). As their names imply, an Alert box lets you know that the Mac OS or your application is doing something that you need to be aware of. Warning boxes are just dialog boxes that tell you something's amiss: usually that you're tying to do something you shouldn't, or that something's gone wrong in your current environment. You can distinguish a warning from a generic alert by the red rim around the outside of its window. Often, a warning will have a more-cautionary icon in the left side of its window than a plain alert (see Figure 3.17).

Figure 3.17

Alerts and warnings are dialog boxes with limited interfaces.

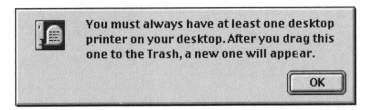

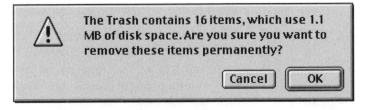

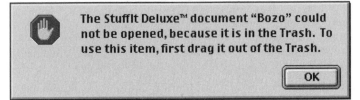

Other universal dialog boxes let you access Mac OS 8's file system from within applications. By using these Open and Save dialogs, you gain access to your hard drive and other desktop resources without having to leave your current application.

Opening Files

In most applications, selecting File➡Open (⌘-O) brings up a dialog box that enables you to open files from your hard drive, or any other volume mounted on your desktop. Although open dialog boxes differ from application to application, they all perform the same basic tasks at a minimum.

JUST A MINUTE

> In most applications, the Open dialog opens to the last used folder you used to open or save a file within the application.

3

To practice using the Open dialog, perform the following steps:

1. Launch SimpleText.
2. Select File➡Open (⌘-O) and the Open dialog box will appear (see Figure 3.18)

Figure 3.18

A basic Open dialog box.

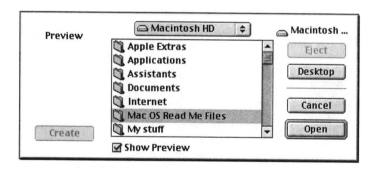

3. Scroll down the menu until you see the folder "Mac OS Read Me Files." Double-click it to show the folder's contents (Figure 3.19)

Figure 3.19

Double-clicking on Mac OS Read Me Files folder in the Open dialog shows the folder's contents.

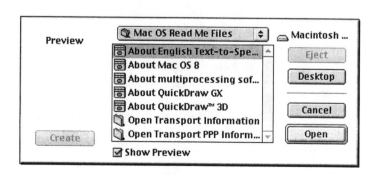

4. Double-click on the file called "About Mac OS 8." The file will open within SimpleText.

To get an idea of the other functions of the Open dialog box, perform the following steps:

1. Place a floppy disk in the floppy drive.

2. Launch SimpleText (if you don't already have it open).

3. Select File➡Open (⌘-O). The Open dialog box appears; open the folder you last used.

4. Click the current folder label, above the scroll box area. You'll notice that the label "Macintosh HD" above the scrolling window is actually a pop-up menu (see Figure 3.20).

Figure 3.20

The current folder label in the Open dialog box is actually a pop-up menu of the folder's path.

JUST A MINUTE

By clicking the current folder label pop-up menu, you see the current path—from the desktop to the hard drive through the various folders that contain the current folder (This even works if you're in a file nested within folders dozens of levels deep.) If you've accidentally double-clicked your way down into a folder and you need to get back to the last level, simply click the pop-up menu and drag down to the folder (or drive) you're interested in.

5. Release the current folder label pop-up menu and click the button marked Desktop. The view will change to show all of the current volumes (disks and drives) on the desktop, as well as any files located there (see Figure 3.21)

6. Click the name or icon of the floppy disk you inserted in your floppy drive (in this example, the floppy disk is called "My Floppy.") The Eject button will become active (undimmed). You can use this button to eject the floppy disk in the floppy drive (if you need to open a file that's on a different disk, for example).

Figure 3.21

Clicking the Desktop button shows all the disks and drives located there, as well as any files.

The Show Preview check box enables you to see a thumbnail-sized image of some sorts of files (see Figure 3.22).

Figure 3.22

Some types of files will display a thumbnail-sized preview in the Open dialog box.

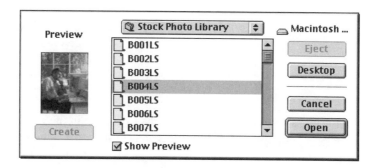

JUST A MINUTE

If a previewable file without a premade thumbnail is selected, the Create button becomes active (undimmed). Clicking this button makes a thumbnail of the document.

Saving Files

Like the Open dialog, the Save dialog opens to the folder you last used in most applications. Navigating through the Finder's file and folder hierarchy is accomplished the same way, and most of the buttons found in an Open dialog box can be found in a Save dialog box, too. Of course, since we'll be saving files with this dialog box, there are a few additional buttons (and skills) you'll need to learn.

To learn how to use the Save dialog box, perform the following steps:

1. Create a new document in SimpleText (File➡New or ⌘-N).
2. Type "This is a test" within the document.

3. From the File menu, select Save (File➡Save or ⌘-S). The Save dialog box will appear, opened to the last view you used within SimpleText (see Figure 3.23).

   (In this example, the Desktop view is shown, since our last exercise left us here; if you're not at this view, click the Desktop button).

Figure 3.23

The Save dialog opens to the last folder you used within the application.

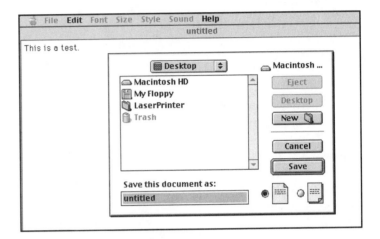

4. Double-click the name of the hard drive in the scroll area (Macintosh HD in this example). The view will change to show the contents of the hard drive.

5. Double-click the Documents folder to display its contents.

6. Name your test file Test File by typing in the text entry field (see Figure 3.24).

Figure 3.24

Name a file by typing its name into the Save dialog's text entry field.

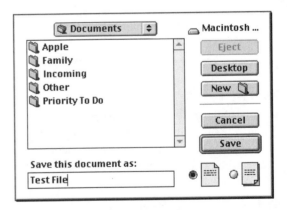

To type the new name, hit the Tab key to select "untitled" and begin typing. (You can also click the mouse in the text entry field and drag over "untitled" if you prefer.)

3

7. Press the Save button (or hit Return, since it is the default button, as indicated by its thick, shaded border). The file will be saved into the currently active folder.

8. To check your work, select File➡Open. The dialog box will open to the last active folder, displaying your file.

9. Hit Cancel to close the dialog box.

TIME SAVER

Mac OS 8 is a lot more stable than its predecessors, but you'll still want to protect yourself from losing your files when your system crashes or you lose power. The best advice we can give you (learned the hard way from what surely adds up to years of lost work between us) is: Save early, save often. You'll probably have to learn this lesson your own way once or twice before you understand its necessity, but as you work on files, get into the habit of hitting ⌘-S every time you think of it.

Now you understand how to save a file into a specific folder. From now on, every time you hit ⌘-S or select Save from the File menu, the file will be resaved into that same location without brining up the Save dialog box.

If you want to save the file into a different location, or save the file under a different name, the Save As... command enables you to do either or both.

To practice using the Save As... command, perform the following steps:

1. Open the Test File document if you've closed it.

2. From the File menu, select Save As... The Save dialog box appears.

3. Change the name of the file by adding "number 2" to the end of the text field. The document's name will now read Test File number 2.

4. Click the New button. A second dialog box will appear asking you to name the new folder.

5. Type "test folder" into the text field.

6. Click the Create button (or hit return) to create the new folder. The Save dialog's view changes to show the (empty) contents of the new folder.

7. Click the Save button (or press return) to save the renamed document into the new folder.

8. To check your work, select File➡Open. The dialog box will open to the last active folder, displaying your file.

9. Hit Cancel to close the dialog box.

10. Select File➡Quit (or ⌘-Q) to exit SimpleText.

Summary

In this hour, you've mastered the basics of navigating the Finder and applications. You've learned to copy and paste text to and from the *Clipboard*, and interpret the contents of *pull-down menus*.

You've learned how to use the *command key* to invoke *keyboard shortcuts* for menu commands, and how to deal with *dimmed* commands, *nested menus*, and *ellipses*. We've also outlined the File and Edit menus in depth, and given you a quick rundown of the other menus you'll be exploring in other hours.

In addition to basic menuing skills, you've also become familiar with the universal dialog boxes, including warnings, alerts, and the Open and Save dialog boxes within applications. You've seen examples of most types of devices you'll find in a dialog box, including *text and numeric entry fields, radio buttons, check boxes, sliders* (and their *thumbs*), *pop-up menus,* and *default buttons.*

Term Review

Command key   The cloverleaf key—located to either side of the space bar—which you use in combination with other keys to invoke keyboard shortcuts.

Default button   A button surrounded by a shaded, thick border, indicating the expected response (often "OK"). You can select this option by hitting the Return key, in lieu of clicking the button itself.

Dimmed   An unavailable menu item which will be gray, rather than black.

Ellipsis   Three consecutive dots (…) that appear on the right side of a menu item, indicating that a dialog box will appear if the time is selected.

Keyboard shortcut   Holding down the Command key (⌘) in combination with the letter shown to the right of a menu task.

Nested menu   An additional menu accessed from the right-arrow indicator of another menu.

Pop-up menu   Menus that appear when you click a button or live area in a dialog box, rather than dropping down from a menu bar.

Pull-down menu   Menus in the menu bar; you click on their title to display their options, then pull (drag) them down to select the appropriate task.

Radio button   A dialog box device that enables you to select from among a series of mutually-exclusive choices.

Thumb   The draggable button on a slider (or scroll bar).

3

Q&A

Q **Why are some of my menu items grayed out?**

A Menu commands become *dimmed* when they're not available for use with your current selection. Usually it's because they're not appropriate actions to take on that particular type of icon.

Q **What do those three dots after menu items mean?**

A They're know as *ellipses* and they indicate that the command has more to it than can fit in a menu. When you select a command with an ellipsis after it, a dialog box will appear that lets you complete your work.

Q **What does the cloverleaf symbol (⌘) mean?**

A It's the symbol for the *Command key*, the key to either side of your space bar that's used to invoke keyboard shortcuts.

Q **Sometimes the files listed in my Open and Save dialog boxes don't match up with what I see when I view my hard drive from the Finder. What gives?**

A Within some applications, the Open dialog box may contain *invisible files*, files used by the Mac OS's internal functions (like moving and renaming files, or creating temporary folders for files being modified). Typically they're hidden by Mac OS 8 to avoid confusing you, but some applications unhide them. Most applications only show their own files (or files that they can access) in their Open dialog boxes. Some have a check box in the Open dialog box that enables you to show all items—even unopenable files—so look for this option if you find the hidden files confusing.

3

Hour 4

The Finder's Menu Bar

In this hour, we'll continue our exploration of the desktop. Specifically, we'll learn to make use of the light gray bar at the top of your screen, known as the *menu bar*.

Of course, you've already used Mac OS 8's menu bar a few times in earlier hours, to perform tasks like viewing control panels and creating new folders. Even back in Hour 1, you used the Special menu to turn off your computer.

The menu bar is the home of many of Mac OS 8's basic features, and the jumping-off point for many others. By the time you've completed this hour, you'll have mastered the basics of navigating the Finder's menus. The menu bar is the light gray strip located at the top of the desktop that displays the titles of Mac OS 8's various menus. But the menu bar isn't just visible when you're looking at the desktop; it's a component of Mac OS 8 that appears within each of your applications as well.

The highlights of this hour include:

- ☐ The tasks you can perform using each of the menus in the menu bar
- ☐ How to use the File menu to open, close, and find files and applications, and to create new folders

☐ How to access a file's Info window

☐ Where to find menu commands for Mac OS 8's copying and pasting features

☐ How to use the Undo command, Mac OS 8's most popular safety net

☐ How to use the Application menu to switch between active programs

Components of the Menu Bar

Although we've spent a fair amount of time playing with the File menu, we've just started learning about all of the menu bar's capabilities. This section will detail the other menus that appear in the menu bar.

Apple Menu

The Apple menu—the menu under the multicolored Apple logo to the far left side of the menu bar—gives you access to many of the utility functions of Mac OS 8, including setting up and selecting your printer, accessing recently used applications and files, and modifying the various control panels that enable you to change the settings of your computer. The Apple menu is so chock full of functionality that we've given it its own chapter, Hour 6. (If you're really curious, or have your heart set on learning the menus in order, feel free to skip ahead. If you stay here with us, though, you'll learn a lot more about menus that will help you understand the Apple menu better once we get to it.)

File Menu

Although it may seem that we've spent a lot of time with the File menu, we've barely scratched the surface of its capabilities.

As we learned before, some menu choices are universal; there's always a "New" command of one form or another in the File menu, and some are dependent upon the sorts of items you're working with. The File menu (and to some extent its next-door neighbor, the Edit menu) is ever-present, more so than other menus in the menu bar.

When you open an application, you'll always see a File menu. Its capabilities and active items will change, sometimes drastically, but it will always be right there next to the Apple menu. (Most applications also have an Edit menu, but we'll cover that in the next section.)

To see how the File menu remains constant, perform the following steps:

1. Double-click the hard drive icon to open its window.

2. Double-click the Applications folder to open its window.

3. Double-click the SimpleText application's icon to launch it.

4

TIME SAVER

To launch SimpleText without double-clicking, you can also drag down the File menu to "Open."

Remember keyboard shortcuts? You can also press ⌘-O to open an application when its icon is selected.

4. SimpleText opens to a new, untitled document (Figure 4.1). Notice how the File and Edit menus appear in the same location as they do in the Finder.

Figure 4.1

Within an application, you'll always see the File menu (and usually the Edit menu, too) just as you do in the Finder.

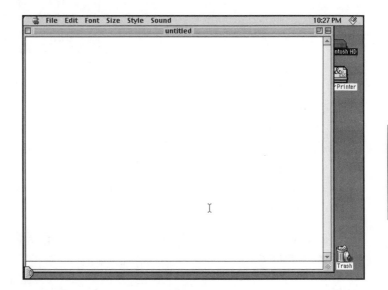

5. Click the File menu. Notice that although the specific items are different, the same basic sorts of options (open, close, and so on) are available here as within the Finder (see Figure 4.2).

JUST A MINUTE

Nearly all applications offer similar menu items in the File menu: Open, Close, Print, Quit, and so on. Even the keyboard shortcuts are usually the same: ⌘-O, ⌘-W, ⌘-P, ⌘-Q. Note that all of these options are tasks that you'd typically perform on files, hence the menu name.

Although we'll cover more details of the File menu later in this hour, here's a hands-on exercise that will teach you a few of the more important commands in the File menu.

Figure 4.2

Within an application, the File menu's options change, but the basic functions remain similar.

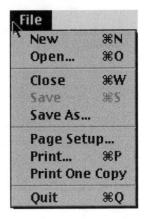

To learn some important File menu tasks, perform the following steps:

1. Create a new folder (using File➡New Folder).
2. Click the new untitled folder and type "Find Me" to rename it.
3. Drag the renamed folder over the hard drive icon and release it. (It will seem to disappear when it's moved inside the hard drive.)
4. Drag down the File menu to the "Find…" command (File➡Find…). The Find File dialog box will appear (see Figure 4.3).

Figure 4.3

Selecting File➡Find… brings up the Find File dialog box.

5. In the dialog box's text field, type Find Me.
6. Press the Find button. A second window will appear that shows your folder. The bottom half of the window shows the path you need to take to reach it; in this case, the folder Find Me is inside the hard drive Macintosh HD (see Figure 4.4).

There are other options of the File menu you can reach from within the finder. *Print Desktop* (available with no items selected) enables you to send an image of your desktop—with or without windows open—to your printer, if you have one available. If you have an active window, the same menu item (now called "*Print Window*") will send a picture of that folder to your printer.

Figure 4.4

A second window appears, showing the location of your "lost" folder.

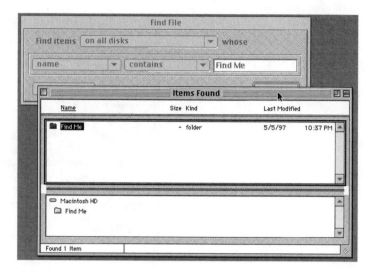

Page Setup also relates to your printer and enables you to specify various settings to be used when files are printed.

Move to Trash does just what you'd expect: if you have an icon selected (except the Trash or hard drive), the Mac OS will automatically move it to the Trash.

Get Info is a useful feature that enables you to view some of the important attributes of your files. To check out Get Info, perform the following steps:

1. Click your hard drive icon to select it.
2. Select File➡Get Info.... A window appears showing you pertinent information regarding your hard drive (see Figure 4.5).

> Try doing the same thing using ⌘-I.

TIME SAVER

As you can see, you can view all sorts of useful information here. The info window for a file, or an application, is slightly different. (If you like, try using Get Info on a few different sorts of files to get an idea of their differences.)

> You can enter any remarks you like in the Comments box, including serial numbers for applications, revision histories for documents, and so on.

JUST A MINUTE

Figure 4.5

*Get Info displays details
about the files you select;
in this example it's the
hard drive.*

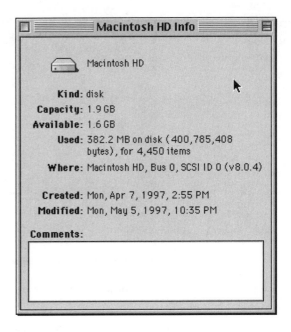

Label enables you to assign a color tag to your files to help you keep track of their purpose
or their origin.

Sharing is the menu item that lets you define who can access your files and folders over a
network. We'll talk about File Sharing in depth in Hour 14.

As mentioned before, *Duplicate* enables you to make a replica of a file (or folder). If you want
to make changes to a file, but you also need to keep a copy of the unedited version, you can
duplicate the file, rename the copy, and work as you normally would.

Make Alias lets you make a shortcut to files or applications that you use frequently, to keep
on your desktop or another easily accessible location. *Show Original* (which is always dimmed
unless you have an alias selected) is also a function of the alias feature of Mac OS 8.

Put Away lets you return a file to its original home if you've moved it onto the desktop
temporarily. It's only active if you've selected a file that's been moved to the desktop.

If you have a file selected (rather than a folder or an application), you'll also see a *Print*
command in the File menu. This command will automatically launch the application that
created the document (if you have it installed on your hard drive) and enable you to print one
or more copies of the file, and then quit the application automatically. We'll talk more about
printing from the desktop in Hour 13.

4

Edit Menu

Much like the File menu, the Edit menu is available within virtually every Macintosh application. Its basic menu choices—Undo, Cut, Copy, Paste, Select all—remain nearly unchanged in every application (although some programs add their own special Edit commands as well as these).

TIME SAVER

Nearly all Macintosh applications use the Finder's keyboard shortcuts for the Edit menu. Unlike the File menu, though, most Edit commands' shortcuts aren't the first letter of the command (⌘-C and ⌘-P for Copy and Paste being the exceptions). Since they're nearly universal, you'll end up remembering them fairly quickly, even without the mnemonics to jog your memory.

The Clipboard

The Edit command—and its keyboard shortcuts—are your interface to Mac OS 8's *Clipboard* feature, the part of the operating system that lets you copy and paste text and graphics from one location to another. Like a layout artist's pasteboard, the Clipboard is a temporary holding place for words, pictures, numbers, or any other piece of a document you want to move from one location to another. (Notice we said "temporary;" when you cut or copy an item to the Clipboard, it only remains there until you cut or copy something else, or exit the current application. If you need more permanent Clipboard-type space, you can use the Scrapbook, a Mac OS 8 feature which we'll discuss in Hour 5.)

Since nearly every Macintosh program has an edit menu, you can also use the Clipboard to move text (or graphics, or... well, you get the point) from one program to another.

JUST A MINUTE

Unless you have a file selected (or you're inside an application), only Select All and Show Clipboard are visible; the rest of the Edit menu's commands are dimmed.

Undo

Undo is the first item in the Edit menu, even though it has little to do with the Clipboard per se. Many Macintosh users feel that the Undo command is the best part of the Mac OS, and we'd be hard pressed to argue otherwise.

To get an idea of the usefulness of Undo, perform the following steps:

1. On the desktop, click the hard drive icon.
2. Hit return to make its name active.

3. Type "New Name" (or any other phrase that you like) to rename the hard drive. (Don't click on the desktop or otherwise deselect the hard drive at this point.)

JUST A MINUTE

If you aren't able to rename your hard drive, it's probably because you have File Sharing turned on. We'll cover this topic more in Hour 14, but for now, you can complete the exercise using any folder or file.

4. From the Edit menu, drag down to Undo (Edit➠Undo). The hard drive's name will change back to its original name.

5. If you select Undo again (or use its keyboard shortcut, ⌘-Z) the name will change back to New Name. You can keep changing back and forth in this manner, as long as you don't deselect the hard drive.

Undo works in the same way within an application. If you've accidentally deleted a key paragraph of text (something that we book authors never do, of course), you can usually use ⌘-Z to get it back, as long as you haven't copied anything else to the Clipboard.

CAUTION

Although Undo can be a lifesaver, never count on it saving your neck. Undo doesn't work with many key Finder-related tasks (like creating new folders or emptying the Trash), and most applications only let you Undo the last task you've completed. If you happen to delete that precious paragraph and then scroll down to begin working elsewhere, chances are the even the mighty Undo can't rescue you from yourself.

Despite its limitations, once you get used to using Undo, you'll come to depend on it; it's very addictive. You'll start wishing that every device you use had a similar feature (your sewing machine, your drill, your oven).

Cut

As its name implies, the Cut command removes any selected item. But unlike truly deleting an object, Cut enables you to place the removed item on the Clipboard for future use.

To use the Cut command, perform the following steps:

1. On the desktop, create a new folder (⌘-N).

2. Rename it "A folder called Fred."

3. Using the cursor, select the words "A folder called" in the icon's title (see Figure 4.6).

Figure 4.6
*Only part of the icon's
name is selected.*

4. In the Edit menu, select Cut (Edit➡Cut). The folder's name changes to simply "Fred."

5. Use the Undo command to change the folder's name back to the long version.

Copy and Paste

Cutting is useful, but you'll probably spend more time copying and pasting information.

The Copy command makes a copy of selected information and places it on the Clipboard. (Unlike Cut, Copy doesn't remove the item from the original.) The Paste command enables you to place cut or copied information from the Clipboard into a new location.

To practice using the Copy and Paste commands, perform the following steps:

1. Create a new folder on the desktop.
2. Select the words "A folder" from the folder we used in the last hands-on exercise.
3. From the Edit menu, drag down to "Copy" (Edit➡Copy).
4. Create a new folder. (Do not click onto the desktop or otherwise deselect the new untitled folder; its title will remain highlighted).
5. From the Edit menu, drag down to "Paste" (Edit➡Paste). The new folder's name will change to "A folder."

Don't forget that you can use the keyboard shortcuts ⌘-C and ⌘-P for Copy and Paste. You'll probably use these commands more than any others—except, perhaps, ⌘-Z—so it pays to memorize them.

Clear

The Clear command doesn't relate to the Clipboard at all. It's merely a stripped-down version of Cut that removes information without placing it on the Clipboard.

Select All

The Select All command is useful for selecting large groups of items without clicking each one individually (it doesn't relate to the Clipboard either, for what it's worth).

From the desktop, Select All will make all its icons active. If you're within a window, all of its folders (or other icons) will be made active.

Show Clipboard

The Show Clipboard command shows you the last thing you cut or copied. To view your clipboard's contents, perform the following steps:

1. From the Edit menu, select Show Clipboard (Edit➡Clipboard). A window appears showing the last item copied or cut to the Clipboard (see Figure 4.7).

Figure 4.7

Show Clipboard displays the last information copied or cut to the Clipboard.

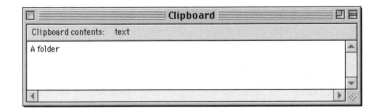

2. With the Clipboard window open, reselect the folder called "A Folder Called Fred."

3. Copy the folder's name to the Clipboard. "A Folder Called Fred" appears in the Clipboard window (see Figure 4.8).

Figure 4.8

The Clipboard window's contents change when new information is copied to the Clipboard.

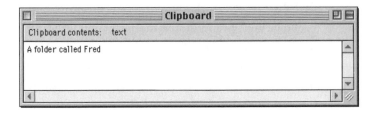

If you're wondering about the Edit menu's last command, Finder Preferences, we'll cover it in Hour 17.

JUST A MINUTE

Application Menu

The Application menu—indicated by the miniature Macintosh icon in the far right corner of the menu bar—enables you to switch between the Finder and any active applications you may be running (see Figure 4.9).

4

Figure 4.9

The Application menu shows active applications and enables you to switch between them.

By selecting any active program in the Application menu, it's automatically brought to the front and made the active window. You can also hide the current application (or all programs *except* the current application) using this menu.

JUST A MINUTE

When you view the Application menu from within an application, its menu bar icon changes to that of the program you're currently using (see Figure 4.10).

Figure 4.10

The Application menu's icon changes to the icon of the currently active application.

Other Menus

Of course, there are other menus in the menu bar that we haven't covered. Here's an overview:

View Menu

The View menu enables you to customize the appearance of your windows and the Finder. We'll discuss this more in Hour 17 "Customizing the Finder and Software" and Hour 8 "Your Filing System."

Special Menu

The Special menu is the home of many Mac OS 8 housekeeping tasks, like shutting down and restarting, and emptying the Trash (as you learned in Hours 1 and 2, respectively.)

If you have a floppy disk mounted on the desktop and selected, the Eject and Erase Disk options will appear. We'll discuss these features in Hour 5.

The Sleep command is a way to save most of your computer's power usage without actually turning it off. If you'll be leaving your system unused for a period of time, you can select the Sleep option. When you return, press any key on the keyboard, and you Macintosh will "reawaken" ready for use in the same state it was in when you put it to sleep. This option originated—and is most useful—on PowerBook portable computers, but it works on most Power Macintosh models as well.

Help Menu

The Help menu offers access to the built-in help system of Mac OS 8. It's also active within all applications and frequently lets you reach their individual help functions. We'll discuss this menu in more detail in Hour 9.

Summary

In this hour, we taught you to use the *menu bar* and its various menus to perform a variety of Mac OS tasks. We've outlined the various tasks each of the menus performs and gone into detail about the File, Edit, and Applications menus' features. You're now proficient at using the *Clipboard* for copying and pasting information from one location to another, and in using the *Undo* command to back your work up one step. Furthermore, we covered using the *Application menu* to switch between active programs and to hide programs temporarily.

Term Review

Application menu   The menu on the far right of the menu bar (indicated by a tiny Macintosh icon in the Finder, and an application's icon when a program is active) that enables you to switch between or hide active applications and the Finder.

Clipboard   Mac OS 8's facility for copying and pasting text and graphics from one location to another; a temporary holding place for any copied or cut piece of a document.

Menu bar   The light gray bar at the top of the Macintosh screen where the Finder's menu resides.

Undo   A menu command ($\mathcal{H}$-Z) that enables you to undo the last action taken within an application or the Finder.

4

Q&A

Q You mention the Application menu, but there's no "Application" on my menu bar. Why can't I find the Application menu?

A You won't find any menu titled "Application" in the menu bar. The Application menu is represented by the tiny Macintosh icon in the right corner of the menu bar. Its appearance changes within applications, where it takes on the icon of the currently running program.

Q I tried using Undo ($\mathcal{H}$-Z) to fix a mistake, but nothing happened. Why?

A Undo doesn't work with some Finder tasks (like creating a new folder or emptying the Trash) and applications typically let you Undo only your last task.

4

Hour 5

Floppy Disks and Hard Drives

You should already know a bit about floppy disks and hard drives because we talked about their icons in Hour 2, "The Desktop." There's much more to these storage devices than just their icons, though, and in this hour, you'll learn all the fundamentals of managing them. Floppy disks and hard drives—in fact, any storage device—are relatively simple things in terms of what they do: they store information. Say you take notes of a class or a meeting on a sheet of paper. You can either transcribe those notes into a file that you store on your hard drive, or you can take the sheet of paper and put it into a filing cabinet. Think of your hard drive as a large filing cabinet. How you keep it organized is up to you, but we'll deal with that in Hour 8, "Your Filing System."

Floppy disks can be a convenient way of carrying files back and forth from school or the office, but they aren't ready to accept data right out of the box. We'll teach you how to properly prepare them.

Getting to know your hard drive may seem a little more complicated because there's so much more stored there. We'll show you how to determine how much space your hard drive has.

Finally, we'll also talk about how you can add additional hard drives and other storage devices to your Macintosh to increase both your capacity and your flexibility in storing data.

The highlights of this hour include:

☐ How to prepare your floppy disks so you can save files on them

☐ How to get floppy disks out of their drive

☐ How to find out how much space your files take up on your hard drive

☐ How the Macintosh makes it easy to add extra storage space

Floppy Disks

The first step to take with a floppy disk is to prepare it to store data. This involves a process called *initializing*, which prepares the floppy to accept data, and *formatting*, which essentially lays out a pattern for storing the data. Anything that stores data, whether tape or hard drive or floppy, must go through this process to work. The hard drive inside your Macintosh was formatted at the factory, and you can buy floppy disks already formatted. However, it's important to know how to do it.

Erasing a Floppy Disk

There isn't a command in Mac OS 8 to initialize a floppy disk, nor is there a command to format one. The only command option you have is to erase the disk. Now, you may rightfully ask yourself, how can I erase a disk that doesn't have anything on it? That's kind of an oxymoron, like jumbo shrimp or rush hour, isn't it? You'll get no argument from us. The fact of the matter is, the Macintosh is smart enough to know when you put the floppy disk in whether it needs to be initialized, formatted, or if it is ready to roll. All you have to do is follow these steps:

1. Insert the floppy disk into the floppy drive. Its icon will appear on your desktop.

2. Go to the menu bar and click on Special➡Erase Disk.

3. A dialog box will ask if you want to completely erase the disk (see Figure 5.1).

Figure 5.1

The dialog box for erasing a floppy disk.

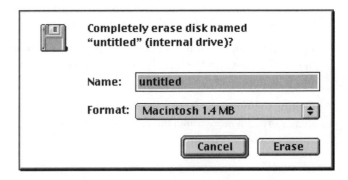

5

4. Click on the disclosure triangle to see your other options. Note that you have the option to name the disk and an option for the disk's formatting at 1.4 MB—either for Macintosh or DOS or ProDOS. Because the Macintosh comes with a software utility for reading floppy disks that have been created on PCs, you can format the disk to be immediately readable on a PC. For now, leave this setting on Macintosh 1.4 MB.

5. Click on Erase. You'll hear a steady tapping and see a dialog box reading "Erasing disk."

JUST A MINUTE
You can use floppy disks from PCs on Macintosh systems, but you can't use floppy disks from Macintoshes on PCs without a special additional piece of software. We'll discuss these and other Windows compatibility issues in Hour 22, "Compatibility with DOS and Windows".

After the floppy disk has been fully formatted, double-click on its icon to open its window. You'll see that it's empty because its status bar will read "0 items, 1.3 MB available" (see Figure 5.2). At this point you say, "Hey, wait, you said it would be 1.4 MB. Where's my other one-tenth of a megabyte?" As Sydney Greenstreet said in Casablanca, "Carrying charges, my boy, carrying charges." It's true. After a disk has been formatted, it steals a little bit of space to keep track of that formatting information. The same goes for every other storage device.

Figure 5.2

After the floppy is formatted, it only has 1.3 MB of space available.

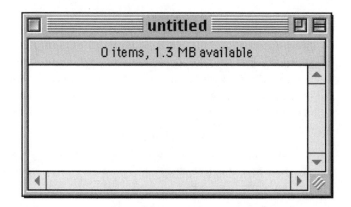

JUST A MINUTE
If you have a floppy disk full of information you no longer need, you can go through this same process to remove the files. Of course, you could also open up the floppy disk's window, highlight everything, and drag it to the Trash, but using the Erase Disk command is faster and easier.

Naming a Floppy Disk

You can rename a floppy disk icon the same way you rename a hard drive icon or an application icon, as we discussed in Hour 2. To rename a floppy disk, perform the following steps:

1. Click on the floppy disk's name.

2. When the border turns white, start typing. (If you only want to change part of the name, just click on the name and highlight the part you want to rename.)

JUST A MINUTE

Your limit for floppy disk names is 28 characters, unlike Macintosh files, which have a naming limit of 31 characters. This pretty much handles most words you'd want to use to name a disk (see Figure 5.3).

Figure 5.3

You can fit some pretty long names in 28 characters.

Sir Arthur Conan Doyle

Ejecting a Floppy Disk

Like most actions on the Macintosh, you have the choice of several ways to accomplish the same thing. Ejecting a floppy is no exception. It's one of the few procedures we know of that gives you not one, not two, but *four* different options. We'll show you all four with these steps (just remember to reinsert the floppy after each one). To eject a floppy disk, perform the following steps:

1. Remember learning about the Trash icon in Hour 2? Besides using it to throw away files, you can also use it to eject your floppy disk. Highlight your floppy drive icon and drag it to the trash. The drive will automatically eject your floppy (the same process works for CD-ROMs).

2. Press ⌘-E on your keyboard. The same thing will happen.

3. Now before you reinsert the floppy disk, go back to the menu bar and click on Special. Notice that the command for Eject is dimmed. As we mentioned in Hour 1, that's the Macintosh's way of telling you an action is no longer an option. Insert the floppy and highlight it. Now complete the process, clicking on Special➡Eject.

4. Insert the floppy again and make sure it's highlighted. Press ⌘-Y on your keyboard. The drive will eject your floppy.

5

JUST A MINUTE

If all else fails, there is one other way to eject a disk, but we only recommend it as a last resort. See the small hole just under and to the right of the floppy drive? If you straighten a paper clip and insert it into this hole, the floppy disk will eject.

TIME SAVER

⌘-Y is the command for the process of unmounting a drive that you're accessing across a network, but it will also work with a floppy disk; you'll learn more about this in Hour 12, "Networking."

Saving to a Floppy Disk

Storing a file on a floppy disk is a simple process. Follow these steps:

1. Double-click on your hard drive to open it.
2. Find the folder named "About the Mac OS" and click on its disclosure triangle.
3. In that folder is a file named "Read Me." Click on this file, keeping the mouse button down, and drag it to your Floppy Disk icon. A dialog box will appear, with an estimate of how long the copying process will take (see Figure 5.3A).

Figure 5.3A

The copy-process dialog box.

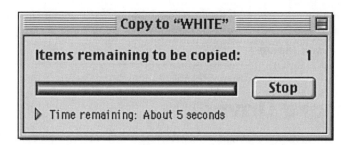

5

JUST A MINUTE

If you try to copy a file that's larger than the floppy's capacity, you'll get an error message telling you there isn't enough room (see Figure 5.3B).

Figure 5.3B

If the file you're copying is bigger than the floppy, you'll get an error message.

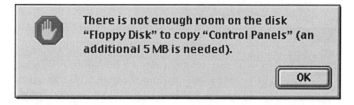

Dealing with a Zip Drive

If you've bought a Macintosh very recently, it's possible that it has what's known as a Zip drive already built-in. Built by Iomega Corp. (www.iomega.com), these drives use cartridges that hold 100 MB (megabytes) of data. The cartridge is not much bigger than a floppy, but it is about twice as thick (see Figure 5.4). Although they hold 100 times more data, they cost more, too—about $20 each, versus less than a dollar for a floppy disk. If you want to take a lot of graphics to work or school on one storage medium, though, they come in handy. (You can also buy external Zip drives, as well as other removable storage devices to plug into the back of your Macintosh.)

Figure 5.4

The Zip cartridge is not much bigger than a floppy disk; it is just a little bit thicker, but holds about 100 times more data.

JUST A MINUTE

If your Macintosh has a Zip drive, the Zip cartridge's icon will appear on your desktop after you insert it into the drive, the same way a floppy disk icon will.

Hard Drives

National Geographic once showed Microsoft founder Bill Gates sitting on a remarkably high stack of papers. He was holding a CD-ROM to emphasize the point that it could hold as much information as the stack of papers he was sitting on (he was held in place by a crane and harness, if you're wondering). But a CD-ROM only holds 640 MB of data. A 2 GB (gigabyte) hard drive holds three times that much data and can deliver it to you much, much faster. That's pretty good for a piece of hardware roughly the same size as a carton of frozen vegetables.

JUST A MINUTE

A megabyte roughly equals 1,000,000 bytes. A gigabyte equals roughly a thousand times that—1,000,000,000 bytes. A byte equals one character, and there are approximately 300 characters on a page of typed text. This means that in a 1 GB hard drive, you could store 33,000 pages of text.

Checking Your Hard Drive's Capacity

It's always a good idea to know how much space is on your hard drive. You may want to install a software application that takes up 78 MB. You may laugh, but that's exactly how many a fully installed version of Microsoft Office for Mac takes up on a hard drive.

To check the capacity of your hard drive, perform the following steps:

1. Highlight the hard drive icon.
2. In the menu Bar, click on File➡Get Info (or press ⌘-I).
3. The resulting dialog box shows you all the details you need to know about your hard drive (see Figure 5.5). Notice that it will tell you not only how big your drive is, but how much space you have left and how much you're using. It'll also show the last time the hard drive was modified.

Figure 5.5

By asking for information about your hard drive, you can see how much capacity you're using and what's still available.

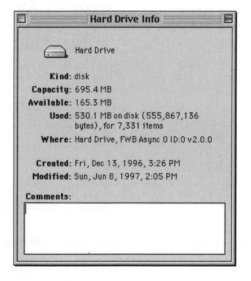

Adding External Hard Drives

At this moment, please stop what you're doing and say a quiet, reverent thank you to whomever originally insisted that Macintosh systems incorporate a technology called SCSI (which is pronounced "scuzzy" and stands for Small Computer Systems Interface) to attach peripherals like external storage drives and scanners. Why is this important? Because if you want to add an external hard drive, all you have to do is turn off your Macintosh, plug one end of a SCSI cable into the hard drive, and the other into the back of the Macintosh, and turn your machine back on. You're done. The Macintosh will automatically recognize that something new has been plugged in, and its icon will appear on your desktop.

Because SCSI is not built into most PCs, you have to add it. This involves buying an add-in card, opening up the case, installing the card, and then installing software to make sure the SCSI card and all the attached peripherals are recognized by the PC's operating system. It's a long involved process, so just be glad you bought a Macintosh.

To initialize the new drive, perform the following steps:

1. Click on your hard drive icon. Find the folder named "Utilities" and double-click on the application called "Drive Setup."

2. Double-click on Drive Setup. A dialog box will appear showing you your storage devices (see Figure 5.6).

Figure 5.6

The Drive Setup dialog box shows which devices are attached to your Macintosh.

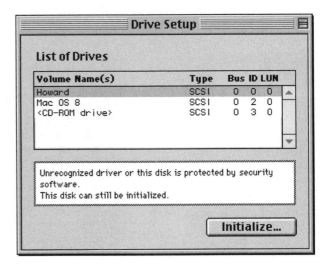

3. Highlight the external hard drive, and then click on Initialize.

JUST A MINUTE

If your Macintosh has what's known as a *tower* configuration—which means it's more vertical than horizontal, you already have room to add more hard drives. These machines have empty spaces called *bays* where you can add more capacity.

Partitioning a Hard Drive

When you format a Macintosh hard drive, the most capacity you can get out of it is 4 GB (if your Macintosh is new, the capacity of its hard drive will probably be between 1 and 4GB). This didn't used to be a big problem, because until 1997 there weren't any drives bigger than

4 GB. However, the more space the drive has to cover to retrieve information, the slower it can be. If you split a drive up into smaller areas, called partitions, you can speed up response time. Each of these partitions would have their own name.

CAUTION

> Partitioning is a rather complicated process. It's possible to partition the hard drive in your computer, but we don't recommend it for beginners.

Changing the Startup Disk

After you've added an external drive, you may want to start up your computer from that external drive, depending on the operating system or files you want to use. Changing your startup drive is fairly easy (provided you've named your drives something easily recognizable) by following these steps:

1. Click on the Apple Menu➡Control Panels➡Startup Disk.

2. In the window that appears you'll see your hard drives and the external hard drive you've added (see Figure 5.7). If you've given them particularly long names, the names will be truncated with an ellipsis.

Figure 5.7

Your choice of startup drives.

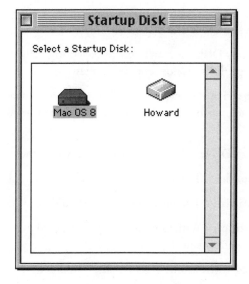

3. Click on the drive or partition you want your Macintosh to start up from and close the window. The next time you start your computer, it will use that newly designated drive.

4. If you want to restart immediately using the newly designated drive, go to the menu bar, click on Special➡Restart. You're on your way. (To change it back, simply reverse the process.)

CAUTION

> Don't forget—you must have a version of Mac OS on any drive you're going to use as a startup disk.

Summary

We began this hour talking about simple floppy disks and hard drive capacity, but we rapidly continued onto more complicated topics—adding external drives and partitioning them, for instance. You'll use this information even if you buy something as simple as an Iomega Zip drive on which to store or backup data.

Because the Macintosh has a SCSI port built-in, you can easily add external hard drives or other devices like CD-ROMs. That'll come in handy later if you outgrow your hard drive and want to add a new one.

Term Review

Floppy Disk   A small storage device originally flexible enough to bend—hence its name— floppy disks are now encased in plastic.

Zip Drive   A new storage drive from Iomega available internally on some Macintoshes and clones, capable of holding 100 MB of data on a single cartridge (available in external versions too).

Hard Drive   The primary location where the computer stores files.

Capacity   The amount of space, measured in megabytes or gigabytes, of a storage device.

Initialize   The process of preparing a disk to accept data.

Partition   A method used to divide a hard drive into smaller sections for better reliability and performance.

SCSI   The acronym for Small Computer Systems Interface (pronounced "scuzzy"), which lets you attach external devices such as hard drives to your Macintosh.

5

Q&A

Q How much hard drive capacity do I need?

A It depends on what you're using your Macintosh for. If you're almost exclusively using it for word processing, you can get by easily with a 2 GB hard drive (if you've bought your Macintosh recently, that's probably the smallest one it'll have). If you're doing a lot of graphics work, however, or downloading sound files or movies on a regular basis, you'll need at least a 4 GB drive. You'll also want to think about removable storage as well.

Q Are floppy disks going to become obsolete?

A If the files we use every day grow beyond the capacity of the floppy disk, yes, it will become obsolete. We don't see that happening any time soon though. Floppy disks are too portable and, for the most part, reliable to disappear. It's still the only way to get information easily between a Macintosh and a PC. If the floppy disk is superseded, the Zip drive is its likely successor.

Q I haven't installed any applications on my hard drive, but it's already one-third full. How did that happen?

A Your Macintosh probably came with a bunch of software already loaded on it, only some of which will have any value to you. Some of what's preloaded, though, you may enjoy. We would recommend that, about six months after you've bought your Macintosh, you open up your Finder, take a good look at the preinstalled software on your hard drive, and delete what you haven't used.

5

Hour 6

The Apple Menu

In Hour 6, we're going to go deeper into the workings of the Macintosh. You'll learn about attributes of the computer; some of them you'll adjust once and never look at again, while you'll use others on a daily basis. Either way, you need to know where they are because they contain vital information that we guarantee will come in handy.

You may be looking at the desktop and thinking, gee, this interface looks so simple. How can there be more? That's the beauty of a *graphical user interface*. It hides what you don't need on a regular basis, but makes it easy to find. Wouldn't it be great if closets worked this way?

Specifically, we're going to take you through the Apple Menu. It's easy to find— it's the Apple logo at the left side of the menu bar. You've probably already clicked on it a couple of times and discovered that under the Apple menu is a veritable encyclopedia of information about your Macintosh. Some of it's already there now, because it was installed by Mac OS 8; more will be added as you load applications.

Almost everything you need to know about your computer can be found under the Apple Menu. There are 22 items listed under the Apple Menu in Mac OS 8. The number will grow as you modify your system.

Important Stuff

The Apple Menu holds important information about your computer's components. You'll have to know some of this information when you go to buy additional components or software for your Macintosh. In addition, the Apple Menu has options that will simplify your work. We go through these one by one.

About This Computer

When you're shopping for software, you'll have to know how much memory your Macintosh has and how much disk space you have left. To check this, perform the following steps.

1. Click on the desktop to make the Finder active.

2. Click on the Apple Menu➥About This Computer (see Figure 6.1). As you can see here, this Macintosh has 40 MB of RAM (random access memory, or built-in memory) and 41.4 MB of virtual memory (we'll talk more about virtual memory in Hour 19, "Memory"). The Mac OS is using 7.5 MB, while SimpleText is using just 528 K (where K stands for kilobytes, which is roughly 1,000 bytes).

Figure 6.1

About This Computer shows you how much space the operating system and your applications take up in RAM.

JUST A MINUTE

Remember how we said that once you learn one part of the Macintosh, that most others behave exactly the same way? This is a great example of that: you'll find an About... choice under the Apple Menu for every piece of software you own. When that application is active, just click on the Apple Menu and scroll down to that line.

Apple System Profiler

Just as About This Computer provides information about your system's configuration, the Apple System Profiler provides more information about your hardware. This is also important to know when you go to add equipment to your computer. Some of it is repetitive, but it's better to have information in two locations than not at all. Unfortunately, it means you have to remember to check both places.

Click on the Apple Menu➡Apple System Profiler (see Figure 6.2). As you can see, it repeats the memory information, but it also reveals the kind of processor you have and its speed, what your startup device is, and its SCSI address. Remember we learned about startup disks in Hour 4 (we'll talk more about SCSI addresses in Hour 24). If you have to call Apple or another company for technical support, the technician may ask you to recite what's in this window. That's why it's important to know where it is.

Figure 6.2

The Apple System Profiler reveals important hardware information.

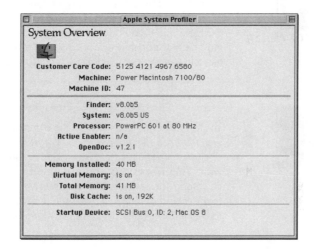

Control Panels

Control panels are aptly named because they *control* specific attributes of your Macintosh—some 52 of them! With them, you can control not only peripherals and software applications, but the appearance of your Macintosh. They're vitally important, so we wanted to call your attention to them here, but we focus on them in depth in Hour 7, "The System Folder."

Chooser

The Chooser is where you *choose* the printer, modem, or network that you want to access (see Figure 6.3). You'll probably only use the Chooser on a regular basis when you're in an office with lots of different printers, a network, or shared modems. If you only have one printer attached to your Macintosh, you can keep its icon on your desktop and not worry about the Chooser. We'll talk more about the Chooser in Hour 12, "Networking."

6

Figure 6.3

Use the Chooser to access networks, printers, and modems.

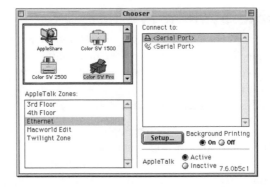

JUST A MINUTE

What you see when you navigate the Chooser will depend entirely on what you have connected to your Macintosh. We've chosen a very simple example, but if you're on a network, you'll have a lot more choices and it may be more confusing. Of course, the bigger the network you're on, the more likely it is that you'll have technical support handy!

CAUTION

The Chooser has been part of the Macintosh almost since the computer was invented. It's not our favorite part of the Macintosh, because it's kind of clunky. It requires an awful lot of clicking and selecting to get what you want. And when *Macworld* conducted usability tests with people who used PCs and Macintoshes, neither group was wild about the Chooser. All that's a kind of long-winded way of saying that if you too find the Chooser to be kind of clunky... you're not alone.

Cool Tools

Not everything under the Apple Menu gives you information or access to other technology. Some of the options are applications that can be real time savers, or make you more productive, or even let you have some fun. Let's look at some of our favorites.

Find File

Remember what we said about closets before—how it would be great if they revealed their hidden contents like the Macintosh does? Well, the time is probably going to come when you store a file on the Macintosh and you just can't find it. Never fear, that's why there's the Find File application—sort of a tracer of lost files. To learn more, follow these simple steps.

1. Before you start, create a file whose title is your first name. Store it anywhere on your hard drive.

2. Click on the Apple Menu➡Find File.

3. In the dialog box that appears, click on the triangle to the right of "on local disks." This gives you the choice of searching on all the disks on the network, all the disks connected to your Macintosh, all the files on your desktop, or just the files in your Macintosh's hard drive.

4. Click on the triangle to the right of "name." This gives you the choices of searching the files attributes.

5. Click on the triangle to the right of "contains." This gives you some Boolean search choices, which let you narrow the search criteria.

6. In the dialog box that comes up, type your name.

7. Now click on More Choices—nine times (see Figure 6.4) to limit your choices by size, kind (alias, extension, control panel, etc.), label (for example, color), date modified or created, version, comments, locked, or folder attribute (empty, shared, mounted). You won't need these for this particular search, of course.

Figure 6.4

You have multiple options for finding files by their attributes.

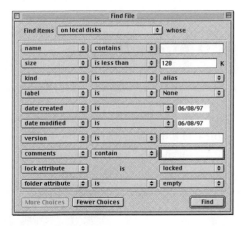

8. Click Find. Your Macintosh will go off and find the file whose title is your first name.

Key Caps

Key Caps is an easy way to add symbols or other characters to your text (see Figure 6.5).

Once you click on Apple Menu➡Key Caps, you can press the Shift key, the Option key, or both at the same time to see your choice of symbols. You can do this by following these easy steps:

Figure 6.5

*With Key Caps, you can
add unusual symbols or
type foreign characters.*

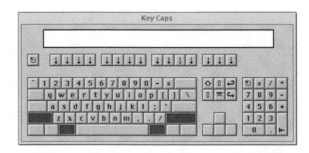

1. Double-click on your hard drive. Open the folder named "Applications," and double-click on the SimpleText application (this is a simple word processing application).

2. Click on Apple Menu➡Key Caps to write the word résumé.

3. Press the Option key. Notice that the accent appears where the letter 'e' usually does (this is not a coincidence, given that e's are frequently accented).

4. Return to your text. Type the first letter of résumé—an 'r.'

5. Press the Option key and then the letter 'e.' It will appear like this: é.

6. Type the next three letters—'sum'—and then repeat step 4. That's it.

AppleCD Audio Player

Did you know that the CD-ROM player in your Macintosh also plays audio CDs, the same way your stereo CD player does? You can even use the computer's built-in speaker (unless you're a real audiophile). We'll talk more about multimedia in Hour 20, "Multimedia," but in the meantime, if you click on the AppleCD Audio Player, you'll get a display that lets you control the CD just as you do your stereo. When there's an audio CD in the drive, its icon will show up on the desktop like any other icon (see Figure 6.6).

Figure 6.6

*The AppleCD Audio
Player lets you play music
CDs on your Macintosh.*

JUST A MINUTE

If you put an audio CD in the Macintosh, it will only appear on the desktop as an audio CD. In this way, it's different than a CD built for computers, which reveals its name. As with floppy disks, you can drag the audio CD icon to the trash to eject it.

6

Calculator

In olden days when desktops were real and not digital, they frequently had typewriters and adding machines on them. The Calculator is Apple's version of the old-time adding machine (see Figure 6.7), for those of us who have forgotten how to multiply in our head and don't trust the results when we scribble on paper.

Figure 6.7

The calculator takes the place of your desktop adding machine.

Use the calculator by clicking on the numbers and symbols. If you prefer to use the keyboard, you can. If you have a numerical keypad, all the keys work the same way, and you can use Enter in place of the = key. The letter c stands for *clear*, and can also be used. However, the Return key cannot be used in place of the Enter key.

Graphing Calculator

This is the Calculator's big husky brother. If algebra wasn't your strong suit in school, this can be your best friend when you're helping with your teenager's homework. It's like a tutor built into your Macintosh, and it's easier to handle than your old math teacher. Follow these steps.

1. Click on the Apple Menu➡ Graphing Calculator.
2. Type z=xy and return (see Figure 6.8).
3. Click on the graph diagrams in the lower-left corner to adjust the values for x and y.
4. To adjust the size of the display, place the cursor over the bar in the middle of the screen. Scroll up or down to resize.
5. To display the keypad, click on Equation➡Show Full Keypad. If you hated algebra, this will immediately bring back very bad memories.
6. To stop the graph, select File➡Quit or press ⌘-Q.

6

Figure 6.8

When you place the cursor over the center bar in the Graphing Calculator, it will turn into a hand to let you adjust the window size.

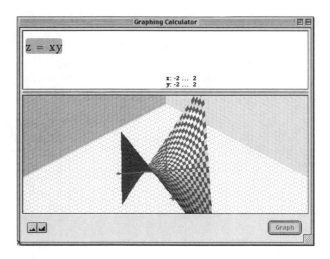

TIME SAVER

The Graphic Calculator offers a full demonstration version. Open the Graphing Calculator and then click Demo➡Full Demo.

Shortcuts

Some of the selections under the Apple Menu give you shortcuts to places you've recently been. These can be real time-savers for getting to applications that you use regularly, but not every day.

Recent Applications

If you select Recent Applications, the Macintosh will show you the last ten applications you launched. Select any one. If you select Recent Documents, the Macintosh will show you the last ten documents you opened. Ditto for clicking on Recent Servers—you'll see the last ten servers you've ever connected to (see Figure 6.9).

Figure 6.9

Under the Apple Menu, you can easily get back into the applications, documents, and servers you've most recently accessed.

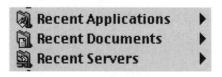

6

TIME SAVER

You can adjust the number of recently viewed applications beyond ten; ten is only the default. Go to the Apple Menu➡Control Panels➡Apple Menu Options. There you can set the number of recently viewed documents, applications, and servers as high as 99 (see Figure 6.10). We'll discuss control panels in more detail in the next Hour, so stay tuned.

Figure 6.10

Use Apple Menu Options to adjust the number of recently viewed documents, applications, and servers.

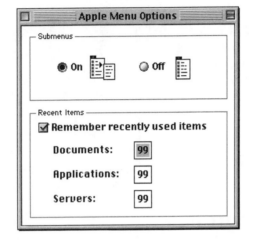

Desktop Printers

When you set up a printer in the Chooser, its icon will appear on the desktop. To print files, just drag them over the icon. This also takes the place of the Print Monitor that appears in earlier versions of the operating system (we'll discuss this more in Hour 13, "Printing"). You can get information about the printer by performing the following steps.

1. Highlight the printer on the desktop.
2. The printing options—start print queue, stop print queue, get printer configuration—will appear.
3. Adjust as necessary.

6

TIME SAVER

You can have multiple printer icons on your desktop. The one with a highlighted border is your default printer. You can rename the icons to reflect what kind of paper the printer holds, rather than its name, as an easy reminder.

Automated Tasks

What you'll find in the Automated Tasks section are prewritten scripts for certain activities on the Macintosh. These are written in AppleScript, a tool for automating sequences of events, which we'll talk about in more detail in Hour 24, "Automation." These scripts handle certain basic activities (see Figure 6.11), like setting up file sharing or creating an alias. Once you've written some AppleScripts on your own, you can store them in this folder for easy access from the Apple Menu.

Figure 6.11

Under the Automated Tasks option are six pre-configured scripts for important features.

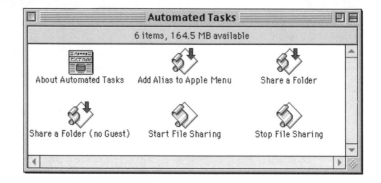

Connect To...

This is a shortcut, brand new to Mac OS 8, that lets you enter a web address that will automatically launch Netscape Navigator or Microsoft Internet Explorer. If you have a web address that you tend to access first (like http://www.espn.com), typing the URL into the box and clicking on Connect will take you straight there (see Figure 6.12).

Figure 6.12

If you have a web site that you like to browse first, type it into the Connect To... box and leave it there.

Fun Stuff

It's not all productivity tools under the Apple Menu. Some of it's just plain fun. Here are some of our favorite examples. Granted, some of them could be characterized as making you more productive, but we don't think of them that way.

6

Scrapbook

In Hour 3, you learned about the clipboard, which holds material that you've cut before you pasted it. Of course, if you cut more material without first pasting the first material you cut, you've lost the latter. Think of the Scrapbook as a clipboard that doesn't lose material you've cut. When you first open it, it holds pictures, but you can add anything you want to it. You can access it whenever you want.

We'll use the example of a digital signoff. On the Internet, people usually sign their electronic mail with their name, affiliation, and a snippet of their philosophy (see Figure 6.13).

Figure 6.13

An example of a signoff for electronic mail that can be kept in your Scrapbook.

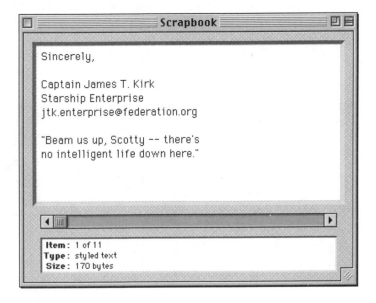

To put your signoff in the Scrapbook, perform the following steps.

1. In SimpleText or your word processing application, type your digital signoff and highlight it.
2. Click on Edit➡Copy.
3. Click on Apple Menu➡Scrapbook and click on the window to make it active.
4. Click on Edit➡Paste.
5. Close the Scrapbook. The next time you want to close an electronic mail with your digital signoff, click on Apple Menu➡ Scrapbook, copy the signoff, and paste it into your electronic mail.

TIME SAVER

The Scrapbook currently contains some examples of clip art. You can use these to spice up invitations, memos, and even recorded sounds for playback. If you obtain more examples of clip art—say, on a CD—put your favorites here and leave the rest on the CD.

Jigsaw Puzzle

The Jigsaw Puzzle is the Macintosh's answer to Solitaire or Minesweeper in Windows. It's a silly, entertaining way of learning how to use a mouse. The default puzzle in the Mac is a map of the world (see Figure 6.14), but you can also paste over other graphics here. It's pretty easy to do, so we suggest when the puzzle opens up, you click on Options➡Start New Puzzle. When the dialog box asks you to choose the size of the pieces, select *small.* And know your geography.

Figure 6.14

If the pieces are small enough, the Jigsaw Puzzle can be as challenging as a cardboard one (for the first two rounds at least).

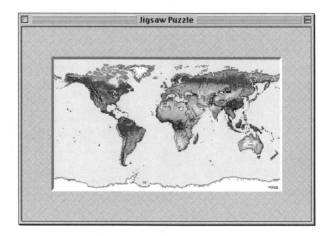

Stickies

These are the digital versions of post-it notes. Just like the paper versions, they come in a variety of colors (yellow, green, pink, purple, and more). You can also resize them (see Figure 6.15) and change the text style.

Just for fun, let's create specialized stickies by following these simple steps.

1. Click on Apple Menu➡Stickies.
2. Click on File➡New Note.
3. Click on File➡Note and File➡Color to assign the color and text style you want. Resize the Sticky to the dimensions you want.

6

Figure 6.15

Two different kinds of Stickies: the default, and one specially created to work as a phone message pad.

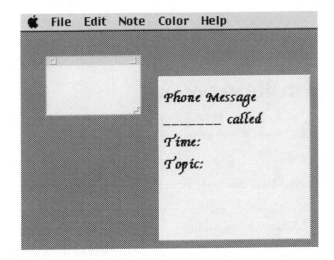

4. Choose File➥Export Text.

5. Click on the Save as Stationery check box.

6. Give the note a name, and click on Save.

7. Your new custom Stickies will now appear under the Apple Menu.

Note Pad

Note Pad is similar to Stickies, except that it uses the SimpleText application and can hold more information. You can write yourself notes, and then open them later in a word processing application. The advantage of Note Pad is that it opens almost instantaneously, while a word processing application can take much longer. If you want to take down important information from someone and you don't want to wait, click on Note Pad and start typing.

Summary

The Apple Menu is a treasure trove of small applications, shortcuts, and tools. Whenever you need to find or launch something in a hurry, the shortest distance between two points is probably found there.

We've just shown you a few of the items that appear under the Apple Menu. When you have a chance, we urge you to test all of them to see what they do. Be adventurous. Clicking on something isn't going to unleash a disaster. The worst that happens is that you learn something you didn't know before (and that's why you're reading this book, isn't it?).

6

Everything under the Apple Menu is there for easy access. In the next hour, we'll talk about the System Folder, and you'll learn how to put applications that you use often under the Apple Menu so you can access them quickly.

Term Review

Apple Menu   The menu under the Apple logo on the upper-left side of the menu bar, under which you'll find important tools and shortcuts.

Chooser   A desk accessory that enables you to access other devices over the network.

Find File   An application that enables you to find files by any number of criteria.

Key Caps   A desk accessory that enables you to easily create characters that appear in foreign languages or special fonts.

Stickies   Digital post-its that enable you to write quick notes to yourself.

Q&A

Q Everything under the Apple Menu seems to be different. How do I find out what's a desk accessory and what's an application?

A Click on System Folder➡Apple Menu Items. Highlight anything you want information on and click ⌘-I (for Get Info). The resulting window will tell you all you need to know.

Q Can I delete any of these menu items? The Jigsaw Puzzle is a bit of a time-waster, don't you think?

A A friend of ours calls such applications *fritterware* because they fritter away your time. Yes, you can delete them. Just follow the instructions in the previous question, and instead of highlighting the item, drag it to the trash. If you change your mind about one of them, you can just ask a friend to copy it from his system—most of them are small enough to fit onto a floppy disk.

Q You didn't talk about OpenDoc Stationery, one of the other Apple Menu items. Why not?

A Apple is a company with a lot of great ideas. It also has some clinkers. OpenDoc is one of the latter. It's a little complicated to explain here, but it falls into the category of *component* software. The idea behind it was that you could buy components like spell checkers and table creators and insert them into applications that didn't have them. Apple worked on it for several years (along with IBM), and still didn't have the kinks worked out of it when it realized that Java, which works on PCs and workstations running the Unix operating system, does the same thing, and better. OpenDoc won't appear in future versions of the Mac OS, so you'll find little use for it.

6

Hour **7**

The System Folder

Now that you've learned about the Apple Menu, we're going to zero in on the System Folder, the place where some of the most important pieces of Mac OS 8 reside. You may be a little skittish about fooling around with them, but relax—we're not going to send you poking into the arcane mysteries of the operating system in such a way that you'll put a hex on your computer (not in an hour, anyway).

However, we are going to show you the most fundamental parts of the System Folder—the ones that will make Macintosh more efficient and, in some cases, even more enjoyable. Think of the System Folder the same way you think of your home's electrical system—you wouldn't start tearing out the wires without knowing what you were doing, but you're perfectly comfortable changing a light bulb or a fuse.

Although there are lots of light bulbs, fuses, and wiring in the System Folder, we're only going to talk about five important areas:

☐ **Control Panels,** which enable you to change certain facets of your Macintosh;

☐ **Preferences,** which enable you to change the way you view your applications;

☐ **Extensions,** which help your Macintosh communicate with other software and hardware;

☐ and the **Startup** and **Shutdown commands**, which, just as they sound, enable you to customize what your computer does every time you turn it on and off.

Simply put, the System Folder is where you make the adjustments to your Macintosh and its applications to make them fit your needs. Frequently, when you install applications, they'll automatically insert important pieces into the System Folder. That way, you know where to find them if you want to adjust them.

The highlights of this hour include:

☐ What the most important elements of the System Folder are

☐ How you can adjust Mac OS 8 even further so that you're even more comfortable with it

☐ How you can adjust your applications so that they are easiest to work with

Control Panels

First, let's talk about control panels. We talked a little about some of Mac OS 8's control panels in Hour 6, because they're accessible under the Apple menu. Because the Control Panels reside in the System Folder, we'll talk about more of them here.

Using these control panels, you can make your Macintosh work and act like no one else's you've ever seen.

We're going to focus on the control panels that enable you to adjust your Macintosh. They all work pretty much the same way (one of the joys of the Macintosh is that once you learn how to do one thing, you should be able to intuitively figure out anything else you want to do).

General Controls

The first control panel on our list is called General Controls. This lists six basic aspects of what you see on your desktop (see Figure 7.1).

Follow these easy steps to make adjustments based on your preferences.

1. Go to the System Folder on your hard drive.

2. Double-click on the folder named "Control Panels,"then on the icon named "General Controls." The Control Panel will display six options for your computer's behavior.

3. The first option relates to your desktop. By clicking in the first option box, you can keep items on your desktop. By clicking in the second option box, you can have the Launcher application appear at system startup (Launcher is a built-in

7

application that lets you keep icons for frequently used applications on the desktop; we'll talk about it in more depth in Hour 11, "Applications."

Figure 7.1

The General Controls Control Panel lets you adjust six facets of your desktop.

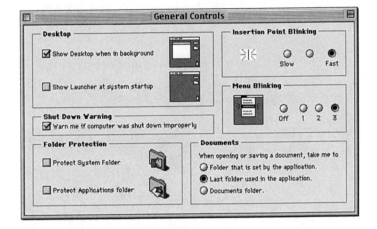

4. The second option (moving down) is the Shut Down Warning. If you click on this option box, an error message will appear when you start up your Macintosh if, when you finished using it the previous time, you didn't use the Special➡Shut Down command.

5. The third option is for Folder Protection. If you don't want anyone fidding with either your System Folder or your Applications Folder, click on these. (File Sharing, which we'll talk about in Hour 14, must be turned off for this option to be available.)

6. The fourth option controls Insertion Point Blinking. This relates to how fast your cursor blinks at the point where you insert text. Click on the various options to get an indication of the speeds available.

7. The fifth option, Menu Blinking, controls the same aspect for drop-down menus. Again, click on the various options to get an indication of which number of blinks you prefer.

8. The sixth option, Documents, lets you adjust which folder is the default when you're opening or saving a document.

9. When you're done, click on the Close box.

JUST A MINUTE

We'll be willing to bet that before too long, you'll deselect item #2, the shut down warning. If your Macintosh crashes, this warning will come up when you restart. At that point, you *know* it was shut down improperly, and you don't need the reminder.

7

Date & Time

You may think setting the date and time to be displayed on your menu bar would be simple, but it's not. It turns out that around the world there are a multitude of ways to display date and time, and the Macintosh lets you set them the way you prefer. Let's walk through each one.

1. As you have previously, go to the System Folder.
2. Double-click on the folder named "Control Panels" and double-click on the Date & Time icon (see Figure 7.1A).

Figure 7.1A

The Date & Time Control Panel.

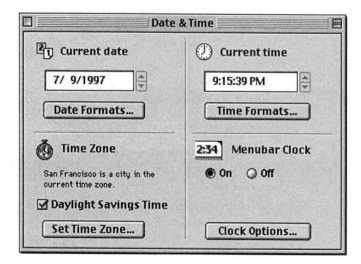

3. You'll see four options. Start by clicking on the Date panel. By clicking on the triangles to the right, you can reset the month, date, and year.
4. Now click on the Date Formats button (see Figure 7.1B). The default is the common style for the United States, as indicated in the button at the top, but you can click on any of the panels marked Weekday, Month, Day, or Year to arrange the date style any way you want. You can choose from a Long Date format on the left or a Short Date format on the right. To see how it will be displayed, as you click, note the changes in the Samples box below. When you're done, click on OK.
5. In the Date & Time Control Panel, click on the Set Time Zone button. The default was selected when you set up your Macintosh, but if you move, you can click on any city from Abu Dhabi in the United Arab Emirates to Zurich Switzerland. This is also an easy way to find out what time it is in a particular city (if you're daydreaming that you're in Paris, for instance, you may want to know if it's time for dinner). Click on OK.

7

Figure 7.1B

Choose from a variety of date formats.

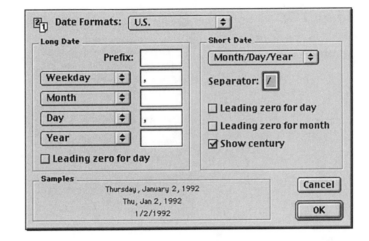

6. In The Date & Time Control Panel, you can adjust the time by first clicking in the time panel and then clicking on the triangles (up for forward and down for back). Now click on the Time Formats button to set the way you'd like the clock to read (see Figure 7.1C). Again, you have several options, including a 12- or 24-hour clock and whether you want the clock to display AM or PM. As with Date Formats, the Samples box at the bottom shows what the time will look like. Click OK.

Figure 7.1C

Choose from a variety of time formats.

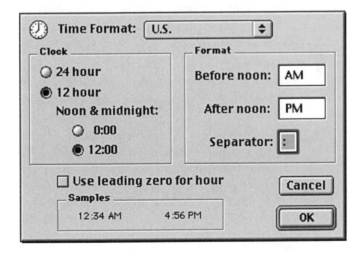

7. In The Date & Time Control Panel, click on the Clock Options button (see Figure 7.1D). By clicking on various settings here, you can display seconds and the day of the week, change the font, size, and color of the clock, and even have it chime (or play a sound of your choosing) on the hour. Click OK.

Figure 7.1D

Choose from a variety of clock options.

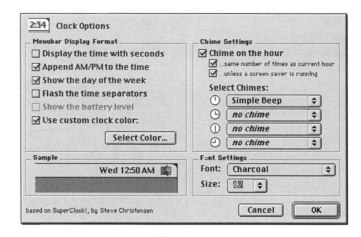

Desktop Pictures

Okay, so much for the serious stuff—now for the fun stuff. Desktop Pictures is great because you can easily adjust it depending on what kind of mood you're in. In previous versions, this control panel used to be called Desktop Patterns, because you could only choose from certain patterns that the operating system gave you. Now, though, you can choose from patterns or pictures. We'll show you how to set this up by following these steps:

1. As you have previously, go to the System Folder.

2. Double-click on the folder named "Control Panels" and double-click on the Desktop Pictures icon.

3. In the dialog box that opens, you'll see a large window that displays the desktop pattern that's currently on your desktop (see Figure 7.2). On the left side of the dialog box, you'll see a button marked Pattern and a button marked Picture. Click on Pattern.

4. Click on the left or right triangles in the horizontal scroll bar and watch the patterns change in the window. To see how it will look on your desktop, click on the Set Desktop button. Don't like it? Click on something else. We've included a few desktop patterns here; imagine how wild they look in color (see Figure 7.3). We've chosen some of the outrageous ones—most of them are quite sedate. The one in the lower-left corner is Howard's favorite (but not Anita's, because she's allergic).

5. If you'd rather choose a Picture, click on that button and then click on Select Picture. This will take you into a list of your folders so that you can find the appropriate file to use as a background.

6. When you've found the pattern or picture you like, click on the close box to select that pattern. You're done... until your mood changes.

7

Figure 7.2
*With Desktop Pictures,
you can choose what your
desktop will look like.*

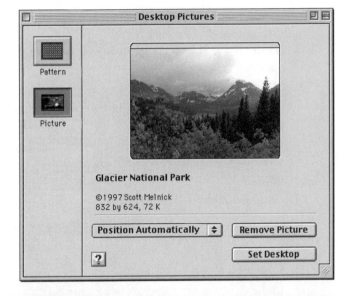

Figure 7.3
*Some samples of the more
outrageous patterns
available—clockwise
from upper right: rocks,
stained glass, bears, and
circuits.*

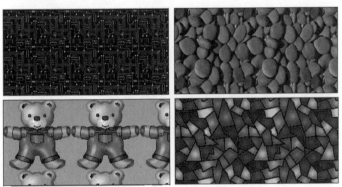

TIME SAVER

> If you have a scanner, you can scan a picture of your family into your
> computer and display it as the background for your desktop. Depending
> on the composition of the picture, it might not be the best design, but at
> least you get a happy picture staring back at you all day long.

Control Strip

We obliquely referred to this back in Hour 2 when we were talking about the desktop. The
Control Strip is a feature that originally appeared only on PowerBooks, but it has migrated
over to the rest of the Macintosh family. It was developed as a way to save screen real estate,

7

which can be pretty limited on a laptop. Sometimes screen real estate can be limited on a desktop computer too. We still haven't figured out a way to describe what the Control Strip looks like. It's not quite a trapezoid, and it only faintly resembles a bathroom scale. However, it's the only thing in the lower-left corner of your desktop. Here's how to figure out what's on it.

1. Click on the Control Strip in the lower-left corner of your screen. See how it springs out to reveal itself?

2. Click on each of the triangles in sequence. You'll see that these are miniature versions of either Apple Menu Items or Control Panels, designed for quick adjustment.

3. Click on the end-tab to snap the Control Strip back in.

You can also adjust the Control Strip. Just follow these easy steps.

1. Return to the System Folder.

2. Double-click on Control Strip.

3. In the dialog box that appears (see Figure 7.4), you can hide the Control Strip permanently, define a hot key sequence to type when you want to see it, and adjust the type font and size.

Figure 7.4

You can adjust the Control Strip to disappear and reappear at will by defining a hot key sequence.

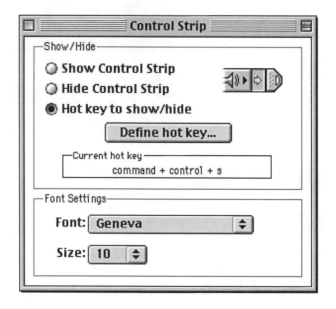

4. After you've defined these attributes, click on the Close box. You're done.

7

JUST A MINUTE

Don't despair that we've only been able to touch on a few of the control panels in the System Folder. Many of them relate to other topics that we'll cover in coming Hours, and we'll revisit many of them at the appropriate time. However, when you feel like exploring, double-click on your System Folder, open the Control Panels folder, and wander to your heart's content.

Extensions

As you become more proficient as a Macintosh user, you'll hear more about extensions (some may also be referred to as drivers). As the name implies, they extend the reach of your Macintosh, enabling the operating system to communicate with other software, hardware, or even a network.

Unfortunately, this is one area where Apple's legendary control over its operating system and hardware can sometimes breaks down. Occasionally, an extension for one device or software will conflict with the extension for another, and your Macintosh may start acting strangely or crashing. Fortunately, the Extensions Manager is a little easier to use in System 7.6. You can adjust the Extensions Manager by following these simple steps.

1. Open the System Folder as you have previously.
2. Double-click on Control Panels.
3. Double-click on Extensions Manager.
4. Go to the lower-left corner of the dialog box and click on the triangle next to "Show Item Information."
5. Click on the Extension labeled "Apple CD-ROM." Now you can see all the information pertaining to your CD-ROM extension (see Figure 7.5).

Figure 7.5

In the Extensions Manager window, you can click on the names of the extensions, like the CD-ROM extension, to learn more about them. Information will appear in the window below.

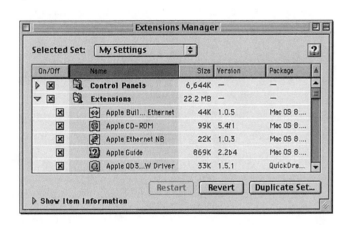

If you think an application you've added to your system is causing trouble, just click on its check mark and restart your machine. If the problem doesn't occur again, you pinpointed the misbehaving product. (For help with the offending product, check its manuals, visit the vendor's web site, or call the technical support line for assistance; we'll discuss this in more detail in Hour 25.)

TIME SAVER

> Always install a new application or a new peripheral one at a time, and make sure that it works with your system before adding any other new application or peripheral. Sure, it's tempting when you get home from the retail store to start loading your new toys, but if you start having problems, you'll find it difficult to track down exactly what's causing the problem.

JUST A MINUTE

> When you start up your Macintosh, you'll see a parade of icons across the bottom of your screen. They correspond to your control panels and extensions. Not all of these have icons, however, so there won't be a one-to-one correlation. An icon with a red X through it means it isn't loading. This is a helpful troubleshooting device if you've just added new hardware.

Startup and Shutdown Items

Let's say that every time you start up your Macintosh, you always launch a particular application—for instance, your word processor or your calendar. Why not use the Startup Items folder in the System Folder to launch the applications? That way, they'll always be ready and waiting for you.

Follow these steps to put applications in your Startup Folder.

1. Return to the System Folder.
2. Click on the Startup Items Folder.
3. Go back to your hard drive and highlight the name of the application or its icon that you want to start automatically.
4. Drag the highlighted name or icon into the Startup Items folder (see Figure 7.6).
5. That's it. The next time you start your Macintosh, that application will open.

You can have a similar process take place when you're done using your computer. That may sound silly—what kind of application would you want to launch when you were done? Well, we know a guy who placed a sound file in his Shutdown Folder, so that every time he was

7

done with work the last thing he'd hear from his Macintosh was Fred Flintstone yelling, "Yabba-dabba-do!"

Figure 7.6

In our Startup folder, we have our electronic mail application and one of our desktop utilities.

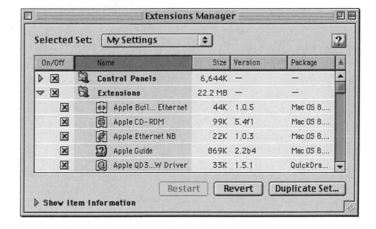

More prosaically, you may also want to launch an AppleScript application to make copies of the files you've just worked on (frankly, we prefer yabba-dabba-do).

To place a sound in your Shutdown Items folder, perform the following steps.

1. On your hard drive, double-click on the System Folder. Then double-click on the folder named "System" (confusing? yes).

2. Among the items in this folder are sounds (their icons look like speakers). Click on any sound you prefer and drag it into the Shutdown Items folder. When you shut down your system, the sound will play. (Later, in Hour 20, "Multimedia," we'll teach you how to create your own sounds, so you can put customized sounds in the Shutdown Items folder.)

Preferences

There aren't too many things on your computer that have such obvious names, but this is one of them (if only there were more). In the System Folder, there's a folder called Preferences, which contains all the documents that control how your applications look.

Currently, they're set at the default, but you can adjust them—when you're in the application. They can only be opened when the application itself is open, and usually by clicking on Edit➡Preferences.

If it's a word processing application, for instance, you'll be able to adjust the default font and type size, as well as request the application make backups for you in case your system crashes. Every one is different (see Figure 7.7).

7

Figure 7.7

Every application's Preferences file looks different. Here is Claris FileMaker Pro on the top and Microsoft Word for Mac on the bottom.

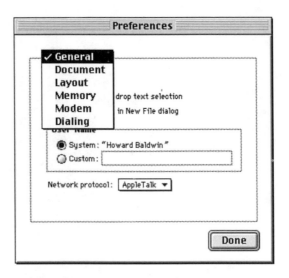

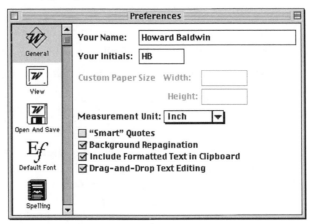

CAUTION

Some Microsoft applications are nonstandard. Microsoft Word for Mac has its preferences under the Tools Menu, as does Microsoft Excel—except Excel calls them Options. Yikes!

To give you an idea of how applications generally work, let's adjust the preferences in the Finder. Remember, you can only adjust preferences within an application, and for this example, the Finder is an application. Just follow these easy steps.

1. In the menu bar, click on Edit➡Finder Preferences.

7

2. In the window that appears (see Figure 7.8), you'll see five attributes to adjust.

Figure 7.8

The Preferences window for the Finder lets you adjust how items appear on the desktop.

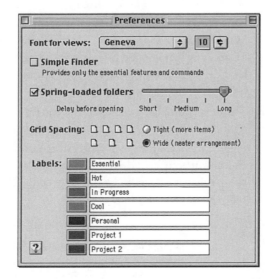

3. Click on the triangle next to the font listed in the "Font for views" section. Pick another font and watch the typeface on your desktop icons change. Slick, huh?

4. Now click on the triangle next to the type size and see how high you can increase the font size. Now you know why the Macintosh is so highly prized by computer users with special needs. Imagine if you had difficulty with your sight—you could crank the type size all the way up to 24 points and not worry about squinting (see Figure 7.9).

Figure 7.9

At 24 points, it's easy to see the Trash can. This might seem silly to you, but not to someone who's sight-impaired.

5. Click on the box next to Simple Finder.

6. Close the Preferences window and move the cursor along the menu bar. See? The choices of what you can do are now limited. Think about using this feature while you're learning the Macintosh to avoid being confused by a lot of choices (once

7

you've read this whole book, though, remove the check mark from the box—you'll be comfortable with everything!).

7. Now open the Preferences window again. Your next choice covers a new feature to Mac OS 8, called *spring-open folders*. We suggest you set this adjustment at *short*. To see how spring-open folders work, drag a file or folder over the Trash or the hard drive. The underlying item will spring open so you can see what's in there before you drop what you're dragging in.

8. The next choice lets you adjust the *spacing* of the icons on your desktop, either tight or wide. Click on these choices to see what you prefer.

9. Finally, there are the *labels*. You can colorize and color-coordinate any icon that appears on your hard drive (see Figure 7.10). Say you want all the folders relating to a particular project to be the same color. Here's where you identify your labels (on your screen, they'll be in color).

JUST A MINUTE

Note that I've made the first color (which happens to be orange) relate to this book. When I go onto the desktop or hard drive, all I have to do is highlight a file, click on File in the menu bar, and scroll down to Labels. Pick the appropriate color, and the file or folder will reflect that color (you might have to be careful, depending on the desktop pattern you've chosen; things could either get pretty garish or completely lost!).

Figure 7.10

You can adjust the labels for your files and folders to be color-coordinated by project.

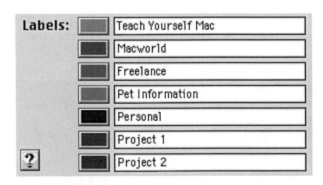

TIME SAVER

Whenever you load a new application, make a point of opening its Preferences file immediately to see how you can adjust it.

Summary

In this hour, we targeted the most important items in the System Folder. These are items that control some of the most important facets of the Macintosh and all its applications—extensions, fonts, and preferences.

Much of what you do with items in the System Folder will depend on your personal preference. You may not even have to deal with them at all. In the case of extensions, for instance, you may not have to adjust them until you're required to do some troubleshooting.

As you go through the System Folder, you'll see some items that you've already worked with up until this point in the book. After you're finished with this book, almost all of the items in the System Folder will be familiar to you, so you may want to return to learn more about them.

Term Review

System Folder   Perhaps the most important folder on your Macintosh, it stores most of what you see under the Apple menu.

Control Panels   As its name implies, these items control certain facets of basic items on your Macintosh.

Extensions   As its name implies, these items control certain facets of items that you attach to your Macintosh.

Fonts   These describe the way characters and other symbols look on the Macintosh.

Preferences   A file belonging to every Macintosh application that includes ways to adjust the application to your liking.

Q&A

Q Just so I'm clear on this, what are the difference between control panels and extensions again?

A There's no hard and fast rule, but generally, control panels enable you to adjust attributes within your Macintosh; extensions work with optional hardware or software outside your Macintosh. One exception is the Control Panel for your monitor, but of course, a monitor isn't optional.

Q Once I've spent some time with my control panels and adjusted the machine to my liking, should I ever have to worry about them again?

A Not unless you (a) are indecisive, or (b) really like fiddling with your computer.

7

Q **Is there any way to turn off that annoying parade of extensions when I start up my Macintosh?**

A Oh, how I wish there were. Unfortunately, that's your confirmation that they're on and working. You have to go into the Extensions Manager to figure out which is which, but it's really a handy way to confirm everything you expect to work will do so.

Q **Can I remove items from the Apple menu that I don't use?**

A Depending on what they are, you can. We don't recommend deleting them, however. Use the Extensions Manager to determine whether they're a Control Panel or an Extension. Then go into the System Folder and find the folders labeled Control Panels (disabled) or Extensions Manager (disabled). Move the item you wanted to delete into the disabled folder so that you have access to it later should you change your mind.

7

Hour 8

Your Filing System

In Hour 7, you learned about the System Folder, where your Macintosh stores all of its important files. Now, we're going to talk about where you're going to store all of *your* most important files—your filing system. Although you could just create files on the desktop and keep them there, you'd eventually end up with a baffling array of icons.

In Hour 2, you learned about folders and files; we're going to build on those skills in this hour. We'll use examples from our work experience at *Macworld* to help you organize your filing system. The work you do is undoubtedly different than ours, but you'll be able to apply these lessons to what you do. We'll provide tips along the way.

If you think of yourself as a disorganized person, take heart. It won't take much to organize your Macintosh's filing system. And if you decide that another way is better, it's easier to reorganize than a paper-based filing system.

The highlights of this hour include:

- ☐ How to set up a filing system that matches your projects
- ☐ How to move files off of your desktop quickly
- ☐ How to navigate your desktop quickly and easily

Organizing Your Desktop

Of course it's presumptuous for us to tell you how to organize your desktop. Everyone has a different working style, and everyone's work is organized a different way. If you're an artist, your work may be organized by client. If you're a teacher, it may be organized by week or quarter. As editors, our work is organized by issue, and then sub-categorized by article.

Although it's fairly easy to rearrange your desktop if you set it up one way and change your mind, it'll be a big time-saver if you take a minute and think about requirements of your particular work. Think about what might be the best way to categorize the information you'll be creating and keeping track of. In the meantime, we're going to use the example of a teacher, both because the Macintosh is so popular in education and because all of us have presumably been through school and can easily apply the lessons to our own situations.

Setting Up Folders

You already know how to create a folder by pressing ⌘-N. If you create the folder while you're in the Finder, it will appear on the desktop as "untitled folder." To set it up on your hard drive, perform the following steps:

1. Double-click on your hard drive icon.

2. Press ⌘-N. The new folder will appear.

3. Name the untitled folder, "My Folder" (you can use your real name if you want, but we'll refer to it as My Folder). To refresh your memory on the easiest way to rename folders, refer to Hour 2.

Setting Up Hierarchies

Now we're going to set up a hierarchy of folders within My Folder. A hierarchy is just a fancy way of saying "structure." The hierarchy will replicate the schedule of a school year; we'll organize it by days, weeks, and quarters. It may sound like a lot, but it will be remarkably easy. We're going to assume that each day the teacher has a lesson plan, so to set up the hierarchy, perform the following steps.

1. Create six untitled folders:

2. In order to keep them in alphabetical order, rename five of the folders for the days of the week this way (the diacritic marks represent spaces) "^^Monday," "^^Tuesday," "^^Wednesday," "^Thursday," "Friday." Rename the sixth folder "^Week 1." Mac OS 8 lets you use spaces to create your own hierarchy.

3. Highlight each of the folders for the days of the week and drag them into the Week 1 folder.

4. Highlight the Week 1 folder.

5. Click on File➡Duplicate (or press ⌘-D). A folder named "Week 1 copy" appears. Repeat the process nine times and rename the folders "^Week 2" through "^Week 9."

6. Repeat the process three more times and rename the folders "Week 10," "Week 11," and "Week 12."

7. Create a new folder named "Fall Quarter."

8. Highlight the weekly folders and drop them into the "^Fall Quarter" folder.

9. Highlight the "Fall Quarter" folder.

10. Click on File➡Duplicate. Repeat.

11. Rename the new folders "^Winter Quarter" and "Spring Quarter." Now you have a year's worth of folders all ready for lesson plans (see Figure 8.1).

Figure 8.1

By starting with the basic structure of your week, you can easily create a year's worth of organized folders.

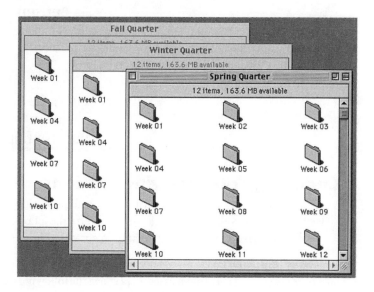

In order to maintain the desired order of your folders, whether you're viewing them by List, Buttons, or Icons, go to View➡View Options, click on "Keep Arranged," and select the "by name" option. We'll talk about viewing options in more detail later in the chapter.

JUST A MINUTE

It may seem logical to keep your word processing files with your word processing application, but the fact is, the two don't go together. You don't need to access your word processing application on a regular basis, but you will need your word processing files regularly. By opening a file, you'll launch its application.

TIME SAVER

Viewing Your Desktop

You can view your desktop in a multitude of combinations. If you prefer to see one folder as a window, and another folder as a pop-up window, and a third as an alphabetical list, you can. You arrange your views by clicking on the View option in the menu bar (see Figure 8.2). We'll show you how to easily set up each of these viewing options.

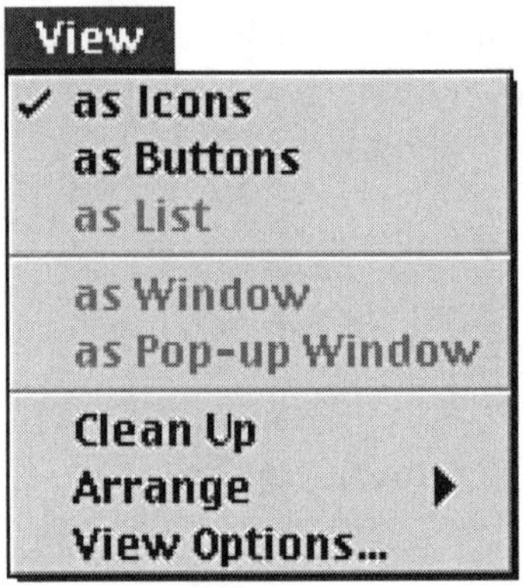

Figure 8.2
The View Option in the menu bar.

Choosing Your Viewing Options

All of your viewing options are set in the menu bar option called View. To arrange your viewing options, we're going to ask you to perform the following series of steps. When you're done, you'll have a view of your desktop in a variety of different ways.

View as Icon

To see the contents of a folder as icons, perform the following steps. Don't close any windows, as each series relies on the previous one.

1. Open the folder named "My Folder."
2. In the menu bar, click on View➡as Icons. The contents of this folder will appear as icons (see Figure 8.3).

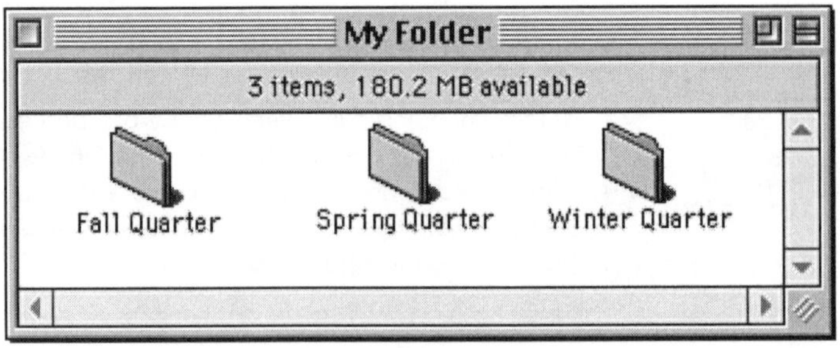

Figure 8.3
Viewing folder contents as icons.

TIME SAVER

Mac OS 8 has some built-in keyboard shortcuts for navigating through windows that will save you time and effort (we'll discuss shortcuts in more detail in the Hour 9, "Help"). To close all folder windows, press option and File→Close or option and click on the Close box. To zoom a window to the full size of the screen, press option and click on the zoom box. To close a window after opening an icon, press Option and File→Open or press Option and double-click the icon.

View as List

To see the contents of a folder as a list, perform the following steps:

1. Double-click on the "Fall Quarter" folder.
2. In the menu bar, click on View→as List (see Figure 8.4).

Figure 8.4

Viewing folder contents as a list.

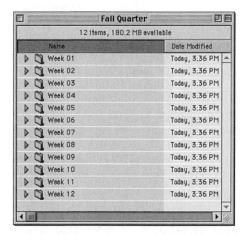

TIME SAVER

To change how items are listed, double-click on the column heading. To expand the contents of a selected folder, press ⌘-right arrow. Conversely, to collapse the contents of a selected folder, press ⌘-left arrow. To move an item to the top level in the window, drag the icon to the window's title bar.

To expand all the contents of a selected folder, press ⌘-Option-right arrow or press Option and click on the triangle. Conversely, to collapse all the contents of a selected folder, do the opposite.

View as Buttons

To see the contents of a folder as buttons, perform the following steps:

1. Double-click on the "Week 1" folder.

2. In the menu bar, click on View→as Buttons.

Here's the final result (see Figure 8.5).

Figure 8.5

Viewing folder contents as buttons.

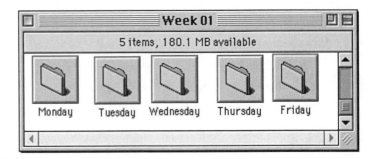

You've set up the days of the week as pop-up folders, the Fall Quarter as a list, and the top folder in the hierarchy (My Folder) as a window. Note that the folders corresponding to the days of the week are dimmed in the Fall Quarter folder to indicate that they're "open" as pop-up folders.

A folder must be open before you can change it from a window view to a pop-up window view. If the folder is closed, those options will be dimmed.

JUST A MINUTE

Choosing More Viewing Options

Depending on how you've set up your view, there's one more option box to explore. To view these options, perform the following steps:

1. In the menu bar, click on View→Icon View Options (of course, if you've chosen to View→as Button, your choice will be "Button View Options").

2. Click on the "Keep Arranged:" box.

3. Click on the down arrow in the selection box to see your choices for the order of your icons, list, or buttons (see Figure 8.6).

8

Figure 8.6

The Icon View Options box and the Button View Options box.

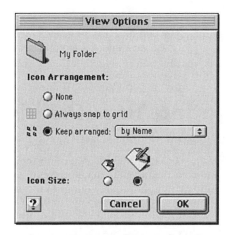

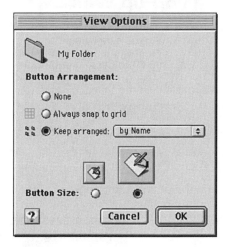

Cleaning Up Your Desktop

You don't have to create pop-up windows if you don't want to. If you're going to be using some folders or files during the course of a work day, you can just move them onto your desktop. When you're finished, and want to clean everything up, perform the following steps:

1. Highlight the folder or file you've been using (if you've been using more than one, highlight as many as you like by holding down the Shift key).

2. In the menu bar, click on File➡Put Away (or ⌘-Y).

3. The folder icons will disappear, but you'll find them returned to their proper location.

> You can also use the File➡Put Away command to unmount file servers or other items selected through the Chooser.

Navigating Your Desktop

There are other ways of arranging your desktop so you can navigate through your folders more easily. The Macintosh has several ways of making the folders you use most frequently readily available. And, even better, it makes it easy to change which folders are at the forefront on the desktop, so that if you're working on one project in the morning and another in the afternoon, you can easily switch views.

Viewing Pop-up Windows

Pop-up windows are new to Mac OS 8. They enable you to put a folder on your desktop while using the least screen real estate possible.

To see the contents of a folder as a pop-up window, perform the following steps:

1. Double-click on the "Week 1" folder.
2. Double-click on the "1Monday" folder.
3. In the menu bar, click on View➡as Pop-up Window.
4. Double-click on the "1Monday" tab. Repeat steps 1–3 for the other days of the week.
5. To make the windows "pop-up," click on their tabs (see Figure 8.7).

Figure 8.7
Pop-up windows appear at the very bottom of your desktop.

Viewing Spring-open Folders

We talked a little bit about spring-open folders in Hour 7. This is a new feature to Mac OS 8 that also aids in navigation through your folders. Let's say you've created that first lesson plan, and you want to insert it into the folder for Monday of the first week of the first quarter. That's a lot of opening and closing just to move one file. To move the file using spring-open folders, perform the following steps:

1. In SimpleText or your word processing application, create a file named "Lesson Plan" and save it on the desktop.

2. Highlight the file and move its icon over the hard drive icon. Don't let go of the mouse.

3. The hard-drive icon will spring open. Still holding the mouse button down, move the file icon over the folder named "My Folder." It too will spring open.

4. Repeat the process by holding the file named "Lesson Plan" over succeeding folders until the folder named "Monday" springs open. Let go of the mouse, and your lesson plan is where it belongs.

TIME SAVER

Apple added another neat tool to Mac OS 8 that lets you navigate through folders even when you're not trying to place a file or a folder within another folder. Click on a folder and hold the mouse button down. As long as you don't move the mouse, after a moment the cursor will turn into a magnifying glass icon. By moving this over folders, they will open and reveal their contents. You can drill down as far as you like as long as you hold the mouse button down. To drill back up, just move the magnifying glass up to the title bar.

Using Aliases to Navigate and Launch

The Macintosh operating system offers another helpful feature for easy access to an application, called an *alias*. You may think that an alias is something criminals use, but in this case, it's a positive thing. An alias is like a shortcut that you leave on your desktop. Use it to access a file or an application that might be stored several layers down among the folders on your hard drive. By creating an alias, you can access it quickly. To make an alias for your folder, perform the following steps:

1. Highlight "My Folder."

2. In the menu bar, go to File➡Make Alias (or type ⌘-M).

3. A folder called "My Folder alias" appears. The type is italic, so you can always distinguish the alias from the real thing (see Figure 8.8).

4. Highlight the name of the folder and delete the word alias.

5. Double-click on the folder and the contents will appear.

Figure 8.8

The name of an alias is always italicized to distinguish it from the original.

Using the Apple Menu as a Shortcut

We're going to help you create one more shortcut, just one more way that you can easily find the folders you work on regularly. Remember in Hour 6 when we talked about the Apple menu? Now we're going to insert the file or application you want to see when you click on the Apple Menu, just by performing the following steps (we're going to use the spring-open folder feature again):

1. Double-click on your hard drive and highlight "My Folder."

2. Click and drag the folder over the System Folder. The System Folder will spring open. Keep the mouse button down.

3. Move the highlighted folder over the Apple Menu Items folder. When that springs open, let go of the mouse button. This will move "My Folder" into the Apple Menu Items folder (see Figure 8.9).

Figure 8.9

For fast access, you can put any folder you want under the Apple menu.

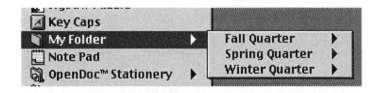

4. In the menu bar, click on the Apple menu and scroll down. You will see "My Folder" in order under M.

5. Click on "My Folder" and navigate through the submenus to get where you want.

Putting folders or files under the Apple Menu is just one more way the Mac OS gives you to make your Macintosh as easy for you to use as possible. Obviously, you don't want to put too much there, or it will get so cluttered as to be unusable. But with discretion, you can build your own library of frequently used information.

Summary

As you can see, Mac OS 8 provides a multitude of ways that you can set up and navigate through your own filing system. This enables you to get where you want as quickly and easily as possible.

Using what you've learned in this hour, you can put items under the Apple menu or put aliases on your desktop. You can hide folders under pop-up tabs and use the spring-open feature to get inside them quickly. Pretty soon, you'll be zigging and zagging through your Macintosh like a pro. That's one of the goals of the Mac OS—adding capabilities so that you don't have to think about your computer—just your work.

8

Term Review

Alias   A shortcut to a folder or file that you use frequently, its name will always be italicized.

Buttons   A way to view your folders and files, as a visual clue that they can be pressed.

Hierarchy   The structure of a folder that holds many other folders and files.

Pop-up folders   A method that shrinks folder titles down to tabs similar to those on manila folders, so that many folders can be visible on your desktop without taking up a lot of space.

Spring-open folders   A method for navigating through folders easily by holding a file or folder over it so that it opens.

Q&A

Q Can I set up different folders to be viewed different ways?

A Certainly. You may want to have the folders that contain very few files set up to be viewed as icons, so you can easily see them. You may want to view other folders, such as your System Folder, as a list so that everything in there is alphabetical. You may want to view your Applications folder as buttons, so you can easily launch the programs.

Q You said that if I move a file from one location and don't re-create an alias, the link will be broken. How do I rebuild the link?

A The easiest thing to do is to go back to the original file and create a new alias. If you can't find the original file, use the Find File command under the Apple menu.

Q Can the pop-up folders that appear at the bottom of my desktop be stacked so that I can keep more down there?

A Unfortunately, no—nor can they be overlapped like some paper-based filing systems. However, if you've got that many pop-up folders, you might consider a way to consolidate them so that you have a happy medium of convenience and screen real estate.

Hour 9

Help

In all the preceding hours (and in all those yet to come), we've provided you with step-by-step information for learning how to use your Macintosh. We've tried to make it as comprehensive as we can, but the fact remains that as you add applications to your computer, you will probably have more questions. In this hour, we won't tell you the answers, but we will show you how to find the answers when you need them.

The Macintosh has one of the best built-in Help systems of any computer. It's called Apple Guide, and it will actually walk you through the steps necessary to solve your problem. Most software applications you buy also have their own specific Apple Guide.

You may even find an added bonus in the form of mini-tutorials. Unlike most Help systems, which only tell you what to do, Apple Guide may also walk you through the process onscreen. When one of these mini-tutorials is available, a button will appear marked "Guide Me." Click on it, and you'll see lots of visual clues to help you along—steps highlighted and options circled in red. Better yet, you won't have to repeat the action later—once AppleGuide walks you through the process, you've actually done it.

Another added Help method is called "Tutorials." If there is a tutorial installed for your application, you can launch it, and it will walk you through the important facets of the software.

The highlights of this hour include:

☐ How to find the Help system when you need it

☐ How to get the most out of your computer's Help system

☐ How to find and use your software application's Apple Guide

☐ What other kinds of help are available in your applications

☐ What other kinds of help are available to Macintosh users

Mac OS Help

Finding Help on the Macintosh is easy, because the word "Help" sits right on the menu bar (see Figure 9.1). Previous to Mac OS 8, a question mark sat on the right of the menu bar, but usability studies revealed that not everyone immediately realized that this was where to access help. The new version reflects that. What you see when you click on it changes depending on which application is active. When you're in the Finder, the Help menu will give you information about Mac OS 8 in general.

Figure 9.1

Clicking on "Help" in the menu bar brings up the Macintosh's help system.

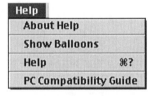

Help
About Help
Show Balloons
Help   ⌘?
PC Compatibility Guide

JUST A MINUTE

At times under "Help," you will see an option named "Tutorial." It will only appear in applications that have tutorials installed. These are additional aids for learning more about your applications.

When you bring up Help specifically for Mac OS, you'll find it is divided into three areas: a topic list, an index, and a search tool called "Look For." We're going to walk you through each area so you can determine the easiest way for you to search for what you want.

Index

The first time you bring up Mac OS Help, it suggests that you click on Index to start, even though that's the second of the three choices. Go figure. The options listed in the Index fall into three categories:

☐ Definitions of specific topics.

☐ Questions that begin "How do I" perform a specific task.

☐ Questions that explain "Why can't I" perform a specific task.

To learn how to use the Index and answer the questions, perform the following steps:

1. In the menu bar, click on the Help➡Help (or press ⌘-?).

2. Click on the box marked "Index" (see Figure 9.2).

Figure 9.2

Mac OS Help's indexed list of topics.

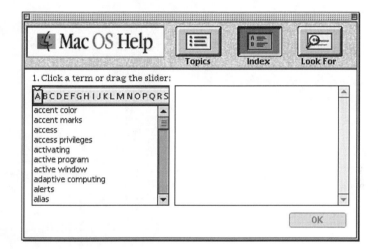

3. Scroll down to "Apple menu" and click on it.

4. In the box on the right, double-click on the question under "How do I" that reads "change items in the Apple menu" (we've already covered this in Hour 5).

5. In the window that comes up, leave "add an item" selected and click on the triangle in the lower right window. Watch as Apple Guide opens the System Folder and draws an arrow to the Apple Menu folder.

6. Click on the left triangle to return to the previous screen, or on the Topics button to return to Help.

To help you understand everything that's possible in a Help topic, let's go through a simple Help topic without options and one that has more options. That way, you'll have experience with various choices that appear.

Let's choose a simple process first. Perform the following steps:

1. In the menu bar, click on Help➡Help and click on Index.

2. Click on the letter "M" on the slider and highlight "mouse."

3. In the box on the right, highlight "adjust the mouse or trackball." Click OK.

4. In the next dialog box, read the text and then select both options: "tracking" and "double-click speed."

5. Follow the instructions shown: click on the Apple Menu, double-click on Control Panels, and then then double-click on the Mouse Control Panel.

6. See how the appropriate portion of the Mouse Control Panel is circled (see Figure 9.3).

Figure 9.3

Mac OS Help gives you visual cues like this circle when you need to make adjustments.

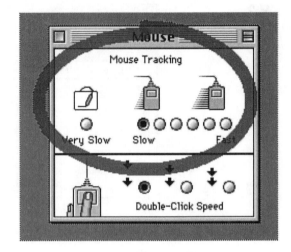

7. Click on one of the speed buttons, then click the right arrow in the Help dialog box.

8. Click on the appropriate double-click speed for your mouse, and you're finished.

You've now adjusted your Mouse Control Panel. If you want to adjust it again later, you can access it by clicking on the Apple Menu➡Control Panels➡Mouse, or by using Help again.

Topics

Now let's look at how you can access Help through the Topics option. The Topics option is very similar to the Index option. In fact, in some cases, you'll find the same material covered. It includes the same "Definitions," "How do I" and "Why Can't I" questions, but it also has a section in which the word "About" precedes specific topics. Also, while the Index lists words, the Topics area lists *concepts*. To see how to get Help through the Topics option, perform the following steps.

1. Click on Help➡Help.
2. Click on the Topics option.
3. In the box on the left, click on "Organizing Your Files."
4. In the box on the right, under the "How do I" list, click on "create a folder." Click OK.
5. Click on the triangles to work through the topic.
6. If you get to the end of the process and you have a question, click on the "Huh?" button. This will provide further clarification or more information. Do this now (the "Huh?" button has been grayed out up until now).
7. You now have a window that offers you more clarification about files and folders: displaying contents, specifying icon sizes, assigning labels, and changing labels. For more information, select one of these and click on the right triangle.

To learn as much as possible about the Macintosh, take some time to wend your way through the Help system in just this way—clicking on "Huh?" and disclosure triangles. Although we've tried to teach you everything about the Macintosh in this book, we certainly can't include the entire Help system!

TIME SAVER

> To return to the main Help menu from any particular topic, click on the disclosure triangle that points upward. If you click on the Close box, you'll have to open Help from the Apple Menu again.

Look For

Now let's look at the options under the "Look For" box. This combines the options of the two other boxes. To learn how to search for particular keywords, perform the following steps.

1. In the menu bar, click on Help➡Help.
2. Click on the "Look For" box.
3. Click in the blank option box on the left to make it active. Type "folders."
4. Click the "Search" button. You'll see choices of "About" topics, definitions, and the "How do I" questions (see Figure 9.4).

Figure 9.4

When you search on a particular keyword, further information appears in the right-hand box.

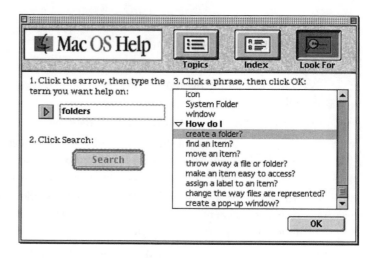

TIME SAVER

If you use Mac OS Help on a regular basis, and prefer to search in a particular way—say, by topics—the Help screen will default to that choice the next time you access Help.

Application Help

You can also get help from within applications. Let's use an application that's already on your Macintosh—SimpleText. It's an easy-to-use word processing application. To access its help system, perform the following steps:

1. Click on your hard drive. Double-click on the Applications Folder.

2. Double-click on SimpleText to launch it. Click on File➥New.

3. In the menu bar, click on Help➥SimpleText Guide.

4. In the SimpleText Guide, click on "Topics."

5. In the box on the left, click on "Text."

6. In the box on the right, click on "change the way text looks?" Click OK.

7. Follow the instructions in the window, clicking on the right-facing triangle at the conclusion of each step.

9

Balloon Help

Balloon Help is a double-edged sword. For a new user, it's an excellent aid when you're trying to find your way around the desktop. As you move the cursor over menu options or icons, a little balloon will pop up, kind of like the dialogue balloons in comic strips. An explanation of what that particular option or icon does will appear. To make it disappear, move the cursor.

When you become more confident with your Macintosh skills, Balloon Help can be somewhat aggravating. Why? Because while you're trying to work, these balloons keep popping up all over the screen, even if you're just moving the cursor somewhere else. After you feel comfortable with your basic skills, we recommend that you make Balloon Help disappear. You can always turn it on again when you purchase a new application to learn more about its capabilities.

Balloon Help within Mac OS 8

To start off, let's see how to access Balloon Help from within Mac OS 8. Perform the following steps.

1. In the menu bar, click on Help➡Show Balloons.

2. Place the cursor over your hard drive to see the Balloon Help pop up (see Figure 9.5).

Figure 9.5
Balloon Help looks like the balloons over comic-strip characters.

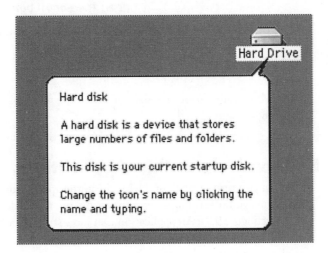

3. Double-click on the hard-drive icon.

4. Move your cursor over several icons to see the message change. Depending on the icon, the balloon can display a specific message or a generic message (see Figure 9.6).

Figure 9.6

Depending on the icon, Balloon Help can give you specific information (above) or general information (below).

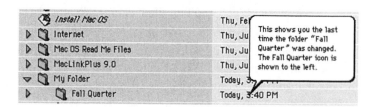

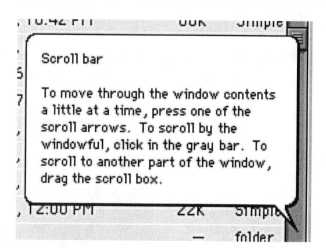

5. Move your cursor over the options in the menu bar to reveal information about those items as well.

6. To turn off Balloon Help, go to Help→Hide Balloons.

Balloon Help within Applications

You can also turn on Balloon Help within the applications that you use. This can be a big help when you're learning a new application, but not all developers take extensive advantage of it (see Figure 9.7). An application that has a strong market presence on the Macintosh is more likely to use extensive balloon help (see Hour 11 for more information on Macintosh applications you're likely to use).

9

Even though an application may not have Balloon Help, though, it will certainly have other Help features (see Figure 9.8). As we mentioned, you can access your application's Help files just by clicking on Help in the menu bar.

Figure 9.7
Not all applications add their own Balloon Help to their Macintosh versions. In Netscape Navigator, balloons only open for the title bar and the close box, not any Navigator features.

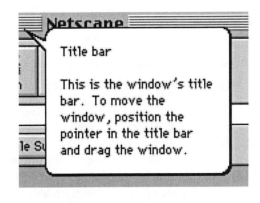

Figure 9.8
Even though Netscape Navigator has limited Balloon Help, it has an extensive Help menu nonetheless.

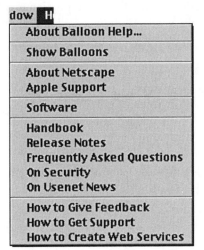

Mac OS Info Center

In Mac OS 8, Apple has added a truly unique method for accessing help called the Mac OS Info Center. It appears on your desktop automatically, and you may have been wondering what it is. It's an innovative way to give you access to fundamental information on your hard drive and to changing information on the World Wide Web. Because Apple is bundling Netscape Navigator with Mac OS 8, it can create this unusual but effective method of delivering information. Most help systems of the future, for applications as well as operating systems, will include this.

What's so unusual about it? When you double-click on the Mac OS Info Center icon, it launches the Netscape Navigator web browser. The difference is that you can now use the browser to browse information stored on your hard drive as well as information that's on the Web. To see how, follow these steps:

1. Double-click on the Mac OS Info Center icon.

2. Note that the main screen for the Info Center says, "You don't need an Internet connection to use the Info Center."

As you can see, there are three help sections to the Info Center: "Show Me What I Can Do," "Help Me Solve A Problem," and "Help Me Explore the Internet." Each section provides help in two different ways: information that's stored on your hard drive (that is, that came with Mac OS 8) and information that's on the web. Why both kinds? Because some information about the operating system is highly unlikely to change, and that can be delivered with your hard drive. Other information may be updated, and this gives you an easy way to go onto the World Wide Web and find out the latest changes.

To access each section, just click on each of the three pictures. We'll walk you through each one.

Show Me What I Can Do

Let's start by clicking on the picture entitled "Show Me What I Can Do." There are three sections of "local" information (that is, on your hard drive) and four sections of web information. Let's go through each one individually.

What's New in the Mac OS?

1. Click the first line, "What's New in the Mac OS? (On the web, anything under- lined is called a "hyperlink." That means that by clicking on it, you'll be automati- cally linked to another page. You'll learn more about this in Hour 16, "Using Your Internet Connection.")

2. This reveals the new features of Mac OS 8. If you're already familiar with System 7, this is a good place to start (you can also see Appendix A of this book).

3. As you can see, the five items listed, Ease of Use, Internet, Multimedia, Perfor- mance, and Appearance, are underlined, meaning that clicking on them will take you to more information about that item. Click on the button marked "Go Back" to return to the "Show Me What I Can Do" section.

Since the purpose of this book is to teach you about all these items (and more), we're not going to go into detail about them here. But it's important to know where to find help if at some point in the future (Heaven forbid!) you find yourself next to a Macintosh without having this book handy.

What Can I Do With the Mac OS?

So that you know where to look for other information, let's look at the next sections as well. Perform the following steps:

1. Click on the hyperlink marked "What Can I Do With the Mac OS?"

2. As you can see, it's divided into five sections, covering Basics, Compatibility, Multimedia, Networking and Internet, and Power. Each of these sections are broken down even further. Each item has a short definition and a hyperlink to more detailed information.

3. Let's look at just one as an example. Under Basics, click on "Finder."

4. Here you get an overview of what the Finder does, along with an explanatory screen capture. Scroll down to the bottom of this window, and you'll find another hyperlink, this one leading to "Mac OS Help." In this way, you can navigate the Help system to find exactly what you're looking for.

5. To return to the previous screen, click on the hyperlink marked "Go Back" or return to the top of the screen and click on the button marked "Go Back." To return to the Mac OS Info Center menu, click on the hyperlink marked "Main Menu" or return to the top of the screen and click on the button marked "Main Menu."

Navigating the Help system works the same way, no matter what section you're in. Clicking on a hyperlink takes you to that page. Once you've done this, you'll find navigating the Web (when you get there) much easier.

Keyboard Shortcuts

We're going to talk about shortcuts in more detail in Hour 24, "Automation," but here's where to find them until then.

1. Go to the Mac OS Info Center main menu. Click on "Show Me What I Can Do."

2. Click on the hyperlink "Keyboard Shortcuts."

3. Note that there are seven hyperlinked items listed: Getting out of freezes, Starting up, Working with icons, Working with windows, Saving files, Taking pictures of your screen, and Working with languages. You can either click on the topic you're interested in, or scroll down to that section.

4. Click on the button marked "Go Back" to return to the "Show Me What I Can Do" section.

In earlier versions of the operating system, you could find keyboard shortcuts under the Help menu. This is much better, because originally, you couldn't print them out. Now they're all in one place, and you can easily print "cheatsheets" to use until you learn the shortcuts.

Information on the Internet

There are four hyperlinks here, each of which will take you to a specific Apple related web site if you have questions. Because web sites change, we can't go into a lot of detail of what you'll find there, but we can talk about the basics of each web site.

- ☐ **Apple Computer's web site** (www.apple.com) is the "home page" for Apple Computer. Consider this the front door leading to all their web pages.

- ☐ **The Mac OS web site** (www.macos.apple.com) focuses on the operating system itself.

- ☐ **Mac OS Late-Breaking News** (macos.apple.com/macos/latebreak/) reveals information about Mac OS 8 that may have become available since you bought your Macintosh. Check here to learn about upgrades, bugs, or other news.

- ☐ **Apple Software Archive** (support.info.apple.com/ftp/swhome.html) lets you download software utilies and upgrades that might come in handy.

Help Me Solve A Problem

Now let's look at the problem-solving information available in your Macintosh's Help system. Go to the main menu for the Mac OS Info Center and perform the following steps:

1. Click on the section marked "Help Me Solve a Problem." As you can see, it's also divided into two parts: one section on Troubleshooting that's on your hard drive, and one section that links to four Apple web sites.

2. Click on the hyperlink named "Troubleshooting." Here you'll find a short primer on what to do if you have problems. Click on the button marked "Go Back."

The larger part of this section gives you links to web sites. The reason is simple: operating systems and application software are complicated things. Problems may crop up despite the best efforts of Apple. If a lot of people start having the same problem, Apple can't easily send e-mail to everyone to inform them. They can, however, put the information on the Internet where everyone can find it. Also, having the information here where you can find it may save you from a long wait calling Apple's technical support. Here's a list of the web sites you can link to from this section of Help.

- ☐ **Mac OS Troubleshooting** (www.info.apple.com/basictroubleshooting) will give you tips on troubleshooting problems you have.

- ☐ **Technical Support Online** (www.info.apple.com/techsupportonline) links you to discussion forums for asking questions of tech support staff, as well as lists of FAQs (frequently asked questions) that may explain your problem.

- ☐ **Tech Info Library** (www.info.apple.com/til) is a compendium of technical information about the components of Apple machines; it may be too much technical detail for the beginner.

9

☐ **Mac OS Late-Breaking News** (macos.apple.com/macos/latebreak/) is the same hyperlink as described above.

Help Me Explore the Internet

Now let's look at the final section. To learn more about the Internet, go to the main menu of the Mac OS Info Center and perform the following steps:

1. Click the section marked "Help Me Explore the Internet."

2. Click the hyperlink marked "Getting on the Internet." As you can see, you have three more hyperlinked sections: "What do I need to get on the Internet?", "How do I set up Internet access?", and "How do I speed up my I access? Click on these for basic information (or better yet, see Hours 15 and 16, "Setting Up Your Internet Connection" and "Using Your Internet Connection").

In this section, too, you have multiple links to items of interest on the Internet.

☐ **Live Home Page** (livepage.apple.com) acts as a starting point for your own Internet exploration, as well as a destination for personalized Internet information; that is, you can request that you be sent updated information on certain topics like sports or technology.

☐ **Internet Search** (livepage.apple.com/search) links you to a search engine for finding what you want on the web.

☐ **Apple Computer's web site** (www.apple.com) is the same "front door" discussed earlier.

☐ **Apple's Education site** (www.education.apple.com) provides resources for parents, students, and teachers, and is included because of the preponderance of Apple computers used in classrooms.

TIME SAVER

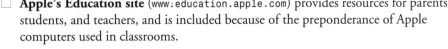

Don't forget that your browser's "back" command is different from the Mac OS Info Center's "back" command. If you want the page you previously looked at, hit the browser's back command. If you want the page previous to the one in the Info Center, click on the "Go Back" button or hyperlink within the screen.

Technical Support

There's nothing more aggravating than buying something brand new and not having it work—especially something like a Macintosh that's advertised as being reliable and easy to use. The fact is, though, that technology is complicated and not everything works the way it's supposed to. There are many facets to the Macintosh, and though you're likely to get a machine that works like a charm out of the box, there's always the possibility that you won't. Don't despair. Help is nearby.

The Help system that we've described within the Macintosh is a guide to learning the system. When there's a problem with the computer itself, though, it's not much—pardon the expression—help. Here are some tips on how to proceed when you need more of a helping hand.

Apple's Web Sites

As you saw with the Mac OS Info Center, Apple Computer really takes advantage of the World Wide Web's capacity as a resource for information. If your Macintosh is connected to the Internet, point your browser to `http://www.apple.com`; you'll find more than you ever wanted to know about Apple. For purposes of this hour, though, you should be aware of `http://www.info.apple.com`, where Apple's technical support information resides (see Figure 9.9).

Figure 9.9

Apple's Technical Support page on the World Wide Web.

TIME SAVER

In order to get to any web address, you can skip *http://*; type whatever comes after the slash marks and you'll still get where you want to go.

(800)SOS-APPL

This is Apple's toll-free technical support telephone number. The call is free, but early in 1997, Apple announced that, like some PC companies, it would start charging for technical support after you'd owned your Macintosh for 90 days. This is why we recommend either studying your manual carefully or going to an Apple web site first—it will save you time and money.

9

There's another reason why we recommend this: whenever there's a big revision to a product—such as System 7.X being upgraded to Mac OS 8, there are bound to be glitches discovered. And if a lot of people upgrade at the same time, technical support lines can be overwhelmed. Technologically conservative folks will wait until the bugs are worked out before upgrading, but not everyone will.

Local User Groups

One of the first things you should do is find a local user group. It will probably be chock-full of Macophiles who would love to help answer your questions. You may need to join first, but the dues will most likely get you a newsletter with important tips, updates on applications and the operating system, and discounts on products. You can find your local user group by performing the following steps. If you have not yet set up your Internet connection, doing this won't be possible. See Hour 15 for details on this. You can also reach the User Group Connection at (408)461-5700.

1. Click on Apple Menu➥Connect To....
2. Type www.ugconnection.org/findagroup.html (see Figure 9.10)
3. "Mac" is the default platform; type your area code in the proper box and click on search.
4. Write down your local user group's contact name.

Figure 9.10

The User Group Connection's page on the World Wide Web.

Connecting Computer Users, User Groups, and Vendors

Don't forget that it's better to give than to receive. If your local user group helps you, consider being a volunteer yourself once you become comfortable with your Macintosh.

Summary

In this hour, you learned that there are really two kinds of Help. There's the kind you use to learn something new about using your Macintosh. There's also the kind you need when something goes wrong.

The Macintosh incorporates a great tool for the first kind, circling or underlining items of interest while walking you through the necessary steps of a process. It also offers Balloon Help for when you're first learning an application and Shortcuts for saving time with keyboard commands.

For the second kind of help, you need to have some patience and maybe even some detective skills. Being in need of technical support is never fun—there are at least some simple ways to start looking for assistance without paying for it. If something goes wrong, web pages and local user groups can be a big help in figuring out what's going on with your Macintosh.

Term Review

Apple Guide The built-in Help system that uses visual clues to help you learn more about your Macintosh and its applications.

Balloon Help Balloons that appear when you hold the cursor over certain icons and commands to explain their purpose.

Keywords A specific word you're looking for when conducting a search.

Shortcuts Commands that enable you to control your Macintosh through the keyboard rather than the mouse.

Q&A

Q It sounds like all these Help systems only tell me what to do, not what to do if something goes wrong.

A That's right, and that's our beef with any Help system. They never take into account that you might get cryptic error messages (for more information on troubleshooting, refer to Hour 24).

Q When something goes wrong with my Macintosh, who do I call—Apple, the company that wrote the software application, the company that manufactured the peripheral, or the store I bought it from?

A It depends. If you can specifically identify what's causing the problem, then you have to start with the company responsible. We suggest going to a web site before calling technical support, because it's possible the company already knows about the problem and has posted a fix that you can easily download and install. Starting with technical support can be time-consuming and expensive.

Q Why can it be expensive?

A You've probably noticed computers are cheaper than they ever have been before. They also have what's known as low *margins*. That means the company charges less, makes less profit, and hopes to make up the difference on volume. The problem is, staffing technical support lines is expensive, so companies have begun to charge for it. Some companies don't let you talk to a technical support representative until you've given them a credit card number.

Q Isn't it the company's responsibility to build products that work?

A Absolutely. But it's also important to read the manual and make sure that you've exhausted your resources before tackling technical support—and we make this recommendation simply because you may find the answer faster that way.

9

PART

II

Improving Your Expertise

Hour

10 Fonts

11 Applications

12 Networking

13 Printing

14 File Sharing

15 Setting Up Your Internet Connection

16 Using Your Internet Connection

Hour 10

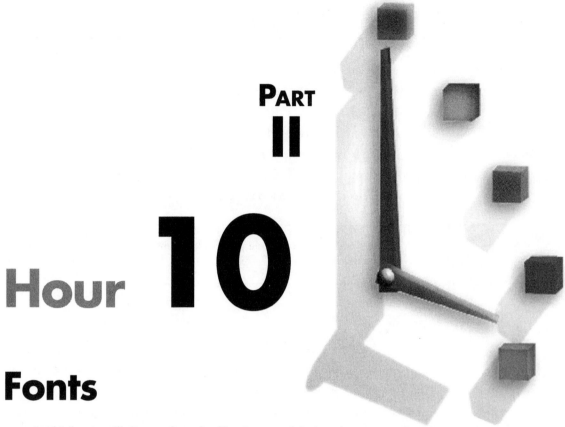

Fonts

In this hour we'll discuss *fonts*, the files that your Macintosh uses to make the type in its documents (and its interface) more appealing.

Fonts are composed of files that describe a *typeface*, a set of typographic characters of a particular design and size.

There's a lot of confusion—even among people who make their living with them—surrounding the terms *font* and *typeface*. Technically, a font is the file the computer uses to create a typeface, and the typeface itself is the style, weight, size, etc. of a set of characters. All but the most technically-savvy Macintosh users, though, say "font" when they mean "typeface." In this Hour, we'll use the terms interchangeably.

To make matters even more confusing, there are a variety of different types of fonts as well. The fonts on your screen are a different sort of font from the ones you use to print to your laser printer, for example. By the end of this hour, you'll be able to sort them all out.

There are many ways to get fonts, and thousands of fonts from which to choose. They all look different, and they serve a variety of needs.

The highlights of this hour include:

☐ How to work with fonts

☐ What the difference is between the various types of fonts

☐ How to add new fonts to your computer, and to your documents

☐ Why you may want to use third-party font utilities

☐ How to use fonts to create good-looking documents

JUST A MINUTE

> We'll discuss how to change your Finder's font in Hour 17, "Customizing the Finder and Software."

Font Basics

The Macintosh was one of the first computers—and certainly the first personal computer—that enabled users to customize the look of the type they created. The Mac OS uses a variety of different types of *fonts* to let you create documents using different type styles.

Mac OS 8 comes with nearly 20 fonts built in; if you own (or buy) a printer, you'll usually get a dozen or so additional fonts. You can also buy fonts from software vendors, or download them from the Internet. Adobe Systems (www.adobe.com/type, 408-536-6000) is one of the most popular commercial distributors of fonts; many other smaller foundries produce extremely popular special-interest or avant-garde fonts. You can also download fonts for free (or a nominal fee) from major shareware sites like *Macworld* Online (www.macworld.com). As a rule, commercial fonts are of a much higher quality than their shareware brethren, but that's not always the case.

Bitmapped versus PostScript Fonts

In the olden days of Macintosh, all fonts were fixed-sized *bitmapped* fonts—each character was made up of a series of dots, forming the shape of the letter or number (see Figure 10.1).

Each bitmapped font came in a variety of sizes—typically 9, 10, 12, 14, and 18 points—in order to give users a choice of sizes to print and view their type with. If you wanted a larger or smaller size (or a size that wasn't offered by your chosen font) you *could* select it, but the result would be a jagged onscreen appearance, caused when the application had to manually enlarge or reduce an existing size.

10

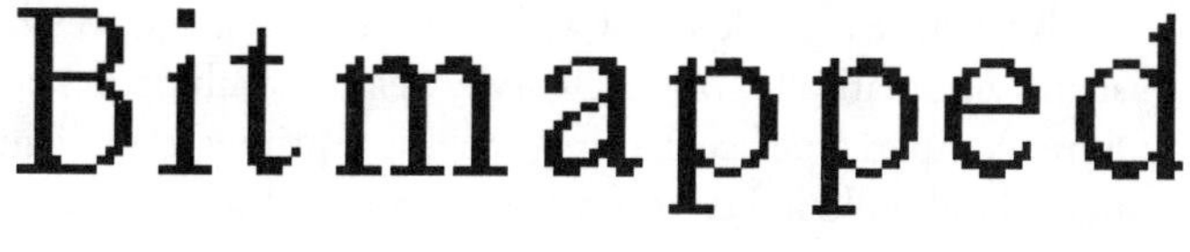

Figure 10.1
A bitmapped character is made up of lots of small, square dots.

Bitmapped

When you print a document using bitmapped fonts, each letter's shape—the specific placement of its dots—is downloaded to the printer. If it looks jagged on your screen, a bitmapped font will also look jagged on your printout. Before the advent of smooth-printing laser printers, a document's appearance was limited by the resolution of the printer, so jagged fonts weren't really all that important; even if they had been able to use smooth fonts, most early Macintosh printers' output would have looked awful by today's standards.

When the LaserWriter came along, desktop publishing was born with the help of *PostScript*. PostScript is a page description language developed by Adobe Systems—the company that you may recognize as the name behind best-selling software packages like PageMaker and Illustrator. (A *page description language*, briefly, is the code that a computer uses to send files to a printer; we'll talk more about this in Hour 13.) PostScript fonts are specifically designed to use PostScript code—rather than dots—to describe their various letterforms' shapes.

Unlike bitmapped fonts, PostScript fonts are scaleable—they don't require a different font file for each typesize. Each font is essentially a miniature program that describes the various lines and curves of all of the letters, numbers, and other characters that a PostScript-capable laser printer can produce.

When you use a PostScript font, the font's built-in intelligence knows how to print each character at any size you specify. It draws the outline of each character (based on the PostScript code that describes its shape) and then fills it in to create the letter's shape (see Figure 10.2). PostScript fonts are sometimes generically known as *outline fonts* for this reason.

Figure 10.2
A PostScript character is made up of a smooth, hollow outline that's filled in.

PostScript

Screen Fonts versus Printer Fonts

PostScript fonts are comprised of two components: the printer (or downloadable font) and the screen font. The *printer font* generates the actual PostScript code that's used to print your document; the *screen font* is the bitmapped font used for displaying the typeface onscreen.

Each typeface is made up of various sizes, styles, and weights. PostScript takes care of the sizing automatically, but each style/weight combination requires a separate printer font. Some complex typefaces have eight or more printer fonts: light, light italic, medium, medium italic, bold, bold italic, heavy, heavy italic and so on.

Even if you're not using bitmapped fonts to print, you still need a separate file for each type size that you want to display. These different-sized font files are grouped together in a *suitcase*, a special folder-like container named for the icon that represents bitmapped fonts (see Figure 10.3).

Figure 10.3

Bitmapped fonts are housed in a special folder-like container called a suitcase.

Helvetica

TIME SAVER

In past versions of system software, these various font sizes were necessary to prevent you from having jagged type onscreen. With Mac OS 8, Apple bundles Adobe Type Manager, a utility that automatically displays typefaces onscreen based on their printer fonts (among other capabilities; we'll talk more about ATM later in this hour). You'll probably want to keep multiple screen font sizes for the fonts you use anyway, though. ATM's process is slightly more time consuming than using the bitmapped font.

JUST A MINUTE

Early bitmapped fonts were used both for displaying type on the Macintosh screen and for printing documents. Because most bitmapped fonts used for printing have gone the way of the dinosaur, you may hear them referred to as *screen fonts*, because they're still the fonts the Macintosh uses to display the typeface on your monitor.

When you buy or otherwise obtain a font, the disk will contain files for both the printer fonts and the screen font suitcase (see Figure 10.4).

10

Figure 10.4

A complete typeface: printer fonts for the various weight/style combinations, and a suitcase containing the screen fonts.

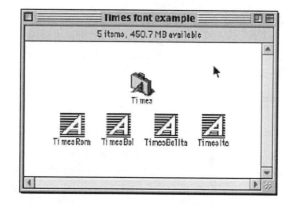

If you double-click on a screen font suitcase, you can see the various sizes and weights of the screen fonts inside it. To investigate the contents of a screen font's suitcase, perform the following steps:

1. Double-click on the System folder to open it.
2. Locate the Fonts folder and open it.
3. Double-click on the suitcase titled "Helvetica." The suitcase's window will appear (see Figure 10.5). You'll be able to see the various point sizes of the screen fonts included in this suitcase.

Figure 10.5

The Helvetica suitcase, open to display its screen fonts.

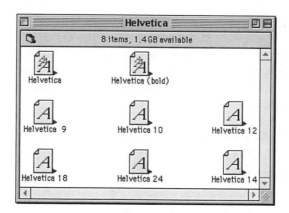

TrueType

In the last screenshot (Figure 10.5) you'll notice two different types of icons: one looks like a file with a single "A" on it, and the other has three cascading "A"s of various colors and sizes. The second icon represents a *TrueType* font.

TrueType fonts were developed as the successor to PostScript fonts, offering a simpler, easier way for most novices to deal with type. To simplify the whole font handling rigmarole, TrueType fonts incorporate both the printer font and the screen font into one file.

Despite their promise, TrueType fonts were plagued by a bad reputation in their early years. Because they were designed for the ease of the layperson—and not built to the exacting standards of the graphic design and typesetting community that generally is the last word on typography—TrueType fonts were shunned for many years.

Apple's inclusion of TrueType fonts in the Mac OS has lent a lot of credibility to TrueType, but if you're going to be creating documents much beyond word processing files or simple page layouts, you'll probably want to rely on PostScript fonts exclusively due to their superior built-in type-handling capabilities and position as a de-facto standard with designers and service bureaus.

Some of the fonts that ship with your Macintosh have a suitcase that contains both the old-fashioned bitmapped screen font and the TrueType version. Sound confusing? It can be, even to old experts like us.

Font Usage

The hardest part of using fonts proficiently is in understanding their various types and functions. In other words, we already have the worst part behind us. This section covers how to install (and remove) fonts, how to avoid common font pitfalls, and how to manage your font resources wisely.

Installing Fonts

Mac OS 8 makes it very simple for you to install new fonts onto your computer. To install a new font, perform the following steps:

1. Insert the font's disk into the floppy drive. (If you've downloaded the font, or it's otherwise already on your hard drive, skip this step.)

2. Drag the font's files over the System folder's icon and release (but do not drag them into the System folder's window, or allow spring-open folders to activate). Mac OS 8 will alert you that these files are fonts, and that they need to be placed into the Fonts folder (see Figure 10.6).

10

Figure 10.6

Mac OS 8 alerts you that it will put these files where they belong.

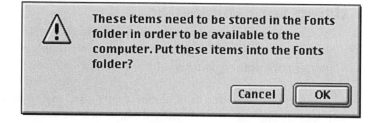

These items need to be stored in the Fonts folder in order to be available to the computer. Put these items into the Fonts folder?

[Cancel]   [OK]

3. Click OK. Now, when you launch an application, the new font will be available for your use.

To remove a font, you'll need to open the Fonts folder and remove its suitcase icon (and its printer font, too, if applicable), and drag the relevant files into the Trash.

TIME SAVER

To get an idea of what a given font looks like, open its suitcase icon, then double-click on any of the font files inside. A window will appear (see Figure 10.7) showing its appearance when set in a sample sentence. TrueType fonts (like the one shown in the screenshot) will show a variety of sizes; regular bitmap screen fonts will display just the size you've opened, so use the largest size available in order to get the best idea of the font's appearance.

Figure 10.7

Double-clicking on a font file brings up a window showing a type sample.

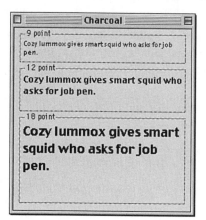

Using Font Utilities

Because fonts can be such a hassle, there are a number of third-party add-ons that help you manage and use type. These font utilities range from simple cataloguing programs that enable you to print out a type sample from each of your fonts (numerous shareware products perform this task, the best being the TypeBook, available for download from AOL and other large shareware libraries) to full-blown utility suites that smooth jagged type, enable you to open different font sets for different purposes, and let you view your fonts in menus in a unified way.

In past incarnations, Adobe Type Manager performed two simple (albeit useful) tasks: smoothing jagged type on non-PostScript printers, and creating smooth screen fonts that enabled most people to toss many of their various screen font sizes.

Nowadays, ATM performs all sorts of font-handling miracles, from its age-old capabilities of scaling fonts for printing and display up through complex font-handling tasks like grouping fonts into sets (so you don't have to keep all of your fonts loaded at one time) and substituting fonts if you don't have the typefaces used to create a document you're working on.

JUST A MINUTE

> Other type utilities, including Alsoft's MasterJuggler and Symantec's Suitcase provide similar capabilities, too, although ATM is arguably the best of the three—and certainly the oldest.

ATM's sibling product, Adobe Type Reunion, is one of a number of utilities that enables you to keep your font menus within applications better. Essentially, font menu managers combine the various weights and styles of a typeface into a nested menu (see Figure 10.8).

10

Figure 10.8

A font menu, with (above) and without (below) a menu manager installed.

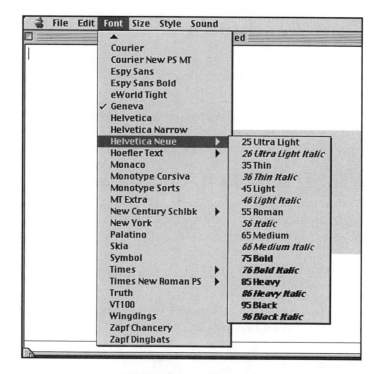

Font Aesthetics

Like many artistic endeavors, your choice of fonts in a document is a matter of personal taste. There are a set of basic guidelines, though, that most designers follow when setting type on the Macintosh.

You may see instances in magazines or advertisements that don't necessarily follow these guidelines. If you really feel strongly about bending (or breaking) the rules, go for it. They're just guidelines, after all.

Serif, Sans Serif, and Others

Most fonts fall into two basic font categories. *Serif* fonts—those fonts that have small flourishes (known as serifs) at the ends of their characters—are typically used for body copy, the main text of most documents. *Sans serif* fonts—those without serifs—are typically used for headlines and other items that need to be easily read, especially at large sizes. (This book, as an example, uses Agaramond—a serif font—for its main typeface, and Futura—a sans serif font—for major headlines.)

Examples of serif and sans serif fonts are shown in Figure 10.9. Serif fonts that ship with Mac OS 8 include Palatino and Times; sans serif fonts include Helvetica and Geneva.

Figure 10.9
Serif fonts have flourishes at the ends of their characters. Sans serif fonts do not.

Serif
Sans Serif

Display fonts are specialized typefaces designed for use in headlines only. They typically look very bad when used at sizes small enough for body copy.

Symbol fonts are collections of icons and other elements that can be created by typing a single keystroke; each "letter" of the font is a symbol. Examples of display and symbol fonts are shown in Figure 10.10.

10

Figure 10.10
Display fonts (above) are best-suited to headlines. Symbol fonts (below) contain icons and graphics that can be created with a single keystroke.

Picking the Right Font for the Job

Although the Macintosh is capable of creating bold and italic styles of type (or both) for every font you have, it's always best to use a specialized font for each. For example, if your font menu offers you the option of Helvetica and Helvetica Bold, choose the Helvetica Bold font to get the best possible appearance. This is especially true for italic fonts—the system's default italicizing of a font simply slants all the characters off to the right. Using the italic version of the font creates a much more desirable appearance (see Figure 10.11).

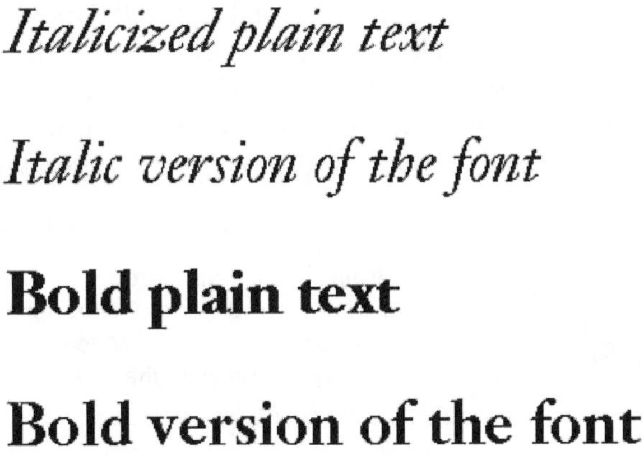

Figure 10.11
Using the proper version of the font will result in a much nicer appearance than simply bolding or italicizing the plain version.

Italicized plain text

Italic version of the font

Bold plain text

Bold version of the font

You'll also want to avoid the pitfall of most novice Macintosh users, which we call Ransom Note Syndrome. Rather than cramming each document with as many fonts as you can, you'll want to keep it simple (see Figure 10.12). Try limiting your fonts to three, at the most: one for headlines or headers, one for main text, and perhaps one for special elements like captions or large blocks of quoted passages.

10

Figure 10.12
Avoid the look of a ransom note by keeping your font selections within a document to a minimum.

When Type **Goes** Bad

Using too many **sizes** or **styles** of **TYPE** in a **document** can lead to an amaturish look.

Dignity—Always Dignity

It's a good idea to keep your type choices down to two or three fonts in each document. This leads to a much more professional appearance.   I

Typesetting, Not Typing

Now that you've mastered the basics of typography aesthetics, there's a few more guidelines you should know.

Like most people, you probably learned how to type on a typewriter, and follow the rule of two spaces after a period for legibility. Unlike typewriters, Macintosh fonts allow different amounts of space for each letter, depending on its size. A capital "W" is wider than a lower-case "l," and the Macintosh understands that. As a result, you don't need to resort to typewriter-specific tricks to make your documents readable; the space after a period, for example, will be wide enough to indicate the visual break.

TIME SAVER

You can simulate the appearance of a typewriter's letterspacing using a *monospaced* font—a font that allows the same amount of space for each letter, regardless of its width. Mac OS 8's Courier is a monospaced font, which we used to simulate the typewriter example above.

Because the Macintosh was built to work as a type-savvy device from the beginning, the Mac OS includes some handy ways to produce professional looking type.

You may be used to using the double-hash symbol (") to indicate the beginning and ending of a quotation, and the single-hash symbol (') as an apostrophe. Although no one would probably be confused by this usage, the Macintosh OS enables you to use true quotation marks by typing a combination of keystrokes (the single- and double-hash marks are best used for abbreviations for feet and inches, by the way).

Likewise, you can create dashes and long hyphens (known in the typesetting jargon as em dashes and en dashes), and ellipses, the three-dot symbol for a lingering thought or a quote broken in the middle of a sentence. Examples are shown below, in Figure 10.13.

10

Figure 10.13

The first example shows incorrect usage of single- and double-hash marks for quotes and apostrophes, and double hyphens for an em dash. The lower example is correctly typeset.

"When setting type, I'd never use non-curly quotes. How unprofessional..."

-- Famous Last Words

"When setting type, I'd never use non-curly quotes. How unprofessional..."

— Famous Last Words

To use keystroke combinations to create typographical characters, perform the following steps:

1. Launch your word processor or SimpleText.

2. Hold down the Option key, and press the key for a left bracket ([ ). An open-quote mark (") will appear.

3. Hold down the Option and Shift keys, and press the left-bracket key again. A close-quote mark (") will appear.

   You can do the same thing with the right bracket ( ]) to create single quotes, or apostrophes. Try it and see.

4. To create a long dash, hold down the Option and Shift keys, and press the hyphen (-) key (located to the right of the zero key on the top row of the keyboard). An em dash (—) will appear.

   You can create a long hyphen (an en dash, which is slightly longer than a hyphen, but not as long as an em dash) by holding just the Option key while typing a hyphen.

5. To type an ellipsis (…), hold down the Option key and press the semi-colon (;) key.

Many word processors enable you to set your preferences to automatically create true quote marks and apostrophes when you type a single- or double-hash mark. We'll talk more about this in Hour 11, "Applications."

JUST A MINUTE

For the last word on Macintosh typography, you'll want to purchase a copy of a small-but-indispensable little book called *The Mac is Not a Typewriter* by Robin Williams, published by Peachpit Press. This venerable book brought the world of Macintosh design kicking and screaming into legitimacy back in the dark ages of the Mac OS. It wouldn't be an

10

exaggeration to say that Robin Williams is largely responsible for raising the consciousness of Macintosh type aesthetics to an acceptable level. She covers specialized topics like letter spacing and proper use of white space, but also teaches the ins and outs of more basic topics like creating accents marks, diacritics, and other special characters right from your keyboard using the fonts you already have.

Summary

In this hour, you've learned the basics of using fonts to enhance the appearance of your documents. We've covered the basic differences between bitmapped and outline fonts, and the components of PostScript fonts, printer fonts and screen fonts. We've also talked about how TrueType simplifies font management.

You now understand how fonts work with your operating system, and how to manage them wisely. You also know how to add new fonts to your system, and the benefits of using third-party utilities to help you get the most from your fonts.

Lastly, we've touched on the basics of type aesthetics, and the methods for creating typeset-quality documents using keyboard shortcuts to produce typographer's quotes and other symbols.

Term Review

Bitmapped fonts   Fonts in which each character's shape is made up of little square dots. Also known as screen fonts or fixed-size fonts.

PostScript fonts   Also known as outline fonts.

Printer font   The component of a PostScript font used to download typographic data to the printer.

Sans serif   A typeface in which none of the letters have serifs.

Screen font   The bitmapped portion of a PostScript font that the Macintosh uses to display type onscreen.

Serif   The flourish (or tail) on the ends of each character in a serif font. The term is also used to distinguish typeface in which the letters have serifs from typefaces in which they don't (sans serif fonts).

TrueType   A simplified type system designed to make type management easier for laypeople.

Typeface   A set of characters of a specific design and size.

10

Q&A

Q I've just downloaded a Type 1 font. What's that? You don't mention it when talking about the different types of fonts.

A A Type 1 font is essentially a PostScript font. Sometimes shareware authors refrain from using the term PostScript because it's a trademark.

Q The type on all of my printouts is very jagged. What's up?

A If you're using a PostScript font, you probably don't have the printer font installed. You may also be using a bitmapped font. For more information about printing problems, see Hour 13, "Printing."

Q How can I get an idea of what a font will look like before I use it?

A Adobe sells a utility called Type Reunion that will let your font menus display each font's name in its own typeface. You can also select the Key Caps utility from the Apple menu, (Apple menu➡Key Caps). By choosing from your installed fronts in the Key Caps menu in the menu bar, you can display the entire character set of each typeface. Holding down the Option and Shift keys changes the display.

10

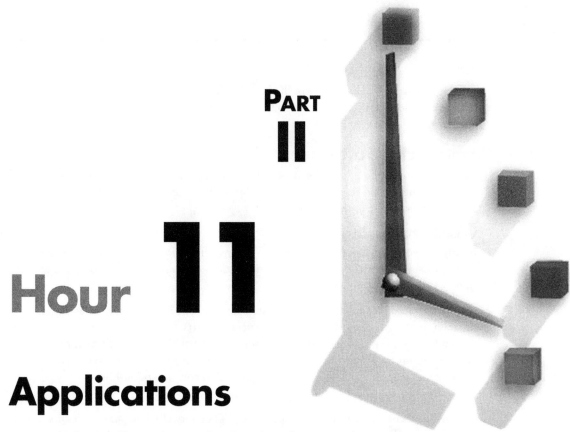

Hour 11

Applications

In this hour we'll investigate applications, the software your Macintosh uses to let you write reports, publish newsletters, communicate with your colleagues, surf the Internet, create digital masterpieces… and just about everything else you can imagine.

The highlights of this hour include:

- ☐ How to differentiate between the major application categories to pick the right package for your needs
- ☐ What types of software you can get for free (or close to free)
- ☐ What the difference is between an application and a utility
- ☐ How to install an application properly

Choosing the Right Applications

You may already have a lot of ideas on how to use your Macintosh. This section will explain briefly the main types of applications available for Mac OS 8. If you don't see the type of application listed here for the work you want to accomplish, don't worry; most software stores will be happy to help your find the right program for your needs. Reviews in the Macintosh magazines listed in Appendix B can also steer you in the right direction, especially if you're trying to decide between two competing products.

Commercial Software

Like most things in life, the majority of worthwhile application programs cost money. (Odd as that statement may seem, some folks actually do give away the fruits of their labors; see the Freebies section later in this hour.)

Word Processing

Nearly everyone—even computer rookies—knows the basic principles of word processing. Not surprisingly, word processors are the most commonly used personal computer application.

A word processor is something like a customizable, flexible typewriter replacement. It's a program specifically designed to help you generate reports, letters, memos, and other written documents. Word processors range from sub-$100 bare-bones text editors through high-powered, multi-megabyte programs (with prices to match) that let you do everything from drawing and graphing to automatic glossary creation and web publishing.

This is probably a good place to mention the principle of using the right tool for the job. You *could* use a baseball bat to swat flies, but it wouldn't be very efficient, and the results you get won't be as satisfactory. Similarly, many word processors enable you to perform page layout, type handling, and graphics tasks, but you'll generally get better results if you use an application that's been designed from the ground up to perform those specific duties. Likewise, a page layout program probably isn't going to provide as proficient a document-editing environment as a word processor can. We're not trying to encourage you to buy more software than you really need, though. If your page-layout demands are limited, your word processor can probably perform them well enough for occasional use.

Microsoft Word is the word processing market leader by a large margin, but it has long been reviled in the Macintosh market for its enormous (some say bloated) size, slow launch times, and cumbersome, Windows-derived interface. Smaller entrants like Corel Corp.'s WordPerfect and Mariner Software's MarinerWrite offer similar (and often better) features at a lower price, but Macintosh users keep flocking to Word because of its historical prominence and ubiquity.

All word processors enable you to change typefaces and sizes, save your files for later revision, cut and paste text, and perform basic text-handling functions like double-spacing and indenting paragraphs. Most include spell-checking features, automatic page numbering, the ability to import graphics from other programs, and search-and-replace features. As we mentioned before, there's really no limit to the tasks some word processors attempt to perform; high-end word processors offer charting functions, annotation and footnoting of text, specialized layouts and formatting, and links to spreadsheets and databases.

11

Nearly all word processors have at least two different cursors: the typical arrow cursor used for accessing menus and toolbars, and an I-beam insertion cursor that enables you to select a new entry point for typing (see Figure 11.1).

Figure 11.1

Most word processors have two different cursors, depending on where you're pointing. The arrow cursor activates menus and toolbar features, while the I-beam cursor lets you click to choose the text insertion point.

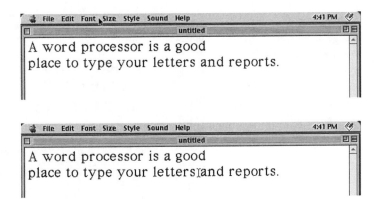

Desktop Publishing

When most people think of the Macintosh, desktop publishing (also known as DTP) is the application category that comes to mind first. And rightly so: desktop publishing made the Macintosh a viable personal computer platform, propelling it out of the realm of a curiosity.

Back in the mid-1980s Aldus Corporation created an entirely new industry with the release of PageMaker (now owned by graphics powerhouse Adobe Systems). The release of PageMaker and the introduction of the original LaserWriter laser printer made typeset-quality printing and page layout possible for the first time on a personal computer. Most early PageMaker documents weren't polished and perfect by today's standards, but in the intervening years nearly every major magazine—and the majority of book publishers and newspapers—have migrated to desktop publishing software and methods.

A few years after PageMaker's debut, Quark introduced QuarkXPress. At first, XPress had a reputation for being difficult to master, but rewarded its devotees with superior color and type handling features. Years later, QuarkXPress and PageMaker are still duking it out for the page layout crown, each revision bringing a slew of new features in a sort of one-upmanship rally. These days, the Quark-vs.-PageMaker debate is more historical than anything else. More high-end designers still use XPress, but it's more likely because that's what they learned to use back in the days when there was a serious differentiation between the products rather than because of any one specific feature.

Page layout packages let you create single- or multipage documents that combine text and graphics in a variety of ways. Most page layout packages enable you to import text from your word processor, and graphics from a drawing, illustration, or image editing program. You usually can make some level of modifications to the text and graphics within the desktop publishing document itself, although its primary purpose is as a container for the other types of content (see Figure 11.2).

Figure 11.2

A page layout/DTP program enables you to combine text and graphics into a newsletter, book, magazine, or other page-style document.

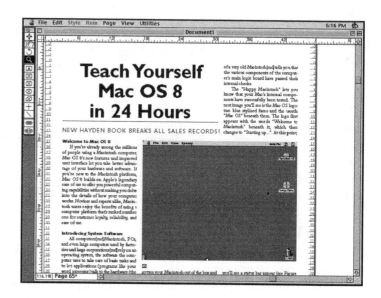

Graphics

Graphics applications include three major types of programs: drawing packages, illustration programs, and image editors.

Drawing packages—like ClarisDraw—are best suited to simple graphic uses, such as floor plans, diagrams, and other drawings composed mainly of basic shapes and lines. They offer simple manipulation tools like object rotation, text placement, and the capability to create lines of various widths and shapes filled with colors and patterns (see Figure 11.3).

Illustration packages go to the next level. Like drawing packages, they enable you to create simple shapes, but also offer complex and creative features like placing text along a curved path, blending two colors within a single shape, skewing objects to create perspective, cutting a hole (or a mask) in one object with the shape of another, and many others.

Like DTP, the world of illustration packages is broken along quasi-religious lines: Adobe Illustrator and Macromedia FreeHand (formerly owned by PageMaker creator, Aldus) are the two major contenders, but other applications—including MetaCreations Expression and Painter, and Deneba Canvas—offer similar features and incorporate special tools that create 3-D style effects or mimic natural media such as watercolors or oil pastels.

11

Figure 11.3
Drawing packages perform best when used for simple graphics.

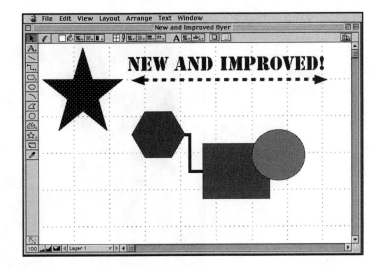

Like word processors and DTP, the line between drawing and illustration packages isn't as clear as it used to be. As simple packages add features and high-end packages become easier to use, there's less and less differentiation between the two categories.

Image Editors

Image editors—like Adobe Photoshop and PhotoDeluxe—enable you to manipulate photographs and other scanned images. Using add-on filters called *plug-ins,* most image editors can create a variety of special effects like changing the image to give the appearance of broken glass or a whirlpool—in addition to performing color correction and basic clean-up tasks like cropping and sizing images (see Figure 11.4).

Spreadsheets

Like the accountant's ledger that their design imitates, spreadsheets enable you to perform data calculations of all sorts, and all modern spreadsheets offer charting capabilities that let you display your numbers in graphical form (see Figure 11.5).

11

Figure 11.4

Image editors enable you to manipulate scanned images or other bitmapped graphics.

Figure 11.5

Spreadsheets let you crunch numbers, and chart them.

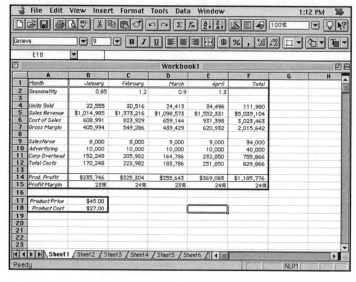

Like word processing, Microsoft monopolizes this category. Microsoft Excel is the only Macintosh spreadsheet with any semblance of market share, although newcomers (like Adrenaline Software's Numbers & Charts and Spreadsheet 2000 from Casady & Greene) offer unique capabilities that have earned them the support of a vocal minority.

11

Software Suites

If you don't know what sort of work you'll eventually need to do, you might want to invest in a *software suite*, a set of integrated applications that offers the capabilities of multiple types of programs in one package (usually at a lower price than if you'd bought each one separately).

ClarisWorks is the leader in this marketplace, combining most of the functionality of full-blown applications for word processing, spreadsheets, charting, presentations, graphics, and Internet access.

These applications leave out many of the high-end features that novices probably won't use, and integration between their applications is helpful for people who need help placing their spreadsheet data or graphics drawing into their word processor document.

Technically, Microsoft Office is a suite that combines Word, Excel, PowerPoint, and Microsoft Mail, but it's geared toward the business buyer, rather than the small office/home office user targeted by ClarisWorks and its ilk. You get the full version of all four applications, but integration is minimal and the applications are no easier to use as a set than they are on their own.

Other Types of Applications

We've covered the major types of applications that most people use regularly, but we've really only seen the tip of the iceberg. The world of Macintosh software is an ever-growing field. Here are a few other categories you might run across:

- [ ] **Database** applications enable you to create searchable repositories (databases) for your information. Claris FileMaker Pro's ease of use and power make it a favorite in the Macintosh database community.

- [ ] **Connectivity** programs include Internet browsers (like Netscape Navigator or Microsoft Internet Explorer) and email packages (like ClarisEmailer or Qualcomm Eudora). We'll talk more about them in Hour 15.

- [ ] **Presentation** packages enable you to make professional-looking onscreen (or printed) slides and other presentation materials for meetings and events. Microsoft PowerPoint and Adobe Persuasion are the major players here, and the differences between the two are subtle.

In the world of *Personal Finance* software, Intuit's Quicken is the undisputed champion. This electronic checkbook has made believers out of former finance-phobics. After a simple setup procedure, you can enter (and even print) checks, reconcile your register, plot your budget, track credit obligations, and plan savings and investments as well. You may also want to check out Intuit's MacInTax program next April, to help you prepare your federal (and some states') income tax return.

11

Of course, you didn't *just* buy your Macintosh to work hard, and you'll be delighted to find the software stores full of all sorts of diversions. Although most major *games* are released first on the Windows platform, their appearance (often a year or more later) on the Macintosh is usually worth waiting for. Macintosh hardware and the Mac OS provide a significant advantage in the quality of the graphics, sound, and performance of many games.

Screen savers—programs that fill your screen with images of swimming fish or destructive doggies after a period of inactivity—can also be entertaining, despite the fact that Macintosh monitors haven't needed saving in years—modern monitor technology makes it nearly impossible for images to "burn in" to a computer screen. Berkeley Systems' AfterDark is a best-seller.

Utilities

Utilities are similar to applications, except that their focus is typically limited to a specific task. (They're so much like applications, in fact, that there's no technical difference; nearly all utilities are merely small applications.) A utility is generally designed to do one thing well (back up your hard disk, decompress files, create macros) whereas an application performs a series of related functions and typically (although not always) creates a document or output of some sort. We're generalizing, of course, but utilities typically *do something* and applications typically *make something*.

A few utilities you'll want to check out:

- ☐ **QuicKeys** is a macro-creation utility that enables you to perform complex operations with a single keyboard shortcut (see Hour 24 for more details). This utility is technically a control panel.

- ☐ **DiskCopy** is a nifty little utility that enables you to make quick and easy copies of floppies.

- ☐ **Retrospect** is the leading dedicated disk backup utility. See Hour 21 for more reasons why you'll want to get very familiar with this one.

- ☐ A **multi-format file opener** (like CanOpener) enables you to open (or at least view) files from other people's machines when you're missing the program that created them. They're also useful if you end up with a corrupted file that your application won't open; sometimes you can retrieve the text from it.

- ☐ A **disk utility package** (such as Norton Utilities) enables you to check your hard drive for problems, optimize its speed, and other storage-related tasks.

- ☐ A **multipurpose utility suite** like Connectix Desktop Utilities offers a bundle of a number of smaller utilities that let you set power settings, control menu options, enhance your Finder windows with additional information, password-protect files, and lots of other basic features.

11

Freebies

Free software: what a marvelous idea! Believe it or not, there are ways of obtaining software packages that perform many of the same functions as commercial applications for free or a minimal fee. Some applications and utilities come standard with your Macintosh; others are included in a package-deal purchase price; still others are available for download from Internet sites like *Macworld* Online (www.macworld.com) or Shareware.com (www.shareware.com) or commercial online services like AOL or CompuServe.

Bundled Software

Some Macintosh models (especially those geared toward the home or education market, and those made by non-Apple systems vendors) include—or *bundle*—applications with their hardware. Many bundled applications are about as useful as their price indicates (you get what you pay for, after all), but some vendors include full versions of commercial applications that you'd probably buy otherwise. Of course, bundled programs aren't really free; the price is included in the cost of your computer.

TIME SAVER

> When pricing a system that includes bundled software, be sure you're getting something you'll really use. Although some bundles are genuine values, many include "lite" or "LE" (limited edition) versions of well-known packages. They may sound compelling, but in reality most bundled versions are hobbled so that you'll need to "upgrade" to the full version in order to do any serious work. If you won't be using that funky image editor or no-name children's software that comes "free" with your Macintosh, it's no bargain. Consider the price of competing systems without bundles before you decide you've gotten the deal of the century.

All Apple systems and Mac OS-compatibles ship with SimpleText. As its name implies, SimpleText is a very limited text editor. Think of it as a lobotomized word processor and you won't be too far off the mark.

SimpleText is most often used to launch ReadMe files included with your system or with third-party software. (There's more on ReadMe files in the next section: Installing Applications.) You can also use SimpleText to write a quick note or any other written document that needs minimal formatting.

Aside from SimpleText, there are relatively few true applications that come with most Macintosh systems. Mac OS 8 systems include Netscape Navigator and Microsoft Internet Explorer for web surfing, and ClarisEmailer Lite for Internet email; we'll be discussing those in detail in Hour 16.

Most included applications fall into two categories: utilities and assistants. Utilities bundled with Mac OS 8 include Disk First Aid, a simple diagnostic and repair tool for your hard drive; and Drive Setup, a disk formatter that allows you to completely erase and reformat your hard drive.

The utilities bundled with Mac OS 8 are shown in Figure 11.6. Other utilities are located in the Internet folder; we'll discuss these in Hour 16.

Figure 11.6

The utilities folder on the root level of the hard drive.

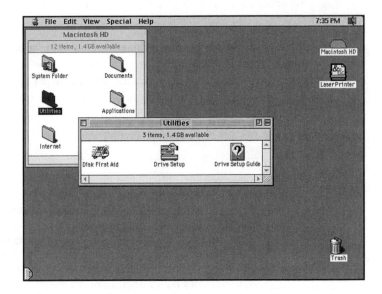

Assistants

Assistants are step-by-step programs that walk you through configuring your Macintosh for various tasks. Assistants provide a secondary interface to Mac OS 8 options that you can otherwise control elsewhere—they're like enormous shortcuts that let you enter pertinent information in one central location; the assistant then enters the appropriate information—based on your answers—into the appropriate control panels, applications, and utilities as needed.

The Internet Setup Assistant, ISP Registration Assistant, and Internet Editor Assistant all help you configure your Macintosh for use online. We'll cover them in Hour 15.

The PowerBook File assistant is used to synchronize files on PowerBook portable systems to your desktop Macintosh.

The most basic setup assistant is the Mac OS Setup Assistant. You probably have already taken a quick pass through this Assistant (Apple sets up all Mac OS 8 systems to launch it immediately the first time they're turned on), but if you haven't gone through it in detail, it's a great place to handle multiple configuration tasks at one time.

11

To get an idea of how assistants work, perform the following steps:

1. Open the Assistants folder on the hard drive (see Figure 11.7).

Figure 11.7

The Mac OS Setup Assistant in the Assistants folder on the hard drive.

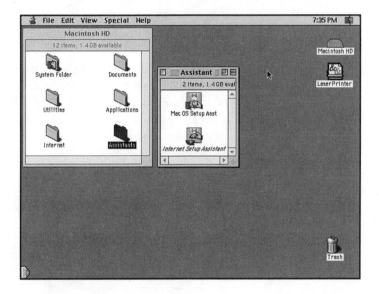

2. Double-click on the Mac OS Setup Assistant to launch it. The Assistant will open (see Figure 11.8).

Figure 11.8

The Mac OS Setup Assistant's first screen.

3. Click on the right arrow (as circled in Figure 11.8 above) to advance to the next screen.

4. The Setup Assistant will advance you through by entering your name and organization name, and by selecting your time, date, geographic location, and language variant (for example, British vs. U.S. English)—all of these data will be used to customize the Mac OS to your needs.

5. The next screen will ask you if you want to use Simple Finder. This feature limits the amount of options you have at the Finder level, which may be good for beginners, but it keeps you from using all of Mac OS 8's capabilities and disables keyboard shortcuts (see Figure 11.9). If you're easily overwhelmed, you may want to turn Simple Finder on; otherwise, leave it off. (This book assumes Simple Finder is disabled.)

Figure 11.9

The File menu, with (left) and without (right) Simple Finder enabled.

File	
New Folder	⌘N
Open	⌘O
Print	⌘P
Move To Trash	⌘⌫
Close Window	⌘W
Get Info	⌘I
Label	▶
Sharing...	
Duplicate	⌘D
Make Alias	⌘M
Put Away	⌘Y
Find...	⌘F
Show Original	⌘R
Page Setup...	
Print Desktop...	

File
New Folder
Open
Close Window
Duplicate
Find...

The remaining assistant questions pertain to your local area network (or LAN). We'll talk more about the remainder of this assistant in Hour 12. (Feel free to complete the rest of the questions, if you want to tackle them on your own, or skip ahead to Hour 12.) For now, though, continue as follows:

6. Click through the rest of the assistant (using the right arrow key) until you reach the final screen, telling you that the assistant will make changes to your Macintosh. Do not quit the assistant or you'll lose the changes you've made.

11

7. Press "OK" to complete configuration with the assistant.

8. Press "Quit" to resume working.

Shareware and Freeware

Shareware (and its variant, freeware) are innovative ways for small software companies (typically one-person shops) to market and distribute their products.

Alas, like bundled software, shareware isn't really free. Unlike commercial software, though, you can obtain shareware without paying anything up front; it's a high-tech version of an honor bar. You can download and use shareware—usually for a specific number of days— to check out how well it meets your needs. After the time limit is up, the author expects that you'll send her the licensing fee (typically ranging from $11 to $50, depending on the type and complexity of the program).

Freeware, on the other hand, really is free. The authors of these programs don't expect you to send them money, and you're under no legal or moral obligation to do so. Some freeware authors ask for a postcard from your hometown, or some other token of appreciation for their efforts if you use the package a lot and find it a useful alternative to a commercial solution (or, more likely, filling a gap where no commercial software exists).

Most major online services offer shareware libraries. *Macworld* Online's shareware library (`www.macworld.com/software/`) contains nearly every type of file you could want. (Unlike many commercial services, *Macworld* Online actually screens its shareware for usability and usefulness.)

11

Installing Applications

Most applications come with an *installer*—a utility that places all of the various pieces of software needed to run an application in the appropriate places (see Figure 11.10).

There are many different types of installers, and they all have different interfaces. Even so, they perform nearly identical functions, and function using the same basic principles. Because we don't assume that you'll have an application to install right away—and because the interface is slightly different for each type of installer—we're simply going to show you some of the basics, rather than walking you through a hands-on exercise.

When installing an application, these are the appropriate steps:

1. By double-clicking on the installer utility's icon, the utility is launched.

2. As the utility opens, its interface screen appears (see Figure 11.11). In some installers, you'll first get a welcome screen, an option to select a destination hard drive, or a ReadMe file outlining special installation instructions.

Figure 11.10

An installer utility, surrounded by its installer files. Some installers hide their files so you can't tamper with them or delete them accidentally.

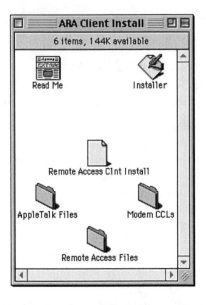

Figure 11.11

An installer utility's interface.

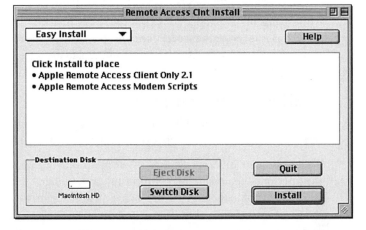

3. To install all of the portions of the application that the vendor recommends, you simply select Easy Install from the drop-down menu (circled in Figure 11.11, above) and click Install. The installer places the appropriate files on your hard drive, and prompts you to restart the machine if any system software components have been added.

4. If you want to pick and choose the files that will be added to your Macintosh, select Custom Install instead. A new interface appears (see Figure 11.12).

Figure 11.12

A Custom Install screen.

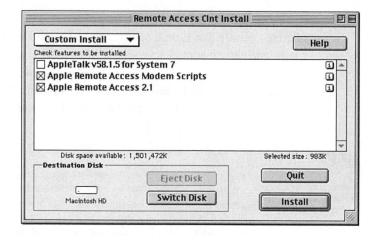

5. Clicking on the check boxes beside the various components will enable or disable them from being installed. The Selected Size amount in the lower-right corner of the screen tells you how much room the selected components will take up on your hard drive. The Disk Space Available file shows how much room is left on your hard drive.

6. Clicking on the information icon (the smaller icon on the right side of each component) brings up detailed information about each piece's function, to help you decide which portions of the software you need to install (see Figure 11.13).

Figure 11.13

An installer information window for a software component.

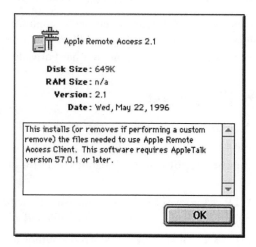

7. If you want to install the software on a drive other than the drive which holds your system software, you'll need to click on the Switch Disk button to select the appropriate destination.

8. After selecting the portions of the program you want to install and verifying their destination, click on the Install button. The installer places the appropriate files on your hard drive, and prompts you to restart the machine if any system software components have been added.

JUST A MINUTE

> The ReadMe files that most installers place on your hard drive aren't space-wasters; they often include valuable information about a product—especially bugs or incompatibilities—that were discovered too late to be included in the documentation. Not only is it a good idea to read them before starting to use a program, you may want to print out a copy and stick it in you manual for future reference, even if there's nothing pertinent there right now.

Summary

In this hour, you've learned what the various types of applications are used for, and how to pick the right one for your needs. We've also covered *freeware* and *shareware* programs—software you can try before you buy.

You now know the difference between an application and a *utility*, and have an idea of which utilities are most useful, and we've walked you through using an installer program to properly place software components on your hard drive for use.

Term Review

Assistant   A step-by-step program that walks you through configuring your Macintosh.

Bundled applications   Programs included in the purchase price of a new Macintosh system.

DTP   Acronym for desktop publishing, the process of creating newsletters and other publications using a personal computer and a laser printer.

Freeware   Shareware for which the author does not charge a fee.

I-beam   The text-insertion cursor in a word processor or image editor.

Plug-ins   Extension modules for graphics applications (especially image editors) that add new tools or give greater functionality to the basic tools.

11

Shareware   Software available for download from online services or the Internet on a trial use basis. Usually written by small software companies (or individuals) and selling for under $50.

Software suite   A group of applications sold as a set. Typically includes a word processor, and other business/productivity applications such as a spreadsheet, graphics, and email.

Utilities   Limited functionality applications designed to perform a specific task.

Q&A

Q I don't have access to the Internet. Where else can I get shareware?

A User groups often sell disks or CDs full of shareware and/or freeware as money-making vehicles, or give it away as part of your membership package. To find a user group near you, see Appendix B.

Q I just downloaded a piece of software from the Internet (or bought a small company's product). It doesn't have an installer. What do I do?

A If a product's installation process is simple and relatively foolproof, vendors often bypass the installer. If there's just one icon on the disk (or in the downloaded file), simply drag it to your hard drive, and double-click to launch it.

If there are multiple files, it's often obvious which is the application and which are the supporting files. Create a new folder within your Applications folder, and move the application and its files into it. If any of the program's files are extensions or control panels, drag them on top of the (closed) system folder icon; Mac OS 8 will automatically place them where they belong, as long as they're system software components. Check for a ReadMe file that might offer additional assistance, too.

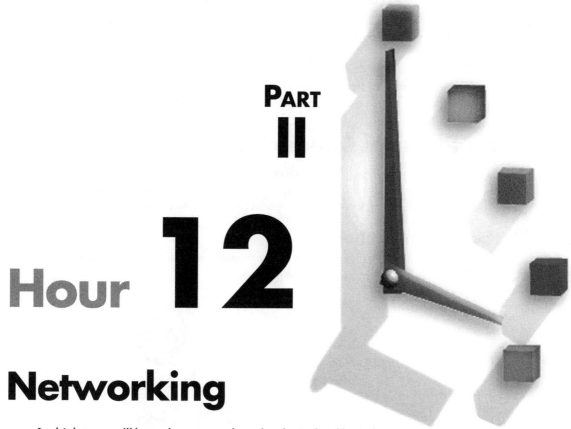

Hour 12

Networking

In this hour, you'll learn about networks—the physical and logical connections between multiple Macintosh systems and/or printers. Networks are the infrastructure over which you can print your documents and share files with other users. (We'll cover these tasks in the next two hours.)

The highlights of this hour include:

☐ How to set up a simple network, such as one connecting your Macintosh to a printer

☐ What types of networks exist, and why you'd choose one over another

☐ How to connect two or more Macintosh systems to each other, and/or to a printer

☐ How to configure Mac OS 8's network software

LAN Basics

The smallest network consists of two devices: two Macintosh systems, or a single Macintosh and a single printer. This second type of LAN (or *Local Area Network*) is by far the most common type.

You can also connect dozens (or even hundreds) of Macintosh systems and printers together using the same basic principles that we'll learn to connect your Macintosh to your printer.

The Physical Connection

On the back of your Macintosh, you'll notice a number of jacks (called *ports*) with icons beside them. You've already used at least one of them to plug in your monitor. Macintosh systems offer two different types of ports for connecting your system to printers and other devices.

Serial Connections

Serial ports enable you to connect your Macintosh to a serial printer or a modem (see Figure 12.1); their icons illustrate these two options.

Figure 12.1
The Serial ports.

JUST A MINUTE

Even though one serial port shows a modem icon and the other shows a printer icon, they're virtually identical. Unless you have some reason to disregard the icons (if, for example, you have two printers and no modem), it's best to plug devices into the appropriate ports, just to avoid confusion. Modem and printer software are set to default to the "correct" port, and you may encounter setup difficulties if you disregard the labels.

LocalTalk Connections

Although direct serial connections (such as those used for printers and modems) aren't technically networks, the printer port is also used for the Macintosh platform's simplest form of networking: LocalTalk. To create a simple LocalTalk network, you'll need to purchase two LocalTalk connectors. PhoneNet brand connectors from Farallon Computing are the most

12

widely-used brand, although other, cheaper knock-offs exist (see Figure 12.2). These connectors contain electronic components that arbitrate the flow of information across the network, and they also provide a connection for the physical wire over which your network data travels.

Figure 12.2

A Farallon PhoneNet connector.

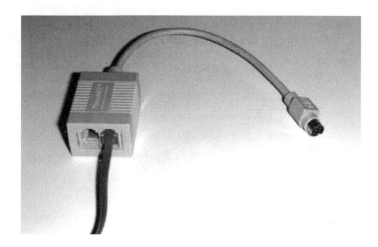

To create a simple LAN, perform the following steps:

1. Turn off all equipment.

2. Plug one PhoneNet-type connector into the printer port of your Macintosh.

3. Plug the second connector into the serial port of your printer.

4. Insert terminators (the plastic pieces that look like phone jack connectors with little rings attached to wires coming out of them) into one of the openings on each of the two connectors.

5. Insert a piece of phone cable (preferably the one that came with the connectors) into each connector's remaining opening, connecting the two devices.

6. Turn the power back on, and you have a network.

That's all there is to it. To connect two Macintosh systems together instead of one printer and one Macintosh, simply plug the second connector into the printer port of the second system.

12

CAUTION

Always be sure that the power is turned off whenever you install or remove hardware from your Macintosh.

JUST A MINUTE

Simple, wasn't it? LocalTalk networking has been around for more than a decade. It was built into the very first Macintosh systems, back in the days when networking PCs together was a difficult, time-consuming process.

It gets even easier from here. To add another device (either a printer or a Macintosh) to your LAN, perform the following steps:

1. Turn off power to all devices.

2. Plug another PhoneNet-type connector (with one terminator) into the new device(s).

3. Remove the terminator from the connector of the computer or printer closest to the new addition.

4. Run a phone cord from the new device's connector to the empty jack on the nearby device's connector.

5. Turn the power back on.

And so on, and so on. To add more devices, repeat the process, being sure to keep a terminator in the connectors at the ends of your chain. This type of network of sequentially linked devices in known as a *daisy chain*. A simple daisy chain LAN—just like the one we set up—is shown in Figure 12.3.

Figure 12.3

A small daisy-chained LocalTalk network.

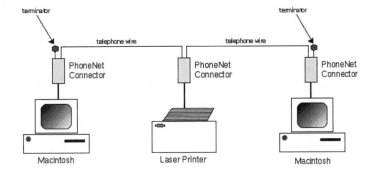

Ethernet Connections

All modern Macintosh systems also offer a second type of networking port: the *Ethernet port* (see Figure 12.4).

Figure 12.4
An Ethernet port.

Ethernet transports data between devices nearly ten times faster than LocalTalk. Its connectors, though, are more expensive, and a true Ethernet LAN requires specialized (and often costly) hardware in addition to the connectors.

The clever folks at Farallon put an end to a lot of the hassle surrounding establishing your own Ethernet LAN when they introduced EtherWave connectors (see Figure 12.5).

Figure 12.5
An EtherWave connector.

Much like PhoneNet connectors, these stingray-shaped connectors plug into the Ethernet port of your Macintosh systems and printers. To connect them, you simply run a piece of cable between the two connectors. Unlike PhoneNet, though, no terminators are required, and instead of regular phone cable, EtherWave connectors use a thicker cable called *RJ-45 cable.* You'll need to know this if the cable included with your EtherWave connector isn't long enough; most electronics supply and computer stores stock RJ-45 cables of various lengths.

12

The Software Connection

Even though the Mac OS has always been much easier to configure than Windows or other PC-based operating systems, there used to be many more steps involved in setting up the software side of things. With Mac OS 8, Apple has simplified matters dramatically.

Using the Mac OS Setup Assistant

In the last hour, we used the Mac OS Setup Assistant as an example of software that's included with your computer. We worked through the first part of the assistant, but stopped short of using it to configure your network. Let's pick up where we left off.

To configure your network using the Mac OS Setup Assistant, perform the following steps:

1. Launch the Mac OS Setup Assistant in the Assistants folder on the hard drive.

2. Click on the right arrow to advance through the previously-used screens for entering your name and organization, selecting your time and date, geographic location, and language variant, and enabling or disabling Simple Finder.

3. Stop when you reach the Local Network Introduction screen (see Figure 12.6).

Figure 12.6

The Mac OS Setup Assistant's LAN introduction screen.

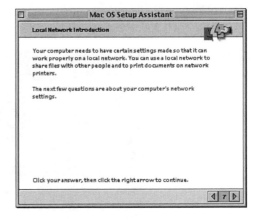

4. Click the right arrow to advance to the next screen.

5. In the next window you'll be asked to select a name and password for your computer (see Figure 12.7).

   If you're only going to have one computer on the LAN, choose whatever name you like. If you'll have company, though, be sure to pick something that can distinguish your Macintosh from the others ("My Macintosh" or "PowerMac" probably are bad choices). For your password, pick something that you'll remember, but that others would have a hard time guessing. After you've entered your name and password, click the right arrow to advance to the next screen.

12

Figure 12.7

The Mac OS Setup Assistant's Name and Password screen.

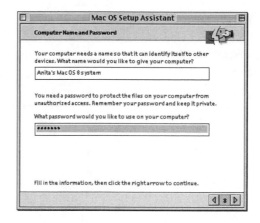

6. The next screen enables you to set up a special folder on your desktop for use when sharing files with others on your LAN (see Figure 12.8).

Figure 12.8

The Mac OS Setup Assistant's Shared Folder screen.

For the folder name, the assistant defaults to the user name you entered earlier, plus "Shared Files," but you can name the folder anything you like.

7. If you won't be sharing files with others, click the No radio button. Click the right arrow to advance to the next screen.

8. The next screen asks you to choose whether your printer is attached via a direct connection or a network connection (see Figure 12.9).

As the assistant notes, if your connection is anything more than a single cable (and yes, LocalTalk connectors count as more than a single cable), you're on a network. Select the appropriate connection's radio button, and click on the right arrow to advance to the next screen.

Figure 12.9

The Mac OS Setup Assistant's Printer Connection screen.

9. The assistant searches your hard drive for printer drivers and your network for printers before moving on to the next screen. After performing this search, it provides a list of all the available printers on your LAN (see Figure 12.10).

Figure 12.10

The Mac OS Setup Assistant's Printer Selection screen.

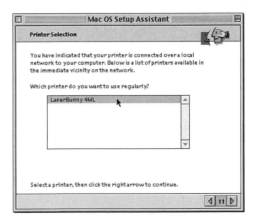

Select the name of the printer you want to use regularly, and click on the right arrow to advance to the next screen.

10. The assistant's last screen offers you the choice of canceling or completing the setup using the parameters you've defined (see Figure 12.11).

11. Click on the Show Details button. A new screen appears (see Figure 12.12).

12. If any of the information on the details screen is incorrect, click on the Cancel button to quit the assistant without making changes to your system. If everything looks fine, click Go Ahead to complete the network setup.

12

Figure 12.11

The Mac OS Setup Assistant's Conclusion screen.

Figure 12.12

The Mac OS Assistant's Conclusion Details screen.

CAUTION

> Don't quit the Assistant before the final screen or you'll lose the changes you've made.

13. Pressing OK enables you to continue with the assistant to set up your Internet access; we'll cover this in Hour 15. For now, press Quit to resume working.

Setting up Manually

The steps we describe here are virtually identical to what the assistant will do for you. The only reason we'd recommend using this manual formula is if you're experiencing difficulties and need to double-check your setup, or you're curious about how the software side of LANs work.

In order for your network devices to be able to speak to one another, you need to enable AppleTalk, the software side of the connection. To turn AppleTalk on, perform the following steps:

1. Open the Chooser (Apple Menu➡Chooser).

2. In the lower-right corner of the window, click the Active radio button next to AppleTalk (see Figure 12.13).

Figure 12.13
Activating AppleTalk in the Chooser with radio buttons.

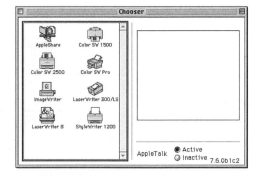

3. Close the Chooser. AppleTalk is now active.

JUST A MINUTE

AppleTalk Zones are smaller LANs-within-LANs that most medium-to-large offices use to simplify matters for their users and the people who administer the network. If you're running a simple network, you won't even know they exist. If your setup includes zones, your LAN administrator or IS department can help you choose the right one. Figure 12.14 shows the Chooser on a LAN with multiple zones.

Figure 12.14
The AppleTalk Control Panel on a LAN with multiple zones.

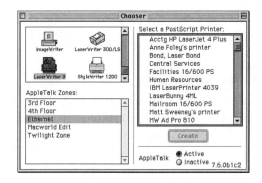

Next, you'll need to make sure that your Macintosh knows where to find your network, physically. To configure this portion of your LAN, perform the following steps:

1. Open the AppleTalk Control Panel (Apple Menu➡Control Panels➡AppleTalk).
2. Choose Printer Port from the pop-up menu (see Figure 12.15). If you're using EtherWave connectors, choose Ethernet instead.

Figure 12.15

The AppleTalk control panel's pop-up menu.

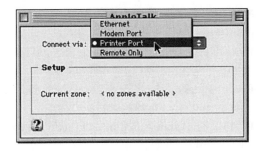

3. Close the AppleTalk control panel.
4. If you changed your connection, a dialog box will appear asking if you want to save your changes. Click Save to enable your new network settings.

Summary

In this hour, you've learned about the differences in the various types of local area network configurations: LocalTalk and Ethernet. You've seen how to install a simple LocalTalk network, and the basics of using the same principles to install an Ethernet LAN using EtherWave connectors.

We walked you through configuring your network software using the Mac OS Setup Assistant, and verifying your settings using a manual approach.

Term Review

AppleTalk   The language that devices use to speak to one another over a LocalTalk network.

Daisy chain   Connecting three or more network devices by linking one device's connector to an open jack on the connector of the next device.

Ethernet   A type of network with higher transfer speeds than LocalTalk.

12

EtherWave   Connectors that enable you to set up a simple Ethernet LAN without using high-end hardware.

LAN   An acronym for local-area network; a group of computers, printers, and other devices located in the same building and connected by cables.

LocalTalk   The hardware portion of a basic Macintosh network, including the connectors and cabling that connect two or more devices.

Network   The physical and logical connections between multiple computers or printers.

PhoneNet   A widely-used brand of LocalTalk connectors that use standard telephone cable to connect networked devices.

Ports   Plugs on the back of your Macintosh, used for attaching your computer to printers and other networked hardware.

RJ-45   The cabling used in an EtherWave Ethernet network, which resembles thick phone cord.

Serial ports   The printer and modem ports on the back of your Macintosh.

Q&A

Q If Ethernet is so much faster than LocalTalk, why doesn't everyone use it for their LANs? Why bother with LocalTalk?

A Most businesses use Ethernet LANs for just this reason. Unfortunately, most low-cost printers aren't Ethernet-capable, and adding Ethernet (if it's even an option) can cost hundreds of dollars. Also, EtherWave connectors are more expensive than PhoneNet connectors (about $100 compared with less than $20). For home and small-office uses, the extra speed isn't worth the added cost.

Q If it's a LocalTalk LAN, why do I use the AppleTalk control panel?

A LocalTalk is the hardware portion of a basic Macintosh network: the connectors and cabling that connect two or more devices (printers, computers, and so on) to one another. AppleTalk is the *protocol*—the language that the devices use to speak to one another over the LocalTalk connection. A lot of people confuse the two terms. Further compounding the problem, Ethernet refers to both the connection and the protocol of the higher-speed LAN.

12

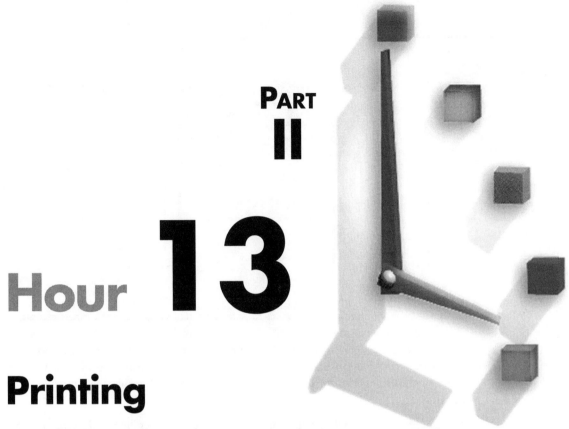

Hour 13

Printing

In this hour, we'll discuss how to use your Macintosh to print documents. We'll cover the basics of configuring Mac OS 8 to recognize your printer properly, as well as show you how to master the Page Setup and Print dialog boxes of both laser printers and inkjet printers (such as Apple's StyleWriter printers).

The highlights of this hour include:

- ☐ How to use the Chooser to access printer drivers
- ☐ How to use the page setup dialog box to get the output you want
- ☐ How to navigate the print dialog boxes of various printers
- ☐ What you need to know about desktop printing

The Chooser

After you've connected your printer to your Macintosh or its network, you need to tell Mac OS 8 where to find it. The *Chooser* is the Mac OS 8 component you use to define the network services you want to connect to, such as file servers (see Hour 23 for more details), or printers. To access the Chooser, select it in the Apple menu (Apple Menu➡Chooser).

A window appears (see Figure 13.1) with a set of printer icons on the left side.

Figure 13.1

The Chooser.

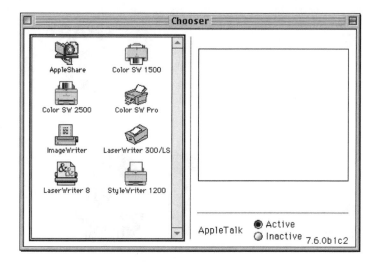

The icons on the left pane of the window represent all of the available *printer drivers*—the software that enables applications to communicate with your printer to print files. Chances are that you'll see a printer icon in the Chooser that looks something like the printer you want to print with.

The method for selecting the printer you want to use varies, depending on the type of printer driver you're using. In general, though, you click the driver's icon, and then click the setup button to complete the process. (We'll discuss the particulars in the following sections.)

TIME SAVER

> If you want to keep your Chooser lean and mean, you can disable the drivers for printers you don't use in the Extensions Manager (Apple Menu➡Control Panels➡Extensions Manager). Printer drivers are located in the Extensions folder, and show up as Chooser extensions in the Kind field (see Figure 13.2). You can disable unneeded printer drivers by deselecting their check boxes in the on/off column.

Setting up Your Laser Printer

To print to a laser printer, use the LaserWriter 8 driver located in the Chooser. LaserWriter 8 is Apple's driver for its own LaserWriter printers, but by using PostScript Printer Descriptions (PPDs), you can use LaserWriter 8 with nearly any laser printer. *PPDs* are documents that contain information about your printer's capabilities, including its resolution, supported page sizes, color capabilities, resolution enhancement features, and more.

13

Figure 13.2

Printer drivers show up in the Extensions folder of the Extensions Manager.

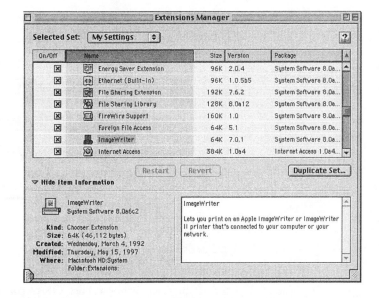

To select the laser printer you want to use, perform the following steps:

1. Open the Chooser (Apple Menu➡Chooser).

2. In the lower-right corner of the Chooser window, be sure that the AppleTalk Active radio button is selected.

3. Click the LaserWriter 8 icon. A list of available printers will appear in the right-hand pane of the Chooser window (see Figure 13.3). (If you're on a large network, many printers will appear; if your home setup includes a single printer, it will be the only choice shown.)

Figure 13.3

Selecting a printer driver in the Chooser brings up a list of available printers in the right-hand pane.

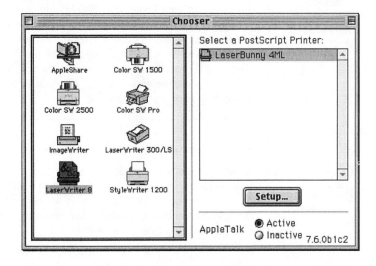

13

4. Click the name of the printer you want to use to select it.

5. Click the Setup button. A new window will appear (see Figure 13.4).

Figure 13.4

The Setup window.

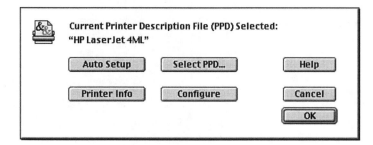

6. Click the Auto Setup button. The Chooser begins its automatic setup process.

7. Highlight the printer's PostScript Printer Description (PPD) in the list.

8. Click the Select button.

9. When you return to the Setup window, click OK to complete the setup process. You'll notice a printer icon to the left of the printer's name in the printer list, indicating that the printer has been set up.

10. Close the Chooser to activate your selection. A printer icon will appear on your desktop, showing that you have an active printer connection.

That's typically all you need to do to use your laser printer. If your printer has options (such as a second paper tray) you may want to click the Configure button to ensure that the Auto setup process has correctly accounted for them.

JUST A MINUTE

If your printer isn't listed in the PPD list, check the software that came with your printer; you'll want to install the correct PPD in the Printer Descriptions folder of your System Folder (System Folder➡Printer Descriptions) so that it will be accessible from the Chooser's Setup window. If you use the Generic PPD, you'll lose access to any special features of your printer, including resolution enhancement, high resolution printing (over 300 dpi), and color, among other options.

TIME SAVER

The Printer Info button (in the Chooser's Setup window) provides you with information regarding the RAM installed in your printer, its color capabilities, its model name, and its name on the network (see Figure 13.5). Click the Update Info button to refresh this information after upgrading your RAM or installing other options.

Figure 13.5

The Printer Info button displays information about your printer's built-in features, configuration, and installed options.

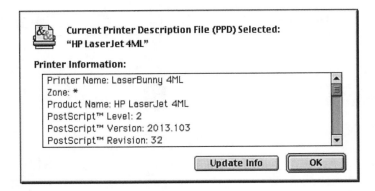

Current Printer Description File (PPD) Selected:
"HP LaserJet 4ML"

Printer Information:

```
Printer Name: LaserBunny 4ML
Zone: *
Product Name: HP LaserJet 4ML
PostScript™ Level: 2
PostScript™ Version: 2013.103
PostScript™ Revision: 32
```

[Update Info]   [OK]

Serial Printer Drivers

If you're not using a laser printer, chances are you're connecting an inkjet printer directly to your Macintosh's serial port. Mac OS 8 ships with a variety of drivers for serial printers.

JUST A MINUTE

If you're using a non-Apple serial printer, it's best to use the driver that came with it. Be sure to place any third-party printer drivers into the Extensions folder (System Folder➡Extensions).

Our example uses the Color StyleWriter 2500 driver, but nearly all serial printers follow similar setup steps.

To enable your serial printer for printing, perform the following steps:

1. Open the Chooser (Apple menu➡Chooser).
2. In the lower-right corner of the Chooser window, be sure that the AppleTalk Inactive radio button is selected.
3. Click the correct printer driver icon. The Setup... button will become active, and you'll be offered the choice of using the Printer Port or the Modem Port (see Figure 13.6).
4. Select the port to which your printer is connected (usually the printer port).
5. Click the Setup... button. A new window appears (see Figure 13.7).

13

Figure 13.6

Selecting a serial printer driver in the Chooser activates the Setup... button and offers you a choice of ports.

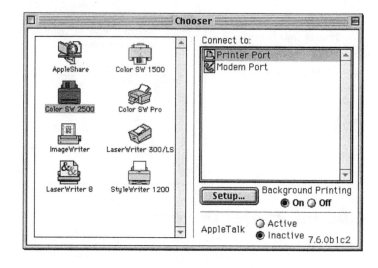

Figure 13.7

Clicking the Setup... button brings up a new dialog box.

6. Click the Share this Printer check box if you want other computers on the network to be able to use this printer. If you select this option, you'll be asked to name the printer and assign it a password.

7. If you want to keep a log of printer usage for your records, click the second check box.

8. Click OK to complete the setup process. You'll notice a printer icon to the left of the printer's name in the printer list, indicating that the printer has been set up. A printer icon will appear on your desktop, showing that you have an active printer connection.

13

When you select a serial printer, the Chooser also displays two radio buttons for enabling and disabling background printing. *Background printing* enables you to print your documents to a file on the hard drive, and return to work faster (the file is then downloaded to the printer as you work). Because you're creating this file on the drive—called a *spool file*—the overall printing process takes longer, but you'll regain use of your Macintosh quicker.

Page Setup

Page Setup enables you to change page attributes and define PostScript options. Our examples will assume that you're using a laser printer, but if you're using a StyleWriter or other serial printer, your choices are much the same. At the end of this section, we'll go over the key differences.

To get a feel for the Page Setup dialog box, perform the following steps:

1. From the Finder, open Page Setup (File➡Page Setup...).

   Its first window—Page Attributes—appears (see Figure 13.8).

Figure 13.8

Page Setup's opening window, Page Attributes.

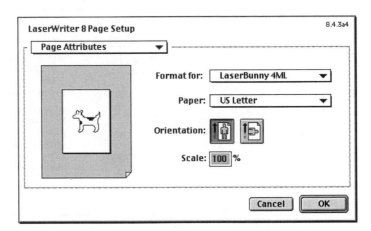

2. To change the active page size, click the pop-up menu next to Paper (currently showing US Letter). For this example, choose Legal. Notice how the size of the page with the dog on it (on the window's left side) changes to reflect your modifications. You'll want to select the paper currently installed in your laser printer, or a size that you can feed manually.

3. To change the orientation of your page, click the graphic buttons next to Orientation. Notice again how the sample page reflects your change.

4. To enlarge or reduce your printed image (compared with its size on the screen), type your desired percentage scaling in the numeric entry box next to Scale. Valid sizes are between 25 and 400 percent. The sample page does not reflect this change.

5. Close the Page Setup dialog box for your changes to take effect.

PostScript Options

Although the main Page Setup window enables you to perform most of the page setup tasks you're likely to need regularly, a second window offers even more capabilities.

To use the PostScript options portion of the dialog box, perform the following steps:

1. Open the Page Setup dialog box.

2. Click the pop-up menu just below the LaserWriter 8 Page Setup label (currently showing Page Attributes).

3. Select PostScript Options. A new window will appear (see Figure 13.9). Notice how your sample page remains true to your previous specifications.

Figure 13.9

The PostScript Options window.

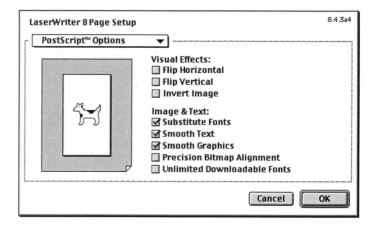

4. Click the Visual Effects check boxes to see what they do. (You can pick any or all of them, and the sample page will reflect your choices.)

5. Click the Image and Text features check boxes to define specific attributes for your printed pages:

   Substitute fonts tell the printer to use its built-in fonts instead of bitmapped fonts (Times for New York, Helvetica for Geneva, and so on). For more about fonts, refer back to Hour 10.

   Smooth Text helps you get better-looking type (if you must use bitmapped fonts) by smoothing out the jaggies. Likewise, *Smooth Graphics* will smooth the jaggy edges of bitmapped graphics.

13

Precision Bitmap Alignment reduces the size of the printed document to adjust for distortions that sometimes happen in printed graphics.

Unlimited Downloadable Fonts provides the best results if you need to print a document with a large number of fonts—especially to a printer with a small amount of RAM. Be aware that your documents will print slower with this feature enabled.

6. Close the Page Setup dialog box by clicking the OK button. To return to your previous setup (without making any of the changes you've defined in this exercise), click Cancel instead.

Application-Specific Windows

If you access Page Setup from within some applications, you'll see a third item in the Page Setup pop-up menu, specific to their own needs. Netscape Navigator, for example, offers a dialog box that enables you to define the headers and footers of web pages you print to show their location, date printed, and other useful information (see Figure 13.10). Other applications offer similar windows.

Figure 13.10

Netscape Navigator's page setup window.

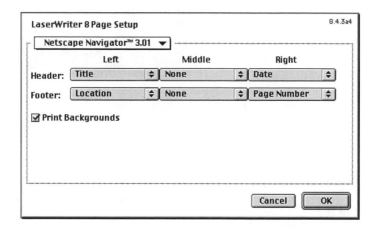

StyleWriter Page Setup

As we mentioned at the start of this section, StyleWriter drivers' Page Setup dialog boxes offer a lot of the same functionality as LaserWriter 8. Here are a few key differences.

First of all, you'll notice that the layout of the dialog box itself is different (see Figure 13.11). You'll see the familiar sample page with the dog and pop-up menus for page size, graphic buttons for orientation, and a numeric entry box for scaling your images, but StyleWriter Page Setup also offers a number of features not offered in LaserWriter 8.

13

Figure 13.11

A serial printer's page setup dialog box is slightly different than that of a laser printer.

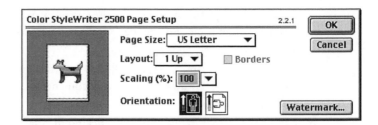

You can, for example, scale your images anywhere between 5 and 999 percent (as opposed to 25 to 400 percent in LaserWriter 8).

You can also print two or four document pages on a single printed page by selecting the Layout pop-up menu. Figure 13.12 shows a 4-up layout with borders between the pages. (LaserWriter 8 enables this feature from the Print dialog box; we'll discuss this later).

Figure 13.12

Setting up a serial printer for 4-up printing.

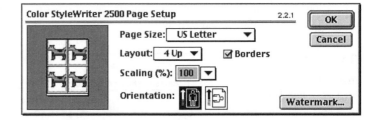

By clicking the Watermark… button, you can place a watermark behind the main image of your document (such as the word Draft in a light gray tint). Figure 13.13 shows the various options you can define: a pop-up menu for selecting the image or text to be used for the watermark, a slider to set the density of the watermark, and a Scaling pop-up menu that enables you to resize the watermark image.

Figure 13.13

The Watermark… button brings up a second dialog box.

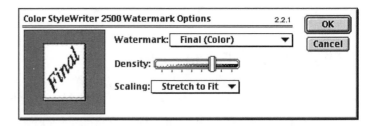

13

Print Dialog Boxes

Like Page Setup, the dialog boxes used to print documents with LaserWriter 8 are slightly different than those used with a StyleWriter (or other serial printer) driver. Our examples assume you're using a laser printer; StyleWriter or other serial printer users will have similar (but fewer) choices.

General Controls

To access the Print dialog box, choose File➡Print Desktop in the Finder. A dialog box appears (see Figure 13.14). You can also access the same dialog box from within any application's file menu, or by typing -P with any file selected or open.

Figure 13.14

The Print dialog box's main screen.

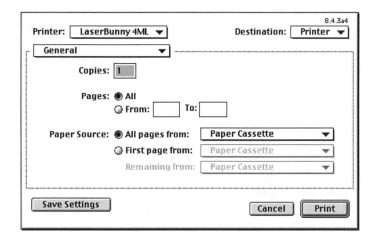

The first screen (called General, as seen in the pop-up window below the Printer field) enables you to define nearly all of the settings you'll use often.

TIME SAVER

If you want to bypass the print dialog box to save time, many applications offer a Print One or Print One Copy command from the File menu. You'll get a single copy of all the pages in your current document, printed with the default parameters.

13

Printer

If you have more than one printer set up and active, this pop-up menu enables you to define the printer to which you want to send your active print job.

Destination

If you need to save your current document to a PostScript file, this pop-up menu enables you to do so. You can define more specific information about this file by using the Save as File screen, which we'll discuss below.

Copies

If you need to print more than one copy, replace the 1 in this numeric entry field with the appropriate number (see Figure 13.15).

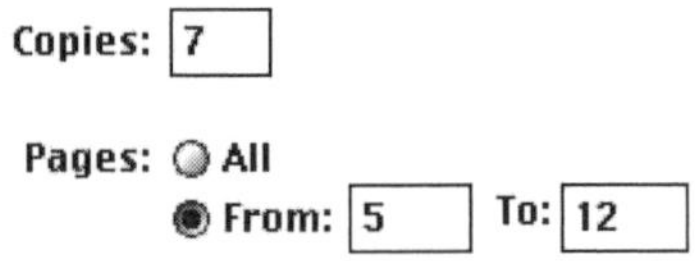

Figure 13.15

The Copies numeric entry field lets you print multiple copies of your document. The Pages fields let you define a range.

Copies: | 7 |

Pages: ○ All
       ◉ From: | 5 | To: | 12 |

Pages

If you want to print all the pages in your document, select the radio button next to All (that's the default). If you only need to print some of them (or even one page), type the appropriate page numbers into the range numeric entry fields (the From: radio button will automatically be enabled).

Paper Source

Paper Source enables you to specify which paper tray you'll use to print your files. Even if your printer only has one paper tray, you'll still use this option to print manually fed sheets. If you want to print the first page of a document on your company's letterhead, for example, and the remaining pages on plain paper from the paper tray, you can. Select First page from: Manual Feed (and place a page of letterhead in your printer's manual feed tray) and Remaining from: Paper Cassette (see Figure 13.16).

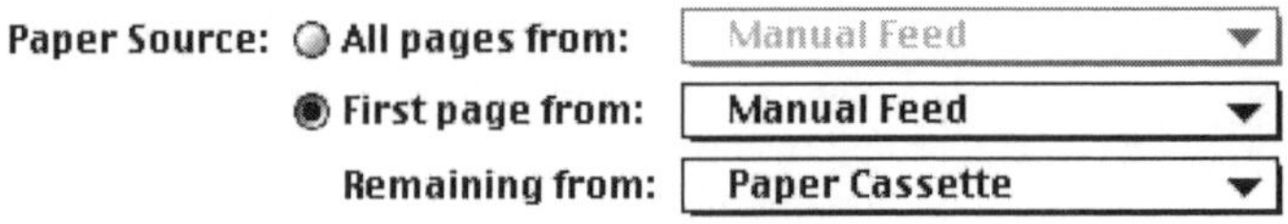

Figure 13.16

Paper Source enables you to print your pages from a variety of locations. You can even set your first page to print from one tray and all the rest from another.

Paper Source: ○ All pages from: | Manual Feed ▼ |
       ◉ First page from: | Manual Feed ▼ |
       Remaining from: | Paper Cassette ▼ |

13

Save Settings

The Save Settings button enables you to record the current settings for use as the default for future print jobs.

The Main Pop-up Menu

By clicking the pop-up menu that currently says General (see Figure 13.17), you can move from the General screen to other areas of the Print dialog box.

Figure 13.17

The Print dialog box's pop-up menu.

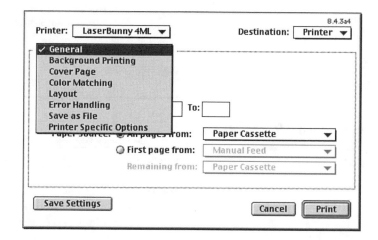

Background Printing

The Background Printing window (see Figure 13.18) enables you to define whether or not your file will spool to the disk before printing (see the StyleWriter page setup section earlier in this hour for a description of spooling). You can also predefine the time at which a file will print, put the document on hold indefinitely, or jump to the front of the print queue by selecting the Urgent radio button.

Cover Page

The Cover Page window (see Figure 13.19) enables you to enable or disable a cover page printout, and define whether or not it should print before or after your document. LaserWriter 8's cover page lists the version of the print driver, the user who printed the file, the current application, the name of the file, the date and time it was spooled, the name of the printer, and the number of pages in the file.

13

Figure 13.18

The Print dialog box's Background Printing window.

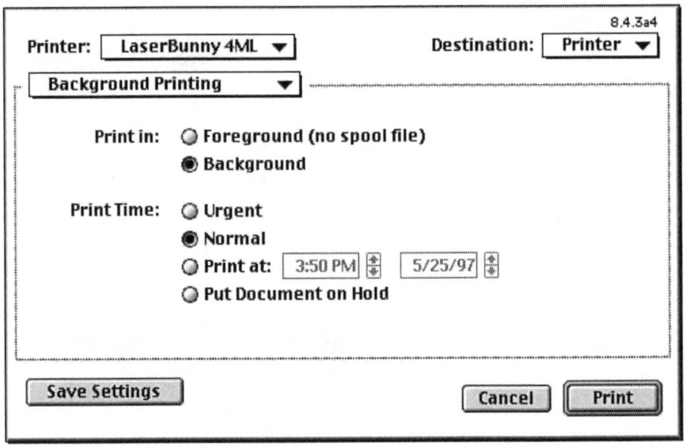

	8.4.3a4
Printer: [LaserBunny 4ML ▼] Destination: [Printer ▼]	

[Background Printing ▼]

Print in: ○ Foreground (no spool file)
            ● Background

Print Time: ○ Urgent
            ● Normal
            ○ Print at: [3:50 PM ⬍] [5/25/97 ⬍]
            ○ Put Document on Hold

[Save Settings]   [Cancel] [Print]

Figure 13.19

The Print dialog box's Cover Page window.

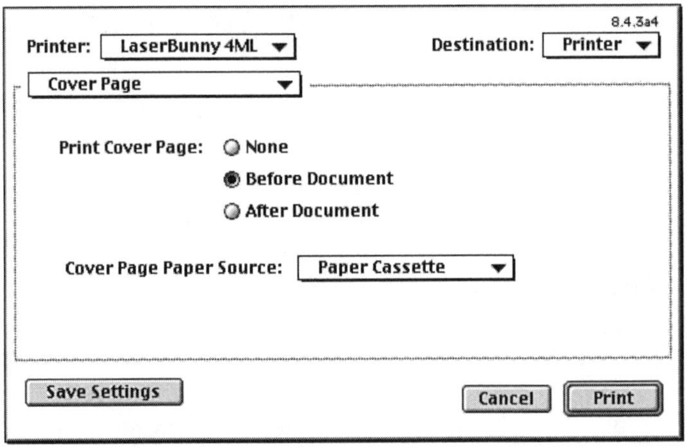

	8.4.3a4
Printer: [LaserBunny 4ML ▼] Destination: [Printer ▼]	

[Cover Page ▼]

Print Cover Page: ○ None
                  ● Before Document
                  ○ After Document

Cover Page Paper Source: [Paper Cassette ▼]

[Save Settings]   [Cancel] [Print]

Color Matching

The Color Matching window (see Figure 13.20) enables you to define the amount of color information sent to your printer. If you're printing a text-only document, it's wise to select Black and White from the Print Color pop-up menu; sending color information will only slow down your print job.

If you're printing illustrations, though, you'll want to select Color/Grayscale—even if your printer doesn't support color—so your file's colors will print as various shades of gray.

13

Figure 13.20
The Print dialog box's Color Matching window.

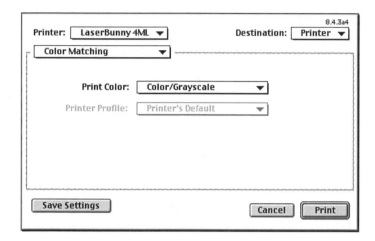

Layout

Like the StyleWriter's Page Setup dialog box's Layout command, this window enables you to print multiple document pages on a single printed page (see Figure 13.21). LaserWriter 8 enables you to combine up to 16 pages on a single sheet, with a variety of borders around the pages to keep them separate. You can also reverse the order of pages, if you like.

Figure 13.21
The Print dialog box's Layout window.

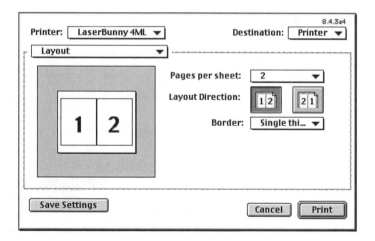

Error Handling

The Error Handling window (see Figure 13.22) enables you to define your preferred method of notification should your print job go awry. *No special reporting* lets you continue working without any notification; *Summarize on screen* presents an alert dialog box briefly explaining what happened; and *Print detailed report* prints a PostScript error log that can be helpful in troubleshooting print problems with a company's technical support staff.

Figure 13.22

The Print dialog box's
Error Handling window.

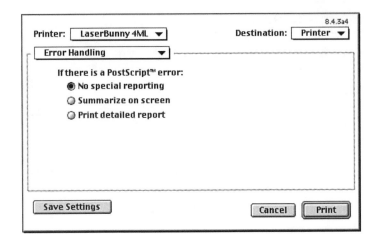

Save as File

Although you can save any print job as a file using the Destination pop-up menu from any
of the Print dialog box windows, the Save as File window (see Figure 13.23) offers more
options, such as the PostScript variant to use, whether or not to include fonts in the file, and
what type of file you'll end up with.

Figure 13.23

The Print dialog box's
Save as File window.

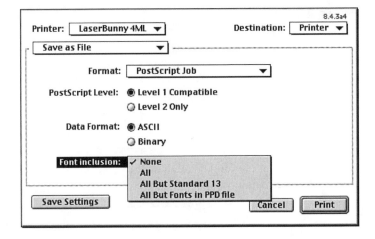

Printer Specific Options

Many printers offer such features as type and image enhancement, varying print quality
(resolution) settings, double-sided printing, and so on. The Printer Specific Options window
(see Figure 13.24) enables you to define these parameters. As a result, it varies drastically from
one printer to another.

13

JUST A MINUTE

If you choose the Generic PPD during printer setup, you'll lose access to any printer-specific features you'd normally access here.

Figure 13.24

The Print dialog box's Printer Specific Options window for the HP LaserJet 4ML.

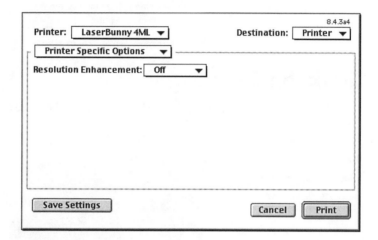

StyleWriter Variants

The StyleWriter print dialog box offers far fewer options (see Figure 13.25).

Figure 13.25

The StyleWriter 2500's print dialog box.

You're able to set number of copies and page ranges, just as in the LaserWriter print dialog box. Your Print Quality choices, however, are limited to Best, Normal, and Draft.

You can select from a variety of paper types: color, black and white, or grayscale images; and notification sounds when there's a printing problem.

The Color button brings up a secondary dialog box (see Figure 13.26) that enables you to define your halftone pattern and pick your Color Sync printer profile. (Your printer's manual can provide information about these features, as well as the Utilities button's functions, which vary from model to model.)

13

Figure 13.26

*The StyleWriter Print
dialog box's color
matching window.*

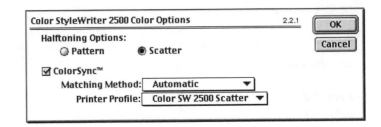

Desktop Printing

When you set up your printer earlier in this hour, an icon appeared on your desktop beneath
the hard drive (see Figure 13.27).

Figure 13.27

*Two desktop printer
icons on the desktop.*

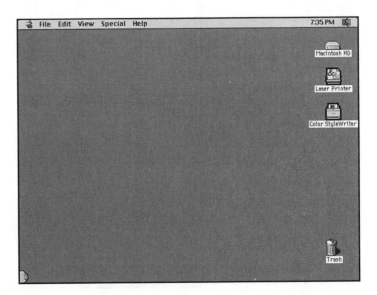

Much as you would imagine, these icons represent the printer that's connected to your
Macintosh. Rather than launching an application to print a file, you can simply drag the file's
icon onto the desktop printer (see Figure 13.28).

After dragging a file to the printer, the usual print dialog box appears. Whenever you print
to a desktop printer (either via a standard dialog box or drag-and-drop) its icon changes to
show an active print job (see Figure 13.29).

13

Figure 13.28

Dragging a file's icon onto a desktop printer.

Figure 13.29

A desktop printer's icon changes to show an active print job.

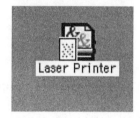

Desktop printers aren't just for drag-and-drop printing. You can also double-click a desktop printer icon to view the *print queue*, a list of jobs waiting to be printed by a particular printer. (see Figure 13.30).

Figure 13.30

Double-clicking a desktop printer shows the active print queue.

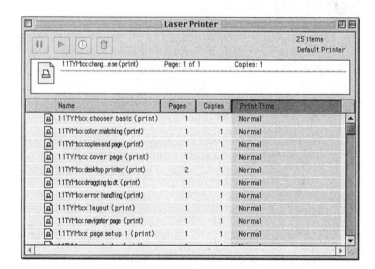

The buttons along the top of the window enable you to manipulate the print queue. The first button (two red vertical lines) pauses the current file (or any file you select in the queue); similarly, the second button (the green arrow) resumes printing of a paused job. The clock button enables you to specify a time for any (or all) of the queued files to print, and the trash can button lets you delete a job from the queue.

You'll also notice that the finder's menu bar gains a new addition when you've got the print queue window open: the Printing menu (see Figure 13.31).

Figure 13.31

The Printing menu becomes active in the finder whenever the print queue is visible.

The Printing menu lets you start and stop the entire queue, change setup information about your printer, specify your default printer, define whether or not you see an alert when manually feeding pages, and obtain configuration information about your printer—including much of the same information you can see in Chooser➥Setup➥Printer Info, plus a list of built-in fonts.

Summary

In this hour, you learned how to print documents. We configured the Mac OS 8 to recognize your printer properly, and explored the various functions of the Page Setup and Print dialog boxes of both laser printers and inkjet printers.

Term Review

Background printing   A feature that enables you to print your documents to a file on the hard drive, and return to work faster.

Chooser   Mac OS 8's facility for letting you choose your printer (and other network services).

PPD   Acronym for PostScript Printer Description, a document that contains information about your printer's capabilities, including its resolution, supported page sizes, color capabilities, and resolution enhancement features.

13

Printer driver   Software Mac OS 8 uses to let your applications communicate with your printer.

Print Queue   A list of jobs waiting to be printed by a particular printer, shown by double-clicking the printers desktop icon.

Spool file   A file created on your hard drive when you print a document, which is downloaded to the printer as you work.

Q&A

Q My desktop printer icon looks different than the ones you show. Why?

A Desktop printer icons vary depending on the model and capabilities of the printer selected. Even within LaserWriter 8, different types of laser printers will have different icons.

Q I've enabled AppleTalk, picked the right driver, but still can't find my laser printer in the Chooser list. What's wrong?

A There are a number of possible reasons why your printer's name won't show up in the Chooser. If you're sure that the printer is turned on and fully warmed up, check to make sure that your network connectors are firmly in place on all ends (if you're using AppleTalk connectors, there are at least four places to check). Some older laser printers—including the Apple Personal LaserWriter—don't work over networks. Be sure to use the correct driver for your printer (not LaserWriter 8) and follow the setup steps for StyleWriter-type serial printers earlier in the hour.

13

Hour 14

File Sharing

If you have more than one Macintosh, you're going to want to network your computers together—even if there are only two of them. In this hour, we'll show you how to set up basic networking from a software standpoint. In the next hour, we'll walk you through the hardware side of connecting your Macintosh.

If your Macintosh is at home, you may think this hour isn't for you. But mark our words, the day is going to come when you'll want to connect your Macintosh to another one. With the price of Macintosh computers decreasing, you may realize it's more efficient to get another one for your work than to wait while your children play games or your roommate surfs the Internet. And you're probably going to want to connect the two so that you can share files and applications without having to load them on both.

You may have heard horror stories about computer networking, but those were undoubtedly about large corporate networks with lots of PCs and machines called servers. The Macintosh's networking scheme is different than that, because Apple envisioned long ago that people would want to network their Macintoshes and share files. Every Macintosh has had built-in networking right from the start. So they made it very easy to do.

The highlights of this hour include:

☐ Sharing files and folders with family and colleagues (or not!)

☐ Setting up passwords and protection so your files can't be changed

☐ Monitoring who's sharing your files

☐ Accessing your Macintosh from another location

Setting Up File Sharing

The interpretation of file sharing is different depending on your perspective. It could mean letting someone else access files on your Macintosh. It could also mean making sure that you can access your own computer's files from another Macintosh across a network. We'll look at it from both angles.

Sharing Files and Folders

To prepare your computer for access (whether for you or for someone else), you have to start with a Control Panel named File Sharing. These two machines will comprise a "network," which defines two or more computers linked to each other. When we say network, we can be referring to two Macintoshes in the same room used by two different people or to two or more machines connected in an office. To set up File Sharing, perform the following steps.

1. In the menu bar, select Apple Menu➡Control Panels➡File Sharing (see Figure 14.1).

Figure 14.1

The File Sharing Control Panel.

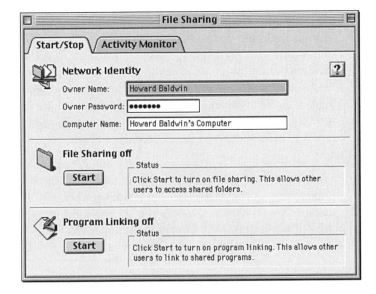

14

2. Type your name next to Owner Name.

3. Type a password next to Owner Password; it will be seen initially as normal text, so don't do this when someone is behind you. Don't worry about it being seen later—once you click outside the box, the characters will change to dots. Make it something you'll remember, but not something people will easily guess.

4. Choose a name for your computer and type it in the box provided.

5. Click on the Start buttons underneath File Sharing. Your Macintosh is ready to be shared.

TIME SAVER

Your password should not be a word that's easily guessed, like "password." Choose something personal that's easy to remember and that has both numbers and letters in it (symbols are good too). One of our favorite tricks is to use residential street addresses, combining the numbers with the first few letters of the street name. Even your closest friend probably won't remember the address of the house you grew up in, but you will.

TIME SAVER

When you type in the name of your computer, it should be something easily recognizable, like "Howard's PowerMac 8600." Don't forget that at some point you'll be accessing your computer through the Chooser from a list of machines on the network. If everyone has a PowerMac 8600, and that's what they type in as their computer's name, no one will know whose is whose!

JUST A MINUTE

If you want to access a specific file that someone is already using, a dialog box will inform you of this and offer you "read-only" access. This means that you'll be able to read the file, but not make changes to it.

Linking Programs

In the File Sharing Control Panel, there's also an option for Program Linking. If you select this option, you make the applications on your Macintosh available to other users on the network. To do this, perform the following steps:

1. Click on your hard drive and select the software application that you want to share. This comes in handy if you want to be able to use your word processing software when you're at a Macintosh that's dedicated to another purpose.

14

2. In the menu bar, go to File➡Sharing.

3. In the dialog box that appears, click on the box next to "Allow remote program linking." Now, others (including yourself) will be able to access this application from another computer (see Figure 14.2).

Figure 14.2

The dialog box that enables remote program linking.

JUST A MINUTE

Later, in Hour 21, "Security and Safety," you'll learn about locking your applications so that other people can't use them. Remember that if you lock your applications, file sharing doesn't work.

CAUTION

When you buy a software application, you buy the right for one person to use it at a time. So if you're using your word processing application and someone else wants to link to it, they won't be able to. If you want to avoid this situation, talk to the software developer about getting what's known as a *multi-user license*—a way for more than one person to use the software at once.

Changing Passwords

You should change your password on a regular basis, just to be on the safe side. To do this, click Control Panels➡File Sharing in the menu bar. In the control panel, type in a new password and hit return. You're done (we'll go into more detail about passwords in Hour 21).

14

Setting Up Users & Groups

So who are you going to let use your Macintosh? You may want some people to see certain files on your Macintosh, and you may even want other people to change certain files on your Macintosh. You may enable your assistant to insert appointments in your calendar, for example.

Mac OS 8 has an easy way for you to adjust who gets to see and change files on your machine. To enable others to use your machine, perform the following steps:

1. Click on your hard drive and access a file you want others to be able to access.

2. In the menu bar, click on File➡Sharing.

3. In the window that appears, you have two options: to prevent the folder from being moved, renamed, or deleted, or to share the folder and its contents (see Figure 14.3).

Figure 14.3

The default window for file sharing.

4. Click on the second box ("share this item and its contents"). The dimmed options will become available, and your name should appear as owner (if not, type it in).

5. Click on the triangle under "Privilege."

6. Because this is your machine, you want to be able to both see and change files. Click on "Read & Write" (don't close the window, though—we're going to use it in the next section).

14

Arranging Access Privileges

The next task in setting up file sharing is setting up access privileges. To do this, you need to go into a control named Users & Groups. There are a couple of ways to do this. To learn both, perform the following steps:

1. From the open window, click on the triangle next to "User/Group."

2. Choose the last option, "Open Users & Groups" (or in the menu bar, click on the Apple Menu➤Control Panels➤Users & Groups) (see Figure 14.4).

Figure 14.4

The Users & Groups Control Panel.

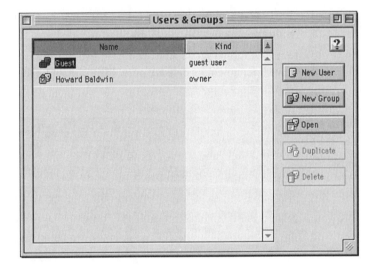

3. Click on the button marked "New User."

4. Click on the "Name" box and type the user's name.

5. Type in a password and click on the box enabling the user to create her own password later (see Figure 14.5). That person can now access your machine.

Designating Groups

If you work with a small group of people within a larger one—say, a department within a corporation—you may want your immediate coworkers to be able to access your Macintosh, but not everyone in your office. At home, you may want to give your spouse access to certain files across the network but keep your kids away.

14

Figure 14.5

After you've put in the appropriate information, the "new user" window is renamed.

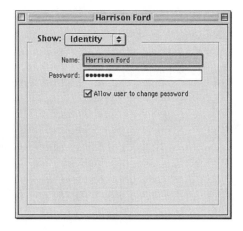

JUST A MINUTE

Setting group-access privileges only prevents access across a network; if you're trying to keep files safe from prying eyes, see Hour 21.

To set up a group of people who can access your Macintosh, perform the following steps:

1. Click Apple Menu➡Control Panels➡Users & Groups to open the control panel.

2. Click on the "New User" button to create users for this group.

3. Click on the "New Group" button to create the group (see Figure 14.6).

Figure 14.6

After you've created the users, you can create the group they should be in.

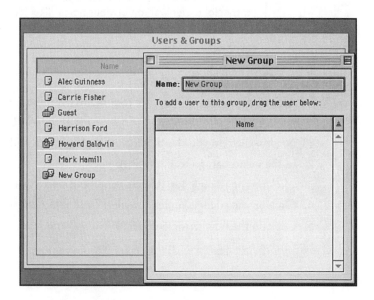

14

4. Drag the names of the users onto the group icon; the user names will not disappear.

5. Highlight the group icon, and then click on "Open" to see the contents of that group (see Figure 14.7).

Figure 14.7

The contents of your group.

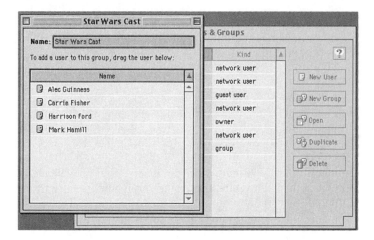

6. To delete a member of the group, highlight that name, and click on File➡Delete.

Time Saver

Rather than give a group access to all the files on your hard drive, create a special folder with an obvious name, like "Shared Folder." Keep all documents that the group needs access to in that folder.

Giving Groups Access

Now that you've created a group, we're going to combine that skill with what you learned earlier. To give your group access to a folder, perform the following steps:

1. Double-click on your hard drive and highlight the folder you want to share.

2. In the menu bar, go to File➡Sharing.

3. Click on the triangle for "User/Group" and select your group.

4. Click on the triangle under "Privilege" and select "Read Only."

5. Click on the next triangle under "Privilege" and select "None" (see Figure 14.8).

6. Click on the close box and you're done.

14

Figure 14.8

Icons for the access privileges change, based on the kind of access users have.

You have now given yourself read-write access, the group read-only access; everyone else has no access privileges at all.

Monitoring Access

You can easily check on who's using files or applications on your Macintosh. In fact, you can even force them to stop using your computer (warning them first is preferable, of course). To determine who's using your Macintosh, perform the following steps:

1. Under the Apple menu, go to Control Panels➡File Sharing.

2. In the control panel, click on the activity monitor tab. This will reveal who's accessing your Macintosh (see Figure 14.9).

3. To notify someone that you want them to stop using your computer, click on their name, and then click Disconnect.

4. In the dialog box that appears, type the number of minutes the other user has before access is denied.

JUST A MINUTE

When other people are using files or applications on your computer, your performance will decrease. That's because it's almost like having two people with two keyboards typing on the same machine.

14

Figure 14.9

The Activity Monitor tab in the File Sharing Control Panel reveals who's accessing your Macintosh.

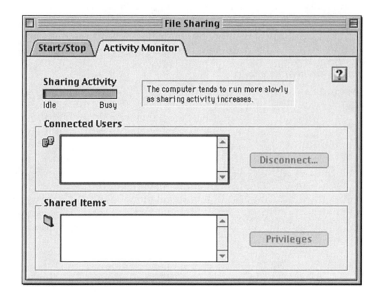

Connecting to Shared Disks

Again, a shared disk depends on your perspective. You may be accessing your files from another Macintosh in your office or home, or you could be on your own Macintosh accessing someone else's files. Happily, the method of connecting to them remains the same.

Getting to Your Mac From Elsewhere

In Mac OS 8, the Macintosh you want to access across the network is no different than any other networked or connected device, such as a printer. As a result, you use the Chooser to access the machine you want. To do so, perform the following steps:

1. From the Apple menu, select Chooser.

2. Click on AppleShare. A list of networked computers will appear in the box on the right.

3. In the box on the right, select the computer you want (now you see why it was important to name them something distinctive).

4. An icon for that computer will appear on the desktop. Now you can access files on that computer (assuming you have access privileges) just like any other external hard drive.

14

JUST A MINUTE

You may have also heard of a process called *remote access*, which lets you use a modem to dial into your computer from another computer. This is somewhat more complicated than file sharing (although they use the same principles), and involves software called Apple Remote Access, or ARA. We'll discuss this in Hour 23, which is devoted to advanced networking.

Summary

Apple has always tried to perpetuate the Macintosh reputation for being friendly. The fact that it so easily shares files is evidence of that. Although it's a little clunky to have to open two control panels to set up access privileges, at least the Users & Groups Control Panel is easily accessible from the File Sharing Control Panel in Mac OS 8 (this wasn't always true).

There is a flip side of file sharing, of course: you need to be careful about protecting files from prying eyes. You probably don't want your kids looking at your financial software for evidence that you really can afford to buy them a pager, for instance. We'll talk more about security measures in Hour 21.

Ultimately, though, it's markedly more simple to be able to get to your files from another Macintosh when you need them, rather than having to put them on a floppy disk or Zip cartridge and carry them to another Macintosh.

And you can always keep track of who's using your machine by checking the activity monitor window. So you don't have to share if you don't want to.

Term Review

Access privileges   By setting these, you can limit what users can do with your files. The three levels of privileges are none, read-only, and read-and-write.

Activity monitor   A window that shows you who's accessing your Macintosh.

File sharing   A capability that gives more than one person access to files (but not at the same time) on a networked computer.

Network   Two machines linked to each other in such a way that they can share files and applications. A network can be two Macintoshes in the same room or two or more machines connected in an office.

Password   A group of no more than 8 characters that limits access to a file or folder.

14

Remote access   A way of dialing into your computer from somewhere else. So that you do this but others can't, you need to have the privileges set properly on your Macintosh.

Users & Groups   A control panel that enables you to give users access to your files and organize them into groups with different levels of access.

Q&A

Q What if I don't want to ever give anyone access to my files?

A Highlight your hard drive icon and, in the menu bar, go to File➥Sharing. In the dialog box that appears, click in the first box, which locks the contents of your entire drive to anyone but yourself.

Q If I do that, how do I access the drive?

A You'll have to use your password.

Q What if forget my password?

A Don't. That's why it should be something simple that you'll remember and someone else is highly unlikely to guess. There's one exception to this: if your Macintosh is on a network, a member of the IS staff may be able to access it. Otherwise, you're stuck.

Q It sounds like if my boss wants to access my Macintosh after I go home, I have to leave it on. So couldn't someone just walk up to it and use the files I don't have locked?

A That's true. That's why you need to think carefully about what you make available to others and what you don't (and what kind of personal material you leave on your computer). You can prevent this by password-protecting your Macintosh (refer to Hour 21 for details).

Hour 15

Setting Up Your Internet Connection

In this hour, we'll cover everything you need to do before you can connect your Macintosh to the Internet. You'll learn where to find the information you need to connect and configure a modem if there's not one already installed in your computer. We'll also cover how to use Mac OS 8's built-in programs to choose an Internet Service Provider and configure your software properly. We'll touch briefly on the method for reentering settings from your old configuration if you've used the Internet prior to Mac OS 8, and using the PPP control panel to automate your Internet activity.

The highlights of this hour include:

☐ Where to find information elsewhere in this book to install and configure a modem

☐ How to use the Internet Setup Assistant to choose an Internet Service Provider (ISP) and log on to the Internet for the first time

☐ How to modify or add Internet settings if you already have an ISP account

☐ How to automate your log-on and log-off sequences for more seamless Internet use

Installing Your Modem

Before you can use your Macintosh to log on to the Internet, you need to attach a modem to your computer. Many computers come with a built-in modem. If your computer is one of these, you're set—move on to the next section, "Using the Internet Setup Assistant."

If your computer doesn't have a built-in modem, you'll need to refer to Hour 18, where we discuss buying and installing a modem, and configuring the Modem control panel.

For fastest Internet access, you'll want to purchase a modem with a transmission speed of at least 28.8 Kbps (kilobytes per second—the standard unit of measure for modem speeds). You can log on to the Internet with slower modems (with speeds of 9600 bps or 14.4Kbps, for example), but you're bound to be frustrated by the slow pace of your connection.

Using the Internet Setup Assistant

After your modem is installed and your settings are properly configured in the Modem control panel, you're ready to begin logging on to the Internet. (If you've accessed the Internet prior to Mac OS 8, skip ahead to the next section, "Updating Your Settings.")

Registering as a New User

To begin the Internet setup process, perform the following steps:

1. Double-click to launch the Internet Setup Assistant in the Assistants folder on your hard drive. Its opening screen will appear (see Figure 15.1).
2. Click the Register button. A new Introduction screen will appear.
3. Read the introduction, and click the right arrow (at the bottom right corner of the window) to advance to the next screen.
4. The next panel (see Figure 15.2) will ask you to enter your name and phone number. Be sure to enter the phone number your computer is connected to, because your settings will be configured based on this information. After you've entered the appropriate information, click the right arrow to advance to the next screen.

15

Figure 15.1

The Internet Setup Assistant.

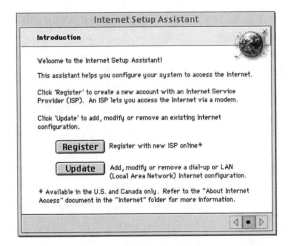

Figure 15.2

The Internet Setup Assistant's Personal Information screen.

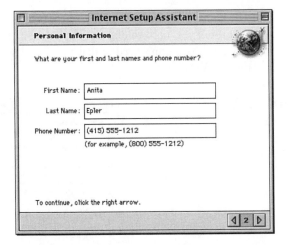

5. In the next screen you'll be asked to reconfirm your modem type (brand and model), port selection (you're probably using the modem port), and phone line type (most domestic service is tone-based; check with your phone company if you're unsure) (see Figure 15.3). After verifying that the information was correctly imported from the Modem control panel, click the right arrow to advance to the next screen.

Figure 15.3

The Internet Setup Assistant's Modem Settings screen.

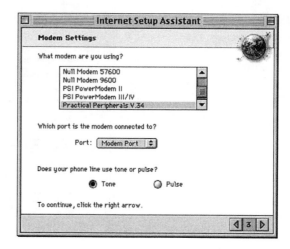

6. The Conclusion screen (see Figure 15.4) offers you tips for selecting an ISP and asks you if you need to dial a prefix before making a call (such as 9 from some offices). If you don't need to dial a prefix, leave the text entry field blank and click the Go Ahead button.

Figure 15.4

The Internet Setup Assistant's Conclusion screen.

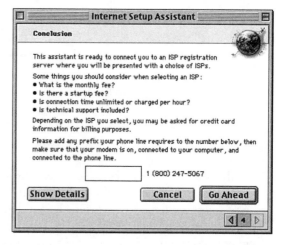

7. The Internet Setup Assistant will dial a toll-free number to connect you to a registration server (you'll hear your modem making noise if you have its speaker turned on). Netscape Navigator launches, and you may receive a warning that you are requesting a secure document (see Figure 15.5). Click the OK button to proceed.

15

Figure 15.5

A Secure Document warning.

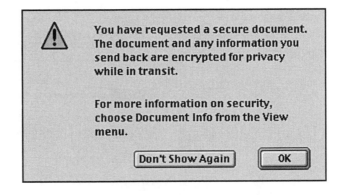

⚠ You have requested a secure document. The document and any information you send back are encrypted for privacy while in transit.

For more information on security, choose Document Info from the View menu.

[Don't Show Again]   [OK]

JUST A MINUTE

When you obtain a secure document from a secure server using Netscape Navigator (or any other web browser), you can be reasonably certain that any information you submit—such as your credit card number and personal data—won't be intercepted in transit. Thousands of people every day transact business over the Internet without incident. If you still aren't convinced of the safety of this procedure, you can forgo the Internet Setup Assistant and contact any ISP for manual log-on instructions. (Articles in back issues of Macintosh magazines—such as *Macworld*—can point you to a reputable ISP in your area; you may also want to ask friends or colleagues whose opinions you trust for a recommendation.) After you've obtained an account, proceed to the "Updating Your Settings" section later in this Hour.

8. You're now logged on to the Netscape Internet Account Server (see Figure 15.6).

   The SELECT> buttons enable you to view information about ISPs through the Internet Account Server. One button will show local Bell (telephone company) ISPs that operate in your area; a second displays long-distance phone companies (such as Sprint) that offer Internet access; and the third button shows national or regional ISPs with local access in your area.

9. Click the button labeled "More Internet Service Provider Choices" (you'll have a chance to come back and view the others later, if you want). A new Navigator page appears (see Figure 15.7) showing one or more ISP's logos.

10. Click one of the ISPs buttons to view information about their rates. A new Navigator page will appear (Figure 15.8).

11. Peruse the information about this ISP. If you want to subscribe to their service, click the "NEXT" button. If you want to return to the previous screen to view other ISP's information, click the "BACK" button and repeat this step.

Figure 15.6

The Netscape Internet Account Server.

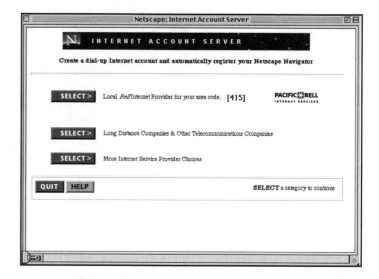

Figure 15.7

The ISP selection screen.

TIME SAVER

Some Macintosh magazines have rated the various ISPs, and nearly every publication has offered step-by-step guidelines on choosing one to meet your needs. The August, 1997 issue of *Macworld* includes a feature on choosing an ISP, including a helpful list of questions to ask regarding features and services.

15

Figure 15.8

A sample ISP informa-tion screen.

15

Depending on the ISP you choose, the assistant's remaining screens will vary. You'll be asked to choose a plan type (hourly or unlimited access) and a billing method (Bell ISPs will often let you put your charges on your regular phone bill; others will want a credit card number). You'll also need to choose a user ID and a password. Pick your user ID carefully; once you begin receiving email at one address, changing it can be expensive (and it's a hassle to let everyone know your new address, just as it is when you move your residence).

12. After you've entered your information, the Setup Assistant will log on to your ISP to check if your account name is already taken, and verify your credit card information. If someone else is already using your chosen name, you can try another (you can also press the Start Over button and try a different ISP, if you prefer). This step can take a few minutes.

13. A new window will appear, showing a service agreement for your ISP. This is a legally-binding document, so you should take the time to read it. After you've read the agreement, click the CREATE button to set up your account. The Setup Assistant will log on to your ISP's server again to create your new account.

14. The next screen contains very important information: the technical support number and web page address, your user name and password, and your email address and password (see Figure 15.9). Write this information down and put it in a safe place.

15. To configure all of the necessary control panels and applications appropriately, click the CONFIGURE button. A progress bar will appear, showing that the Setup Assistant is downloading your account information from your ISP's server to your Macintosh.

Figure 15.9

The final Setup Assistant screen reminds you to write down important information about your account.

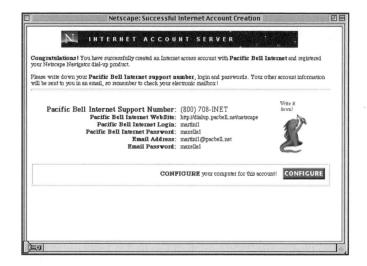

16. The Internet Dialer utility will appear on your screen, indicating that you're ready to dial in to your ISP (see Figure 15.10).

Figure 15.10

The Internet Dialer appears on your screen, letting you know you've completed the setup process.

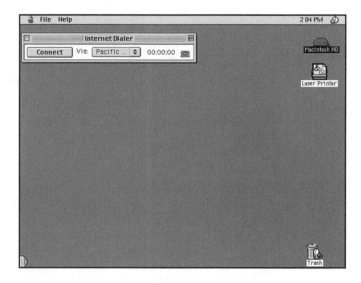

17. Close the Internet Dialer window for now. (We'll log on and use your new account in the next hour.)

Updating Your Settings

If you've been accessing the Internet with previous versions of Mac OS, you can use the Internet Setup Assistant to help you update your Internet settings.

JUST A MINUTE

If you've used the Apple Internet Connection Kit for your Internet access, all of your configuration settings were automatically imported to their proper locations when you upgraded to Mac OS 8. You may want to follow these exercises anyway, to ensure that everything transferred properly.

To update your settings, you'll need to obtain the following information from your records or from your ISP:

☐ Your user name

☐ Your password

☐ Your ISP's dial-in number

☐ Your ISP's domain name server address(es)

After you have gathered the necessary information, you're ready to configure Mac OS 8 to use your existing Internet account. To do so, perform the following steps:

1. Launch the Internet Setup Assistant from the Assistants folder. Its main screen will appear (see Figure 15.11).

Figure 15.11

The Internet Setup Assistant.

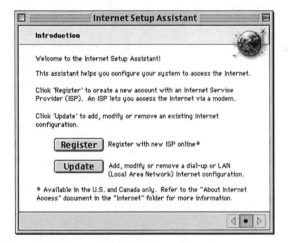

2. Click the Update button. An introduction screen will remind you of the items necessary to complete this process. Click the right arrow (in the lower-right corner of the window) to proceed to the next panel. The Internet Configuration screen appears (see Figure 15.12).

3. Unless you're modifying existing Internet settings, you'll want to click the Add Internet Configuration radio button to select it. (If you're updating an existing

account, click the Modify Internet Configuration button instead.) Click the right arrow to proceed to the next panel. The next screen appears (see Figure 15.13).

Figure 15.12

The Internet Configura-tion screen.

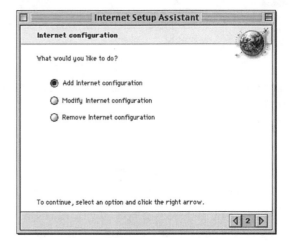

Figure 15.13

The Configuration name and connection type screen.

4. Enter the name of this configuration in the text entry field. Unless you're accessing the Internet via a LAN connection, leave the radio buttons at the default. Click the right arrow to proceed to the next panel. The next screen appears.

5. You'll be asked to reverify your modem settings as defined in the Modem control panel. Click the right arrow to proceed to the next panel. The next screen appears (see Figure 15.14).

6. This screen asks for your important log-in information: the dial-up number of your ISP, your user name, and your password. Enter them, and click the right arrow to proceed to the next panel. The next screen appears.

Figure 15.14

The Configuration information screen.

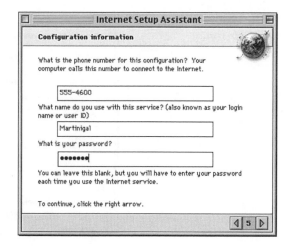

7. Unless you're connecting via a LAN connection, you probably don't have a dedicated IP address. (IP stands for Internet Protocol; an IP address is a unique number ID assigned to computers that hook directly to the Internet via a dedicated, full-time connection.) Click the No radio button in this window, then click the right arrow to proceed to the next panel. The next screen appears (see Figure 15.15).

Figure 15.15

The Domain Name Servers screen.

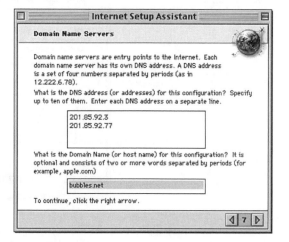

8. In the text entry fields provided, type the DNS address(es) and Domain Name of your ISP. Click the right arrow to proceed to the next panel. The next screen appears (see Figure 15.16).

9. In the text entry fields provided, type your e-mail address and e-mail password. Click the right arrow to proceed to the next panel. The next screen appears (see Figure 15.17).

Figure 15.16

The E-mail Address and Password screen.

10. In the text entry fields, type your e-mail account name (usually it's your e-mail address with "mail." immediately after the @ sign) and your ISP's mail host's name. Click the right arrow to proceed to the next panel. The next screen appears.

Figure 15.17

The E-mail Account and Host Computer screen.

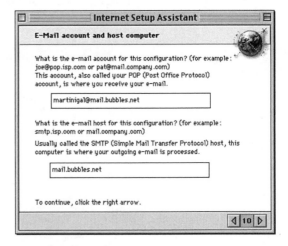

11. In the text entry field, type the name of your ISP's news host (usually it's the domain name proceeded with "news."). The next screen appears (see Figure 15.18).

12. The Conclusion screen offers you three options. You can press Cancel to leave your configuration unsaved; click Go Ahead to save your new configuration; or click Show Details to bring up a new screen (see Figure 15.19), where you can check your configuration information prior to saving it.

15

Figure 15.18

*The Setup Assistant
Conclusion screen.*

Figure 15.19

*The Setup Assistant
Conclusion Details
screen.*

13. Click Go Ahead. The Setup Assistant automatically saves your configuration details to all of the appropriate control panels and applications.

Automating Log-on and Log-off

Mac OS 8 automatically knows to use your predefined settings to log on to the Internet whenever you use your email software, web browser, or other Internet software. If you want to disable this option, or modify your dial-up settings, perform the following steps:

1. Open the PPP Control Panel (Apple Menu➡Control Panels➡PPP). Its window will appear (see Figure 15.20).

Figure 15.20

The PPP Control Panel.

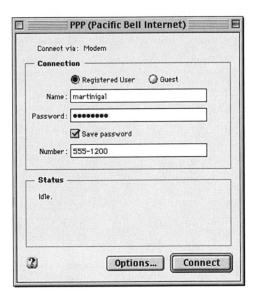

2. You'll see that your log-in name, password, and ISP's dial-in phone number have been preconfigured by the Internet Setup Assistant. Click the Options button. A new window appears (see Figure 15.21).

Figure 15.21

The PPP Control Panel's Redialing window.

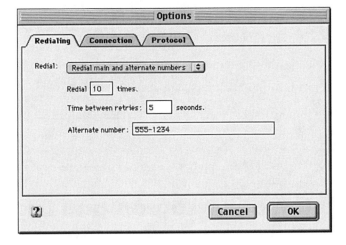

3. Choose your redialing preferences using the pop-up menu and text entry fields. Click the tab marked Connection. A new window appears (see Figure 15.22).

4. This panel enables you to define your automation settings for logging on or off your ISP's server. Checking the "Connect automatically when starting TCP/IP applications" box enables the Mac OS to dial up whenever you open your email

15

application, web browser, or other Internet application. If you want to disable this feature, uncheck this box.

Figure 15.22

The PPP Control Panel's Connection window.

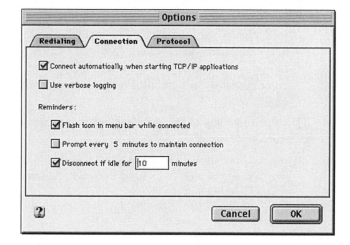

5. The Reminders section enables you to specify how long to remain connected after the computer senses you haven't been active, and gives you the option of flashing an icon in the upper-left corner of the menu bar to remind you that you're online. You can also ask Mac OS 8 to prompt you at predefined intervals in order to maintain your connection. Enter your preferences, and click OK.

6. Close the PPP Control Panel.

7. Click Save in the resulting dialog box to save your changes.

Summary

In this hour, you learned where to look for more information about connecting a modem to your Macintosh, and used the Internet Setup Assistant to log on to the Internet and choose an Internet Service Provider. If you already had an existing ISP account, you learned how to configure Mac OS 8 to recognize your current settings. We also went over the use of the PPP Control Panel to automate your dial-in and log-off processes.

Term Review

Kbps   Kilobytes per second, the standard unit of measure for modem speeds.

ISP   Internet Service Provider, a company or agency that offers access to the Internet for a fee.

PPP   Point to Point Protocol, an industry standard method of establishing remote connections between computers and Internet hosts.

Q&A

Q Why can't I find my modem in any of the pop-up menus?

A Your modem script isn't installed in the Modem scripts folder (System➡Extensions ➡Modem Scripts); scripts are files that tell Mac OS 8 which features and capabilities your modem offers. Check on the CD Extras folder on the Mac OS 8 CD for additional modem scripts, or contact your modem's vendor. You can use the generic script—a nonspecific file that will work with nearly all modems—in the meantime.

Q I don't like any of the ISP choices the Internet Setup Assistant provides. Am I stuck with these?

A No. You can choose and use any ISP with Mac OS 8's Internet applications. Feel free to shop around. You'll need to obtain the same information from your ISP that we described in the "Updating Your Settings" section earlier in this hour.

15

Hour 16

Using Your Internet Connection

In this hour, we'll put your Internet connection to good use. We'll teach you the basics of what you can expect to find online, and then log you on to the Internet for a tour of the World Wide Web, electronic mail, and Usenet newsgroups. We'll show you some handy shortcuts built in to Mac OS 8 to help ease your connection process, and we'll teach you how to log off when you're done online.

The exercises in this hour assume that you've already set up your system to use the Internet, as outlined in Hour 15.

The highlights of this hour include:

- ☐ What you need to know about the Internet before you log on
- ☐ What each of the main uses of the Internet are, and how they differ
- ☐ How to connect to the Internet if you aren't configured for automatic connections
- ☐ Which applications you'll use to browse the World Wide Web, read electronic mail, and read Usenet newsgroups
- ☐ How to use Mac OS 8's built-in Internet shortcuts
- ☐ How to log off when you're done online

Understanding the Internet

Although the Internet has gotten a lot of publicity over the past few years, it's not new. Back in the late 1960s, the Department of Defense set up a computer network known as ARPAnet that enabled government agencies and universities to exchange information easily. In time, ARPAnet evolved into the Internet as we know it today.

The government has long since given up administering this worldwide computer network, which encompasses millions of computers. In fact, no single company or organization owns or administers the Internet; it's supported—both financially and administratively—by the companies, schools, organizations, and service providers that use it.

Today, the Internet is used for all sorts of commercial and entertainment pursuits, in addition to its long-standing military and educational purposes. Most Internet usage can be broken down into four main categories: the World Wide Web, electronic mail, Usenet news, and other smaller features.

The World Wide Web

The World Wide Web (WWW) is the portion of the Internet generating the most interest lately. Using a graphical method of finding and using information, web documents (known as pages) often include links to other documents. These *hypertext* links are the web's main feature; if you're reading a document on one web page about dogs, you might find a link to a page about greyhounds, for example. Clicking on this link would take you directly to the greyhound web page, which might, in turn, provide a link to a web page about dog racing, and so on. Mac OS 8 ships with both Netscape Navigator and Microsoft Internet Explorer, two *web browsers*, applications used to view web pages.

Electronic Mail

Electronic mail (known more frequently as *email*) enables you to exchange text messages with anyone whose email address you know (you've probably seen email addresses in the form of *worker@company.com* or *student@school.edu*); it works much such as the U.S. Mail in that way. Email, though, is much faster and more convenient (and doesn't waste paper!). In addition to basic text, most email applications let you attach other documents (such as word processing or graphics files) to your messages. Mac OS 8 comes with ClarisEmailer Lite for sending and receiving electronic mail.

Usenet News

Usenet newsgroups are similar to electronic bulletin boards: people around the world *post* (or add) messages to them constantly. Newsgroups cover virtually every topic of interest—more than 14,000 in all. You can use your web browser to read newsgroups, or download a dedicated news reader program from the World Wide Web.

16

Other Uses of the Internet

File Transfer Protocol (FTP) enables you to exchange files with other computers on the Internet. Many shareware libraries (as we discussed in Hour 11) operate FTP servers to let you download all sorts of software. You can access FTP servers with your web browser, or download a dedicated FTP application such as Fetch. FTPed files can include software (such as the shareware applications we discussed in Hour 11, or upgrade "patches" for commercial applications) documents (such as manuals or Read Me files for programs, or government publications), or nearly any other type of file. FTP site addresses usually take the form *ftp.company.com;* Apple's FTP site, for example, is *ftp.apple.com*

Telnet is another Internet service that enables you to access other computers remotely. Many libraries, for example, offer Telnet servers for their members. Mac OS 8 doesn't offer any Telnet capabilities, but you can easily download the NCSA Telnet application from most major software archives.

IRC (which stands for Internet Relay Chat) enables you to talk with other Internet users around the world, in real time. As are newsgroups, IRC is broken into affinity groups known as channels. Mac OS 8 doesn't provide any IRC software, but you can download a number of programs from most shareware sites, including *Macworld* Online (`http://www.macworld.com`) or Shareware.com (`http://www.shareware.com`). The Yahoo! IRC page (`http://www.yahoo.com/Computers_and_Internet/Internet/Chat/IRC/`) contains resources on IRC etiquette, as well as links to sites featuring downloadable software.

Netiquette, FAQs, and Other Net.Miscellany

The Internet is a complicated social structure, with a culture and vocabulary all its own. Just as you wouldn't visit a foreign country without learning some of the language and customs beforehand, it's unwise to plunge headlong into the Internet without a guidebook.

Netiquette is a contraction, made up of net (short for Internet) and etiquette. The term Netiquette covers all sorts of topics, from how to behave on IRC, to how to properly post an article to Usenet newsgroups, to basic rules of discourse in email.

Just such as general etiquette, there are numerous guides to Netiquette. Your ISP may provide you with a file containing basic Netiquette guidelines, and most of the best etiquette guides can be found on the World Wide Web by searching on the word "Netiquette" in any search engine. (We'll cover search engines later in this hour). Each Netiquette guide is a bit different (remember, there's no governing body for the Internet) so you'll probably want to read a few to get a consensus.

Every etiquette guide worth its salt will tell you that the first rule of using Usenet newsgroups is to read the *FAQ* for each group you're following. FAQ stands for Frequently Asked Questions, and it's a file containing—you guessed it—the inquiries posted most often.

If you learn nothing else about Netiquette, remember these basic rules:

1. Read the FAQ before posting to a newsgroup.

2. Quietly watch in newsgroups for a while before jumping in. This process is known as "lurking" and it's highly advised to determine the lay of the land.

3. Remember that tens of thousands of people will see any news post you make. Choose you words wisely.

4. Restrain yourself from "flaming" (insulting, degrading, or harassing) other people, in email, newsgroups, or anywhere else, no matter how asinine or contrary they're being. You can't win (trust us).

5. The Golden Rule holds true on the Internet, just as it does in life. Treat others as you would be treated, and you'll enjoy online life a lot more.

Logging on to the Internet

OK, enough preaching. Let's get back to work!

Back in Hour 15, we set up your machine to automatically log on to the Internet whenever an Internet application needs it to. If you bypassed this step for some reason, we'll teach you how to log on to the Internet manually. (If you followed our directions in Hour 15, you can skip to the following section.)

To log on to the Internet manually, perform the following steps:

1. Launch the Internet Dialer by double-clicking on its icon in the Internet folder on your hard drive. A small window will appear (see Figure 16.1).

Figure 16.1

The Internet Dialer.

2. Click on the Connect button. If your modem's speaker is turned on, you'll hear it dial your ISP's server.

3. After you connect to your ISP, the Internet Dialer's button changes to Disconnect and its timer begins keeping track of your time online (see Figure 16.2). You're actively connected to the Internet, and ready to use your Internet software.

Figure 16.2

The Internet Dialer, while connected.

16

Minimize the Internet Dialer's window so you'll be able to access it when it's time to log off, or drag it to one corner of your screen so you can keep an eye on how long you've been connected.

Using Your Internet Software

This section's exercises assume that you've either configured your Macintosh to automatically connect to your ISP when an Internet application is active, or that you've completed the previous exercise and are actively connected to the Internet.

Web Browsers

As we mentioned earlier in this hour, Mac OS 8 ships with two different web browsers: Netscape Navigator and Microsoft Internet Explorer. Our exercises assume that you're using Navigator, since it's the default web browser for Mac OS 8. If you prefer Explorer, feel free to use it. The screens will look slightly different, but you'll be able to follow along.

Originally, web pages were entirely text-based; their hypertext links were merely highlighted words within a document. When you clicked on these colored words, they would take you to another related page, either on the same computer or at another site somewhere else, anywhere in the world.

Today's web pages include hypertext links, as well as a number of more sophisticated elements, including graphics, animated pictures, full-motion movies, and a variety of sounds. Links can be words, pictures, buttons... in fact, nearly anything you see on a web page can be a link to another page.

Because these links are so easy to follow, and because they can take you literally around the world, you can get lost pretty quickly. Thankfully, every browser keeps a log of where you've recently traveled (Netscape Navigator's Go menu, for example, shows a list of your recent sites), so you can retrace your steps if you get too far off track.

But enough talk. Let's put this information to work.

To log on to the World Wide Web, perform the following steps:

1. Launch Netscape Navigator by double-clicking on its icon in the Internet folder (Internet➡Netscape Navigator). The PPP software automatically dials your ISP, and displays a status window letting you know how the connection is proceeding (see Figure 16.3).

2. After you're connected, Navigator's window appears, and it automatically logs you on to the default web page (see Figure 16.4).

Figure 16.3

The PPP Status window.

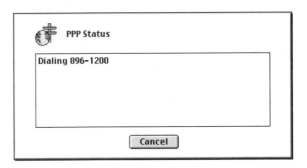

JUST A MINUTE

You may hear the term "home page" when discussing the World Wide Web. Within Netscape Navigator, the term applies to the page set up to load when you launch the browser; colloquially, though, Home Page means any company, person, or organization's main page on their web site.

Figure 16.4

Navigator's default web page.

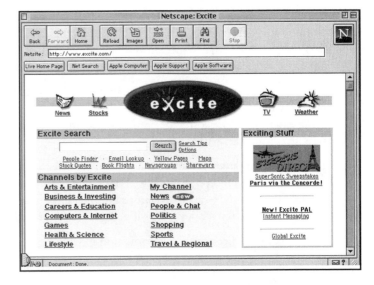

Apple has an arrangement with Excite, a search engine and news provider, to provide Apple-specific content at this location. (A *search engine* lets you type in one or more words to search on, and brings up links to relevant pages on the web.) It's specified by default as your opening page. You may find it convenient to leave it this way, but if you prefer to log in to some other page when you first launch Navigator, you can do so by selecting Options➡General Preferences and typing the web address in the Browser Starts With text entry field.

16

If you've just finished using the Internet Setup Assistant, your screen may look different. Go to the Options menu, and be sure that Show Toolbar, Show Location, and Show Directory Buttons are checked. If they aren't selected, drag down the menu to select them (see Figure 16.5).

Figure 16.5

Navigator's Options menu.

To explore the World Wide Web, perform the following steps:

1. From the Bookmarks menu, select Apple. A submenu will pop out (see Figure 16.6).

Figure 16.6

The Bookmarks menu.

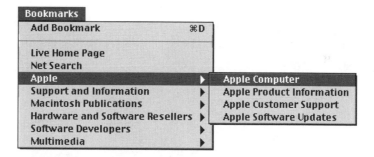

2. Select Apple Computer from the submenu. A new web page appears (see Figure 16.7).

JUST A MINUTE

Your page may look different than the one in Figure 16.7; in fact, it almost certainly will. One of the best features of the web is that it's a constantly changing entity. Some people and organizations update their web pages on a daily, or sometimes hourly basis. You'll also notice that the Location: text field shows a different string of text than on the previous page. The location field's content is known as the page's web address, or *URL* (an acronym for uniform resource locator).

Figure 16.7

The Apple Computer home page.

3. On the left side of the window, you'll see a series of document titles. Click on the one that says Product Information. A new page appears (see Figure 16.8).

Figure 16.8

Apple's Product Information web page.

16

JUST A MINUTE

Notice again how the web address changes to show the new page's location. All of the blue underlined words on this page are actually hypertext links to other pages. The buttons on the bottom are also links, as are the photographs. Clicking any of these buttons will link you to yet another page on the Apple web site.

16

4. When you've had your fill of following links, select Open Location… from the File menu (or use its keyboard shortcut, ⌘-L). A dialog box appears (see Figure 16.9).

Figure 16.9

Navigator's Open Location dialog box.

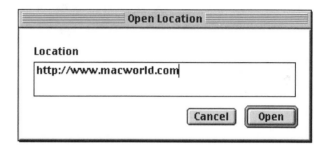

5. Type the following URL into the text entry field: `http://www.macworld.com`. Click on the Open button to load the new web site (see Figure 16.10).

Figure 16.10

Macworld *Online's web page.*

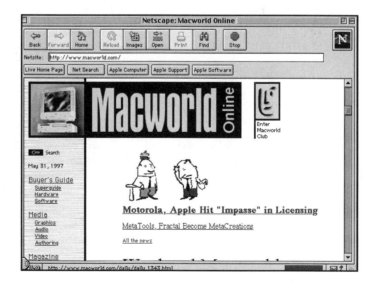

Instead of using the Menu or its shortcut, you can also type an address into the Location text entry field; highlight the current page's address and type. Hit Return to load the new page.

Such as the Apple pages, you'll see a variety of link styles on *Macworld* Online, including text links, buttons, and image links. If you want to save this web page's location for future reference, Navigator's bookmarking feature can add this page (and any other) to your Bookmarks menu.

To add a page to your Bookmarks menu, perform the following steps:

1. From the Bookmarks menu, select Add Bookmark (Bookmark➡Add Bookmark, or ⌘).

2. Click again on the Bookmarks menu's title. You'll see that the current page has been added to the list (see Figure 16.11). You can now access this location from any other location by selecting its menu item.

Figure 16.11

Macworld *Online's web page now appears in your Bookmarks menu.*

Apple has preloaded your Bookmarks menu with lots of helpful locations, including the web sites of all of the major Macintosh magazines, many of the top mail-order catalogs, major software and hardware vendors, and key support and information sites that specialize in Macintosh topics.

But there's more to life than just your computer, and so it is with the World Wide Web. To use a search engine to find pages that match your interests, perform the following steps:

1. Select File➡Open.

2. Enter the following web address: http://www.yahoo.com.

   A new web page appears (see Figure 16.12).

Figure 16.12

Yahoo!'s search engine web page.

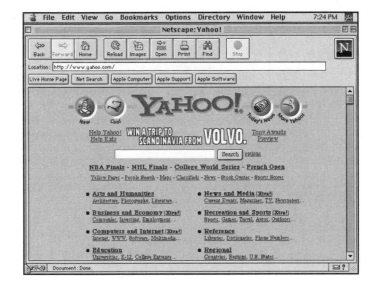

3. In the text entry field, type "SF Giants."

4. Click on the Search button. Yahoo! brings up a list of web pages that have something to do with the San Francisco Giants (see Figure 16.13). You can click on any of the blue links to jump immediately to those pages.

Figure 16.13

Yahoo finds numerous pages that tell you all about the Giants.

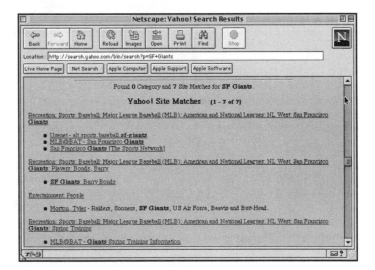

5. When you're done reading about your favorite topics, quit Navigator.

JUST A MINUTE

Yahoo! is just one of many search engines you can choose from. Netscape Navigator includes its own built-in search facility (actually a link to the Excite engine), which you can access by clicking Net Search button. Netscape's own web site (`http://www.netscape.com/escapes/search`) offers links to many others.

TIME SAVER

You can access most web sites without typing the `http://` before the address. In fact, you can often type just the domain name (such as "Apple" or "Macworld" or "Yahoo"). Try it with your favorite sites.

Of course, these exercises represent just a small fraction of Navigator's capabilities and things to see and do on the World Wide Web. To learn more about using Navigator, select Handbook from the Help menu. A complete guide to Navigator's features is covered there, including a hands-on Tutorial (see Figure 16.14).

Figure 16.14

Selecting Help➡ Handbook brings up Navigator's tutorial and reference page.

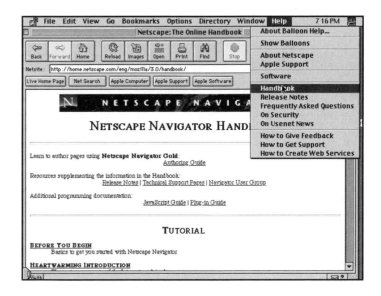

Email Clients

Mac OS 8 ships with ClarisEmailer Lite, which enables you to send and receive electronic mail. To launch the ClarisEmailer Lite application, double-click on its icon

16

(Internet➧InternetApplications➧ClarisEmailer➧ClarisEmailer Lite). Emailer Lite's browser appears (see Figure 16.15).

Figure 16.15

Emailer Lite's browser.

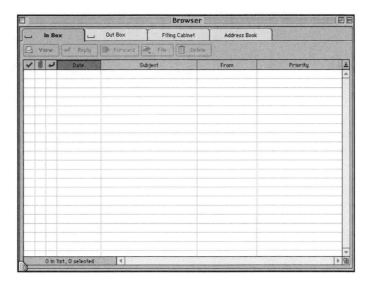

Because you have not retrieved any mail, your browser's In Box is empty. Click on the other tabs (Out Box, Filing Cabinet, Address Book) to get an idea of their appearance.

We won't go into great detail about using Emailer Lite, because Apple has included a separate manual on its use along with Mac OS 8.

If you plan to use email frequently, though, you may want to consider upgrading to the full edition of ClarisEmailer. Details about the full version's features can be found on the web at `http://www.claris.com` and you can download a free trial version from most major shareware sites.

News Readers

Usenet is an interactive set of bulletin board-type newsgroups covering over 10,000 different topics, ranging from classic cars to molecular biology. As you might expect, a fair number of these groups are dedicated to geeky topics such as computers and their operating systems, but most everyone will find a Usenet newsgroup (or a dozen!) that they're interested in reading regularly. Each newsgroup is made up of dozens (or hundreds) of electronic messages called *articles*. To access Usenet newsgroups, you can use your web browser.

To access Usenet from Navigator, perform the following steps:

1. Launch Navigator.

2. From the Window menu, select Netscape News.
   A new window appears (see Figure 16.16).

Figure 16.16

Netscape News.

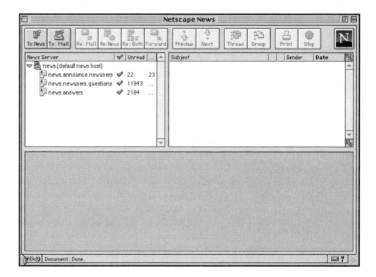

3. To view the contents of a newsgroup, click on its name in the left pane. Articles contained in that newsgroup will appear in the right pane (see Figure 16.17).

Figure 16.17

Articles (right) of a newsgroup.

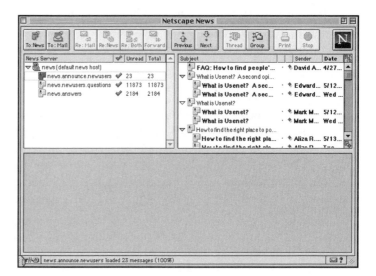

16

4. To read an article, click on its title in the list on the right pane. The text of the
   article will appear in the lower pane of the window (see Figure 16.18).

Figure 16.18

*An article's text appears
in the lower pane when
its title is selected from
the right pane.*

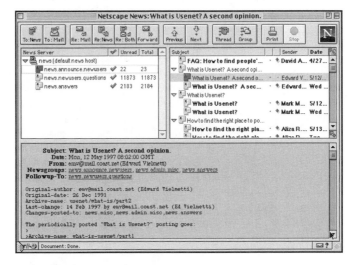

By default, Navigator has subscribed you to three newsgroups: news.announce.newusers,
news.newusers.questions, and news.answers. All three of these groups are good starting
points for your reading, as they not only will help you learn to navigate through newsgroups,
but you'll also learn some important facts about Usenet and its use.

To see a list of all newsgroups, perform the following steps:

1. From the Options menu, select Show All Newsgroups. Netscape will access your
   ISP's news server, where all of the Usenet groups listings are stored. (Depending on
   the speed of your connection, this could take many minutes.) A listing of all the
   available newsgroups on your ISP's server will appear in the right pane of the
   window (see Figure 16.19).

2. Although this list may look pretty dull, it actually gets a lot better. Scroll down
   until you see a listing that says "Rec.* (612 groups)."

3. Click on the disclosure triangle to the left of this listing to display its contents.
   You'll see a list beginning with rec.animals.wildlife (see Figure 16.20).

4. Some of the titles in this list also have disclosure triangles. Click on the disclosure
   triangle to the left of "rec.arts.*" to display its contents. As you can see, this process
   goes on and on.

5. To subscribe to a newsgroup, note its name (you may want to write it down on a
   piece of paper) and select Show Subscribed Newsgroups from the Options menu to
   hide the list of all groups.

Figure 16.19

A list of all the newsgroups on an ISP's news server appears in the left pane.

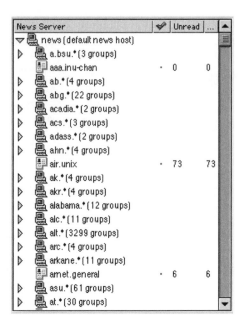

6. From the File menu, select Add Newsgroup. A dialog box appears (see Figure 16.21).

Figure 16.20

The rec. hierarchy of Usenet news.*

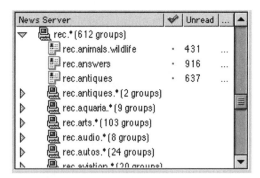

7. Type your desired newsgroup's name in the text entry field, and click OK. Its name will now appear at the bottom of your subscribed newsgroups.

We've really just scratched the surface here, again. For more information on using Navigator as a newsreader, select About Usenet News from the help menu.

16

Figure 16.21
The Add Newsgroup
dialog box.

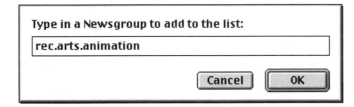

Type in a Newsgroup to add to the list:

rec.arts.animation

Cancel   OK

Dedicated newsreader programs do a better job than web browsers for reading Usenet news. We recommend that you download one from a shareware site (NewsWatcher is a popular one).

Mac OS Shortcuts

Mac OS 8 also comes with some built-in shortcuts to help you get onto the Internet quickly each time you want to use it.

By now, you've probably noticed the Mail and Browse the Internet icons on your desktop. Both of these are simple, iconic shortcuts that launch your preferred applications for web browsing and email (most likely, Netscape Navigator and ClarisEmailer Lite). They work just such as aliases (see Figure 16.22).

Figure 16.22
Internet shortcut icons
on the desktop.

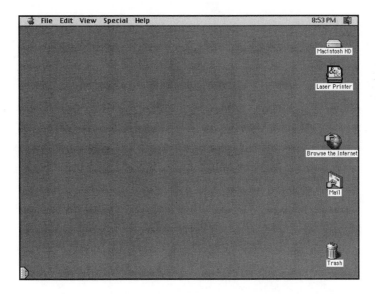

Another handy Internet shortcut can be found under the Apple menu. Selecting Connect To... brings up a brief dialog box where you can type the URL of any web page. Clicking the Connect button launches Navigator, and opens the specified page (see Figure 16.23).

Figure 16.23

The Connect To... dialog box will automatically launch Navigator and connect to the specified page.

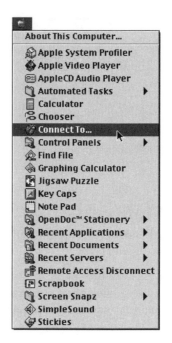

Logging Off

If you set up your PPP Control Panel in Hour 15 to automatically disconnect you after a period of inactivity, you don't really need to do anything to log off. If you want to log off immediately, though, you can.

To log off immediately from your Internet connection, perform the following steps:

1. Open the PPP Control Panel (Apple Menu➡Control Panels➡PPP). Its window appears (see Figure 16.24).

2. Click on the Disconnect button to terminate your connection. When you are logged off, the Status area will read "Idle."

16

Figure 16.24

*The PPP Control Panel
as it appears with an
active connection.*

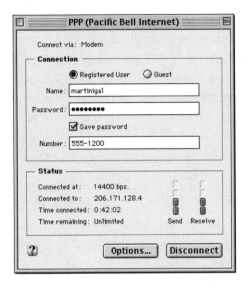

JUST A MINUTE

If you've used the Internet Dialer to log on, you can press its Disconnect button instead.

Summary

In this hour, we've covered the basics of the types of activities and information you can find on the Internet. You've learned how to manually connect to your ISP if you're not set up to log on automatically, and you've taken a brief tour through Mac OS 8's built-in Internet applications. You've learned how to work your way around the Internet's main offerings, including web pages, email, and Usenet newsgroups. You've also explored the Internet shortcuts built in to the operating system, and learned how to log off of the Internet when you're done online.

Term Review

FAQ   An acronym for Frequently Asked Questions—a file you'll want to read for any Usenet newsgroup before you post.

Flaming   Insulting, degrading, harassing, or otherwise rude behavior online.

Netiquette   Etiquette standards of the Internet.

FTP File Transfer Protocol—a method of moving files from one computer to another over the Internet.

Hypertext Live links from one WWW document to another.

Search Engine A web site (or page) that enables you to type in one or more words to search on, bringing up links to relevant web pages.

URL Uniform Resource Locator—a web address.

Web browser An application used to view (browse) web pages.

WWW Acronym for World Wide Web—the graphical, page-oriented portion of the Internet.

Q&A

Q **Everything seems to go very slowly when I'm online. How can I speed up my Internet access?**

A You could buy a faster modem to speed up your access rate. Also, the Internet is generally busiest during and immediately after business hours; try logging on at some other time. It may also be due to the fact that you're accessing slow servers. They may be very popular, image-intensive, or running on slow computers or Internet connections.

Q **Where can I find out more about what's on the World Wide Web?**

A The Mac OS Info Center document "Exploring the Internet" has lots of facts on finding information on the web. You can also use the default Apple Home Page on Excite as a launching point for further Internet exploration.

PART

III

Customizing Your Macintosh

Hour

17 Customizing the Finder and Software

18 Hardware

19 Memory

20 Multimedia

21 Security and Safety

22 Compatibility with DOS and Windows

23 Advanced Networking

24 Automation

Hour 17

Customizing the Finder and Software

In this hour, we'll walk you through the various control panels, preference dialog boxes, and Finder menus used to customize how your Macintosh looks and behaves. We'll also show you Finder customization tricks, and offer you ways to easily localize your system for international locales.

The highlights of this hour include:

- ☐ Using control panels to customize how the Finder—and your software—looks and behaves
- ☐ How to use the Finder Preferences dialog box to control other aspects of the Finder's look and feel
- ☐ Using the View… menu and Labels for better organization
- ☐ How to adapt your system for non-U.S. locations

Customizing the Finder's Interface

Mac OS 8 provides you with numerous ways to customize the appearance and behavior of the Finder. The Appearance and Desktop Pictures Control Panels, along with the Finder Preferences dialog box, provide most of the major interface-altering controls; a number of other control panels offer less-noticeable enhancements; and the View menu provides further ways to customize the Finder's organization.

Appearance Control Panel

The Appearance Control Panel enables you to define most of Mac OS 8's most noticeable global visual preferences, such as accent and highlight colors, and behaviors—such as those of collapsing windows. Items you define here affect not only the behavior of windows and fonts in the Finder, but Mac OS-influenced appearances within applications, too. Specifically, this control panel enables you to manipulate the colors of scroll bar thumbs, progress bars, and text-entry box highlights.

To use the Appearance Control Panel, perform the following steps:

1. From the Apple menu, select Control Panels➡Appearance.

    The Appearance Control Panel opens to its main screen, Color (see Figure 17.1).

2. Within the Color screen, scroll through the Accent Color choices.

Figure 17.1

The Appearance Control Panel's first screen, Color.

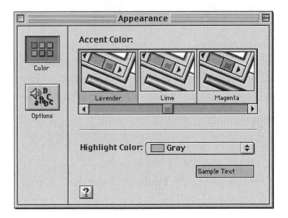

3. To select an Accent Color, click its picture in the scrolling window. Its panel will change to a darker gray to indicate that it is selected.

4. To choose a new Highlight Color, click the pop-up menu and drag to the appropriate choice (see Figure 17.2).

Figure 17.2

The Highlight Color pop-up menu.

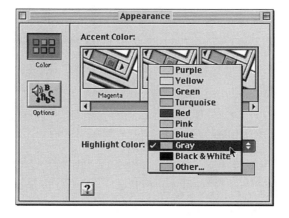

TIME SAVER

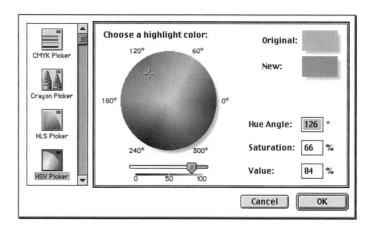

If you don't like any of the predefined highlight colors, you can create your own. Drag the pop-up menu to Other...; a Color Picker window appears (see Figure 17.3).

The default color picker enables you to select highlight colors by clicking the cursor within the color wheel; you can control the color's brightness using the slider at the bottom of the panel. The scrolling list on the left side of the panel enables you to choose from six different color models. Our favorite is the Crayon Picker (see Figure 17.4) which lets you select from 60 different crayon-like shades, including Chlorine, Dirt, and Fire.

Figure 17.3

The default Color Picker.

Figure 17.4

The Crayon Picker.

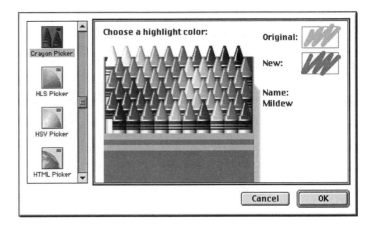

The Appearance Control Panel's second window enables you to control the system font—the font used for menus and dialog boxes—and the behavior of collapsing windows.

To set collapsing window preferences, perform the following steps:

1. From within the Appearance Control Panel, click the Options button on the left side of the window. (If you closed the control panel after our last exercise, reopen it by selecting Apple Menu➡Control Panels➡Appearance.)

2. To enable Window Shade-style window collapsing (by double-clicking in the title bar), be sure a check mark appears in the appropriate check box. If you leave this check box empty, you'll still be able to use Mac OS 8's collapse box; this feature is primarily used to ease System 7 users' transition to Mac OS 8.

3. To disable the "whooshing" noise heard when collapsing windows, uncheck the appropriate check box. Leaving this box checked will enable Mac OS 8 to continue playing the sound.

4. Close the control panel for your changes to take effect.

To revert to a System 7-style appearance, perform the following steps:

1. From within the Appearance Control Panel, click the Options button on the left side of the window. (If you closed the Control Panel after our last exercise, reopen it by selecting Apple Menu➡Control Panels➡Appearance.)

17

2. Click the System Font pop-up menu, and drag to Chicago. (Charcoal is the default Mac OS 8 font.)

3. To disable the Mac OS 8 appearances within applications, uncheck the "System-wide platinum appearance" check box.

JUST A MINUTE

Unless you're having compatibility problems with Mac OS 8 appearances within applications, you'll want to leave the "System-wide platinum appearance" check box turned on. (The *platinum appearance* is the new, 3-D, predominantly gray look of Mac OS 8; disabling this check box will enable some older applications to continue to use System 7-style appearances).

4. Close the Control Panel for your changes to take effect.

Desktop Pictures Control Panel

The Desktop Pictures Control Panel enables you to alter the Finder's background, known as the Desktop. To change your desktop appearance, perform the following steps:

1. Open the Desktop Pictures Control Panel (Apple Menu➡Control Panels➡Desktop Pictures). The opening screen, Pattern, will appear (see Figure 17.5).

Figure 17.5

The Desktop Pictures Control Panel, displaying the Pattern screen.

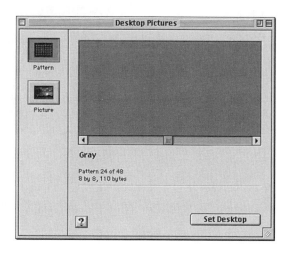

2. Within the Pattern screen, scroll through the pattern choices.

3. To select a repeating pattern or color scheme, double-click its picture in the scrolling window. (You can also single-click it and then click the Set Desktop button, if you prefer.) Your desktop will change immediately (see Figure 17.6).

Figure 17.6

Double-clicking a desktop pattern automatically changes the Desktop.

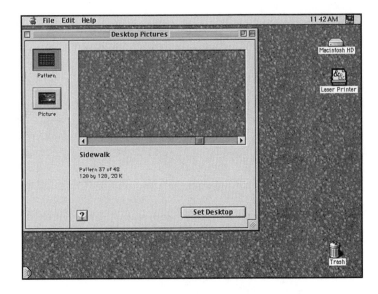

4. If you prefer your backdrop to be a single image, rather than a pattern, click the Picture button on the left side of the panel. The Picture screen appears, showing your current desktop pattern (see Figure 17.7).

Figure 17.7

The Desktop Pictures Control Panel's Picture screen.

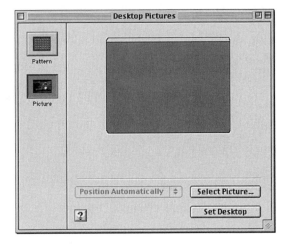

5. Click the Select Picture… button. An Open dialog box appears, showing the contents of the Sample Desktop Pictures folder (see Figure 17.8).

17

Figure 17.8

The Sample Desktop Pictures Open dialog box.

6. Click the Show Preview check box to view the picture before selecting it, if you like.

7. Scroll through the list of pictures, and click the title of the picture you want to use as your desktop picture.

8. Click the Open button to import the image into the control panel.

9. Click the Set Desktop button to change your desktop picture.

10. Close the control panel.

TIME SAVER

If you want to use one of your own scanned photos instead of the samples, you can use the Open dialog box to select it from anywhere on your hard drive. If it is smaller than the number of pixels on your screen, you can use the pop-up menu in the Open dialog box to scale it to fit, center it, or repeat it multiple times across your monitor.

Other Control Panels

Three other control panels enable you to customize some portion of Mac OS 8 appearances and behaviors.

The *General Controls* Control Panel (Apple Menu➡Control Panels➡General Controls) enables you to define the blinking rate of your insertion point cursor and menus (see Figure 17.9).

It also enables you to define whether the Desktop shows behind the currently active window when you're using applications; which folder your Open and Save dialog boxes default to; whether or not you want to receive a warning when your system was turned off improperly; and whether or not you want to protect your System and Applications folders from being modified or thrown away.

Figure 17.9

*The General Controls
Control Panel.*

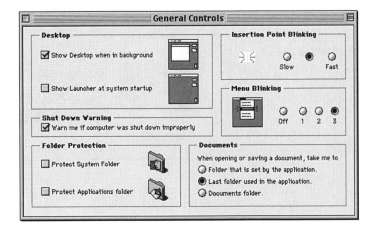

In addition to letting you set the current date and time, the *Date & Time* Control Panel (see Figure 17.10) enables you to specify your preferences about the clock that's displayed in the upper right hand corner of the menu bar.

Figure 17.10

*The Date & Time
Control Panel.*

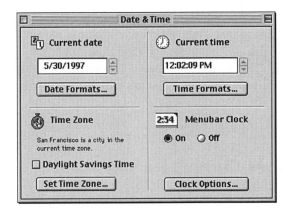

By clicking the Time Formats... button, you can define whether you want 12-hour or 24-hour timekeeping, and whether or not Mac OS 8 should display a zero before single-digit hours (such as 04:00). You can also change the color separating the hour and minutes to a different symbol (such as a dash or a slash) and change the AM and PM designators (to A and P, or a.m. and p.m., for example).

Clicking the Clock Options button enables you to set all sorts of clock-related preferences. You can change the color, font, and size of the clock display, as well as enabling chimes for the hour (or portion of the hour). You can also opt to display the day of the week or seconds with the default hour and minutes, if you choose.

17

The *Monitors & Sound* Control Panel contains a sub-panel for defining your system alert, the "beep" or other noise you hear when the Macintosh requires your attention. You can choose from a variety of predefined sounds, and modify the volume of your alerts (if you want to keep your mistakes relatively private).

Finder Preferences

The Finder Preferences dialog box enables you to define a number of different parameters about your system's appearance and behavior. We've actually already visited the Finder's Preferences dialog box, back in Hour 3. Let's revisit its use.

To change your Finder Preferences, perform the following steps:

1. From the Finder, select Edit➥Preferences...
   The Finder Preferences dialog box will appear (see Figure 17.11).

Figure 17.11

The Finder Preferences dialog box.

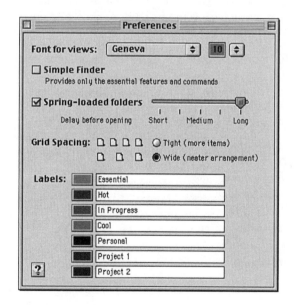

2. To change the font used to display the names of folders and files in the Finder, click the pop-up window and drag to your chosen font. All of the fonts currently installed in your Fonts folder (System folder➥Fonts) will be listed.

3. To change the Finder font's size, type a number into the highlighted numeric entry box, or click the pop-up arrows next to it for preselected sizes.

4. To enable the Simple Finder—where you only see limited menu options and commands—click the check box. (Our exercises will assume that Simple Finder is turned off, though.)

5. To disable spring-loaded folders, click its check box to remove the check mark. To alter the delay before opening a spring-loaded folder, drag the slider's thumb to a new location.

6. To change your grid spacing—the space between your icons—click the appropriate radio button.

7. To change the name of Finder labels, type new names in the text fields to the right of each color swatch. To change the colors themselves, click the swatch to bring up the Color Picker, and select a new color as described earlier in this hour. (We'll talk about using Labels later in the hour.)

8. To implement the changes you've made, close the Preferences dialog box.

The View... Menu

The View menu offers numerous striking departures from previous versions of the Mac OS in terms of defining behavior preferences. We covered this topic extensively in Hour 8, "Your Filing System."

To customize your views, perform the following steps:

1. Open any folder.

2. Select View➥as Icons

3. Select View➥View Options. A dialog box appears (see Figure 17.12).

Figure 17.12

The View Options dialog box, from a window viewed as icons (the dialog box for a window viewed as buttons is nearly identical).

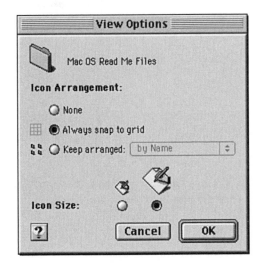

17

4. Configure the dialog box to suit your view preferences.

5. Close the dialog box.

To customize the views in a different way, perform the following steps:

1. Open any folder.

2. Select View➡as List.

3. Select View➡View Options. A dialog box appears (see Figure 17.13).

Figure 17.13

The View Options dialog box, from a window viewed as a list.

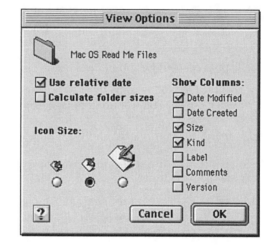

4. Close the dialog box for your changes to take effect.

JUST A MINUTE

You can select the columns to be displayed in the list window, as well as the icon size displayed on the left side. This is also where you can disable Mac OS 8's relative dates feature, which lets files modified within two days display "Today" or "Yesterday" in their date modified fields, rather than the actual date.

Other Finder Tricks

Here are a few more basic tips and tricks to help you customize your working environment under Mac OS 8.

Using Labels

The Labels feature has been around for many versions of the Mac OS, but most beginning users don't take advantage of it. That's a shame, because it can be a powerful (and fun) organizational tool.

To get an idea of Labels' usefulness, perform the following steps:

1. Within the Finder, open the Mac OS 8 Read Me Files folder on the root level of the hard drive.

2. View the windows as a list (View➡as List).

3. Select View➡View Options; click the Label check box to select it; and click the Kind check box to deselect it.

4. Click the file entitled "About Mac OS 8" to select it.

5. Label the file Hot by using the Labels feature in the File menu (File➡Labels➡ Hot). The file's icon will turn red, and its space in the label column will read Hot.

6. Label the file "About QuickDraw™ 3D" in the same way. The file's icon will turn red, and its space in the label column will read Hot.

7. Select the file "About English Text to Speech" and label it In Progress (File➡Labels➡In Progress). Its icon will turn pink, and its label will read In Progress.

8. Select View➡Sort View➡by Label (or click the Label column heading in the window). The Label column turns darker gray to indicate it is the active sorting parameter, and the labeled files group together at the top of the list (see Figure 17.14).

Figure 17.14

Labels can be used to keep files grouped by project or urgency, and sorted within windows.

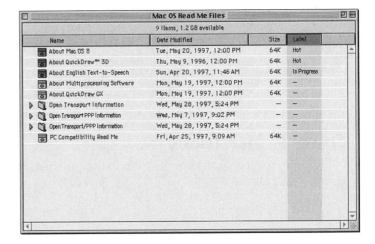

17

Creating a Customized Launcher

In Hour 8, you learned to create pop-up windows—self-closing, tabbed windows that rest at the bottom of your screen. You also learned to view windows as buttons. Both of these methods can be combined to create a customized application launcher.

To create your own customized application launcher, perform the following steps:

1. On your hard drive, double-click the Applications folder to open its window.
2. Select View➥As buttons.
3. Drag the window's lower-right corner to the left as far as it will go.
4. Select View➥Clean Up.
5. Select Arrange➥by Name.
5. Click the window's zoom box—this will maximize its height to fill the length of your monitor and its width to the proper size to show one button wide.
6. Drag the window's title bar to the bottom of the screen to create a pop-up window (see Figure 17.15).

Figure 17.15

A narrow pop-up folder viewed as buttons can serve as a custom application launcher.

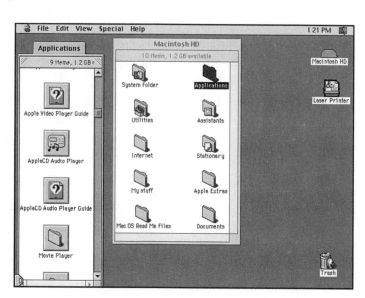

To launch an application using your newly-created custom launcher, perform the following steps:

1. Click the pop-up window's tab to open the window.
2. Scroll until you see the button for the Apple Audio CD Player.
3. Click the Audio CD Player's button. The Audio CD Player will launch, and the pop-up window will automatically close.

International Customization

Four Mac OS 8 control panels help you customize your system for optimal use in foreign (non-U.S.) locales. All of them can be found by selecting Apple Menu➡Control Panels.

The *Text* Control Panel (see Figure 17.16) enables you to specify the language behavior conventions for the Finder—and any applications that use the Finder's preferences—for tasks such as sorting order and case conversion.

Figure 17.16

The Text Control Panel.

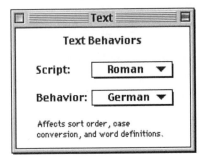

The *Numbers* Control Panel (see Figure 17.17) enables you to choose your preferences for number and currency handling from a preset list, or define your own custom preferences if they're not among the menu choices.

Figure 17.17

The Numbers Control Panel.

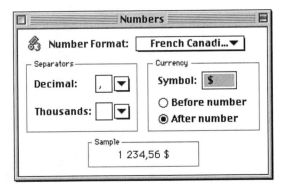

The *Keyboard* Control Panel (see Figure 17.18) enables you to choose one or more keyboard configurations from a preset list. In non-U.S. countries, keyboard configurations are often different than the ones we use here, to accommodate different alphabets; this control panel enables you to select from a number of preset keyboard layouts.

17

Figure 17.18

The Keyboard Control Panel.

The *Date & Time* Control Panel's Time Format button brings up a second screen (see Figure 17.19) that enables you to choose from preset international time formats.

Figure 17.19

The Date & Time Format window's pop-up menu.

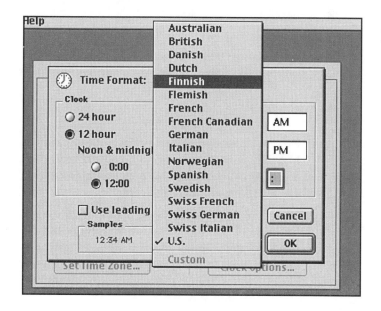

For more information about international software, visit `http://www.macos.apple.com/multilingual/`.

Summary

In this hour, we took you though step-by-step methods of using the Appearance and Desktop Picture Control Panels to customize your workspace, as well as outlining the uses of other control panels for less-obvious interface modifications. We also revisited the Finder Preferences dialog box, and the View… menus covered in previous hours.

You've learned how to use Labels for better organization, used skills from previous hours to create a custom application launcher, and covered the basics of customizing your system for non-U.S. locations.

Term Review

Color picker A dialog box that enables you to choose a color—such as a highlight color or a label color—from a color wheel, sliders, or a representation of a box of crayons.

Desktop pattern A solid color or repeating pattern used as the Finder's background.

Desktop picture An image used as the Finder's background.

Labels A Mac OS feature that enables you to define and sort files and folders into groups by project or priority.

Platinum appearance Mac OS 8's three-dimensional gray-toned look and feel.

Relative dates A Mac OS 8 feature where files modified within two days display "Today" or "Yesterday" in their date modified fields, rather than the actual date.

Q&A

Q **I've got a photograph of a sports car as my desktop picture, but all of the highlight colors I try seem to clash with it. Is there an easy way to choose a highlight color in the color picker that exactly matches the color of the sports car, without using trial and error?**

A Within the Appearance control panel, drag the Highlight Color pop-up menu to Other…; a Color Picker window will appear (see Figure 17.3 earlier in this hour). Hold down the Option key, and the cursor will turn into an eyedropper. Drag the Eyedropper over the area of the photograph (or any other object) you want to match. Click to sample the color into the color picker, then close the color picker window for your selection to take effect.

17

Q I really don't like the appearance of Mac OS 8—I miss System 7.6—but I need its new features. How can I make my system look and feel more like it did in the old days?

A Alas for you homesick folks, there's not really much you can do to disable the Platinum appearance within the Finder. You can set your Finder font to Geneva 10 (File➡Preferences➡Font for Views in the finder) and your dialog box font to Chicago in the Appearance Control Panel (Apple Menu➡Control Panels➡ Appearance➡Options), but that will only take you part of the way. In some applications, you can disable the new look by disabling System-wide platinum appearance (also in Apple Menu➡Control Panels➡Appearance➡Options), but any applications revised to take advantage of Mac OS 8's new features will probably invoke the new look automatically, anyway.

To revert to old System 7-style behaviors, you can disable spring-loaded folders (in Finder Preferences), and enable double-clicking windows to collapse them (in the Appearance Control Panel). You'll also need to disable the relative dates feature in the View Options dialog box of any window that's viewed as a list—including your entire hard drive.

17

Hour 18

Hardware

In this Hour, we're going to talk about some of the hardware you'll be attaching to your Macintosh, either immediately or in the near future. One of the big advantages of the Macintosh is the smooth way it lets you add hardware without necessarily forcing you to be technical.

Some of the hardware we'll be talking about you may have already connected to your Macintosh—like the monitor, for instance, or your modem. That's okay. We'll show you how to adjust these peripherals using some of the control panels we referred to back in Hour 6, "The Apple Menu."

The highlights of this hour include:

☐ How to connect and adjust your monitor and what kinds of monitors are best for certain kinds of work

☐ What kind of input devices you can use with your Macintosh, and how you can adjust them

☐ What you get from other input and output devices, such as CD-ROM drives, modems, scanners, and digital cameras

☐ How to determine whether you need to install internal cards that in turn let you add other peripherals

Monitoring Monitors

After your Macintosh, your monitor is your most important purchase. For one thing, your computer won't work without it. For another, you'll be staring into it almost every moment you use your computer, so it's important to get a quality monitor.

This isn't always easy. The monitor that's on display at the computer store may not have the same quality as the one that's in the box, even if they're the same model. The key is to buy a reputable name brand at a store that has a sensible return policy.

One important thing to test that will not vary from monitor to monitor: the controls. Some companies pay lots of money to brilliant engineers to come up with adjustment controls that only a brilliant engineer can appreciate. At least make sure they seem comfortable and logical before you buy.

Types and Sizes

Monitors generally come in four sizes: 15", 17", 19", and 21". These measurements correspond to the diagonal distance across the screen. Because of a recent lawsuit, however, monitor manufacturers have been forced to disclose maximum viewing area. The glass may indeed measure 17" diagonally, but you may not be able to adjust the desktop to fill the entire space. As a result, you can't take advantage of the maximum viewing area.

What's the major difference between these four sizes of monitors? Price is one. The cathode ray tube inside every monitor represents about half of its cost, but there's no easy way to improve it and reduce the cost, the way you can with CPUs or hard drives. Screen real estate is another. If you tend to fill up your desktop with icons and applications, a larger monitor gives you more room to spread them out. If you work with spreadsheets or graphics documents, being able to see most (or all) the file at once is a time-saver, because you don't have to scroll back and forth.

You may also have seen larger monitors advertised. These can be as expensive as your computer itself (or more!), and work well in conference rooms where presentations are frequently given. They can also be nice to have for playing games and enjoying the maximum amount of screen real estate, but most likely if you can splurge on one of these monitors it's because you just won the lottery.

Whatever you choose, remember that monitors are like well-tailored clothing: once you find something that fits you perfectly, you can't substitute something smaller. It may be worth spending money on a 17" monitor when you first buy your computer rather than to skimp and get a smaller monitor that you outgrow almost immediately.

 18

JUST A MINUTE

Monitors also have an adjustable measurement known as resolution. Resolution depends on the number of pixels (picture elements) on your screen and is expressed by two numbers, one representing the number of horizontal pixels, and the other representing the number of vertical pixels. Your monitor may be capable of displaying 640 x 480, 800 x 600, or 1024 x 768.

Connecting Your Monitor

You've probably already connected your monitor to your Macintosh, since we've been walking you through exercises that require a display, but on the off chance that you haven't, we'll tell you how it's done. It's pretty easy, thanks to the icons that you'll see on the back of your computer. There's one that actually resembles a monitor, with two straight vertical lines on either side of what looks like a picture tube. Plug the cable coming from the back of the monitor into that socket, plug in the monitor, and you're done.

Adjusting Your Monitor

Remember when we were talking about screen real estate? You can adjust your monitor to get more work space on your screen. The icons will be smaller, which is something to consider, but you'll have more room. To adjust your monitor, perform the following steps:

1. In the Menu Bar, click on Apple Menu➡Control Panels➡Monitors & Sound.
2. Click on the box labeled Monitor (see Figure 18.1).

Figure 18.1

The Monitors & Sound control panel.

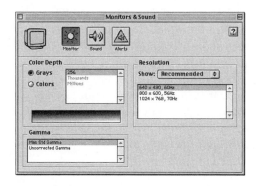

3. Your monitor will be set to its default resolution, which will probably be 256 colors at a resolution of 640 x 480 pixels (the 60Hz next to the pixels refers to what's known as the "refresh rate," the number of times per second that the display is redrawn).

18

4. To adjust the monitor, click on the next resolution available. See how the picture changes? That's because there are more pixels on the screen, but the information is being displayed using the same amount of pixels. As a result, it seems smaller.

5. In the Color Depth box, click on thousands of colors. This enables you to display more than 256 colors on your screen (if your monitor doesn't support this many colors, this option will not appear).

6. The final area of the Monitor control panel, Gamma Color versus Mac Standard Color, is primarily used by high-end graphics professionals for color correction.

7. Close the control panel now. We'll return to it later in Hour 20 when we discuss multimedia.

TIME SAVER

Monitors generally use one of two kinds of technologies. One is called *shadowmask* and the other is *aperture grille*. (Aperture grille is sometimes referred to as Trinitron, a Sony trademark.) Although it's a bit of a simplification, generally users who work with fine lines, such as engineers, designers, and accountants, need shadowmask technology because it's sharper. Users who work with color and illustrations, as in prepress and desktop publishing, need aperture grille technology because it's brighter.

Investigating Input Devices

You may be asking yourself, what the heck is an "input device"? Simply put, it's anything that lets you input data into your Macintosh. These devices range from the simple—your keyboard, your mouse—to the more complex—tablets, trackballs, scanners, and digital cameras. We'll talk about each of them in succession.

Keyboard

The primary adjustment you can make to your keyboard is changing the nationality of the keyboard. To change the default country settings for the keyboard, perform the following steps:

1. In the Menu Bar, click on the Apple Menu➡Control Panels➡Keyboard (see Figure 18.2).

2. Scroll down to U.S. English and select that box. Close the Control Panel.

3. On the right side of the Menu Bar, a flag representing the country you've chosen will appear.

18

Figure 18.2

The Keyboard Control Panel.

Mouse

You might look at your mouse and wonder how many different ways there are to adjust something with only one moving part. You can, however, adjust the speed at which the cursor blinks and the speed at which it travels across the screen. To make these adjustments, perform the following steps:

1. In the Menu Bar, click on the Apple Menu➡Control Panels➡Mouse (see Figure 18.3).

2. Click on your preferred speed (very slow, or anywhere between slow and fast).

3. Click on your choice of double-click speeds. Close the box.

Figure 18.3

The Mouse Control Panel.

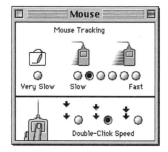

Trackpad

You may also notice a control panel named Trackpad. This is for adjusting the input device found on a PowerBook. If you have a desktop computer, you won't be able to access this control panel. If you have a PowerBook, and you want to adjust the trackpad, perform the following steps.

1. In the Menu Bar, click on the Apple Menu➡Control Panels➡Trackpad (see Figure 18.4).

Figure 18.4

The Trackpad Control Panel.

2. Click on Tracking Speed to adjust how fast the cursor will move compared to how fast your finger moves on the trackpad.

3. Click on Double-Click Speed to adjust how slowly or quickly you want to tap on the trackpad.

4. Click on the options under "Use Trackpad for" to set your clicking and dragging preferences. Click on the Close box.

Tablets

If you are a graphic artist, you may want to use a tablet (see Figure 18.5). These let you write on the tablet with a tool known as a *stylus*. It resembles a pencil but lets you draw on the screen as if you were drawing on a piece of paper. This gives you more freedom than if you were using a mouse. Some people who have trouble with repetitive-stress injuries (RSI) may also use a tablet instead of a mouse.

Your tablet will probably install its own control panel so you can adjust it accordingly. See the manufacturer's manual for more information.

Figure 18.5

A typical computer tablet.

18

Scanners

Scanners are becoming more and more popular for two reasons. First, they're much cheaper than they used to be: you can get a perfectly adequate scanner for several hundred dollars, while several years ago, you couldn't buy one for less than $1,000. Second, with the proliferation of the World Wide Web and personal web pages, scanners are an easy way to get graphics into your computer.

What scanners do simply is "digitize" graphics, where they're photographs or a picture or a page full of type. They break down the image you see with your eyes, translating it into a digital format that the computer can understand. Like monitors, they have resolution measurements, which translate into pixels.

Also like monitors, you can choose from a wide range of models. If you're just archiving family snapshots, you can choose a much less expensive scanner with a lower resolution than if you're working with fine art work.

As with tablets, scanners come with specialized software that you have to load onto your Macintosh (see Figure 18.6). Consult your scanner's documentation for information on getting the best results from your scanner.

Figure 18.6

Scanners let you digitize photographs for storage on the Macintosh.

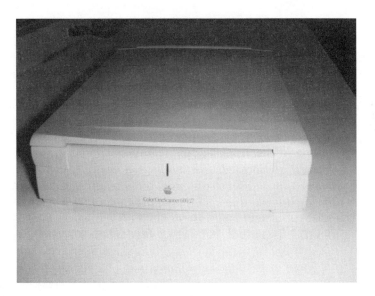

Digital Cameras

For the same reasons that scanners have become more popular, so too have digital cameras. For as little as $200, you can record a digital image, rather than one on film, and download it into your computer. For instance, you could take a picture of the family at a reunion, download it to a computer, load it into an email message, and send it to someone on the other side of the world who can't be there.

Digital cameras are remarkably simple, and if you're going to store family memories in a digital scrapbook rather than a paper one, this may very well be one of your next purchases (see Figure 18.7). Remember, though, that most pictures take up about 200K of space on your hard drive, so you'll have to think about archiving them on some sort of removable storage device for the greatest efficiency.

Figure 18.7

A digital camera image of a digital camera.

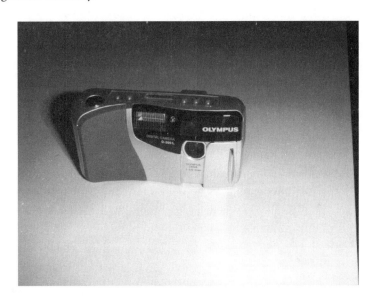

Surveying CD-ROM Drives

Ever since 1993, Macintosh computers have been built with CD-ROM drives (it stands for compact disc, read-only memory). They've become so commonplace that you don't even have to consider adding them anymore. They're used primarily for software distribution, for games, or for reference material—anything that requires a lot of data on a simple, easily transported media.

What Speed Rating Means

All CD-ROM drives have a speed rating, ending in X. The X refers to the original speed at which CD-ROM drives transferred data, which was 150Kb per second (the same as your audio CD). To get the rate of your CD-ROM drive, multiply the number by 1.5. For instance, if you have a 16X CD-ROM drive, it theoretically goes 16 times faster than the original CD-ROM drives (as with most hardware, your mileage will vary).

Is this number important? Probably not. CD-ROM developers want their product to run on as many CD-ROM drives as possible, so they may only build them to work with a drive as fast as 4X. In our tests, the only time you'll benefit from faster drives is if you're loading software

18

from a CD onto a drive or looking up reference material. If you only do this occasionally, it's probably not worth it to invest in the fastest drive. If you want a faster drives to play games, check with the game developer to see which speed they've optimized the game for.

New Speeds Available

If this confusion over speed wasn't bad enough, now some CD-ROM drive vendors are claiming speeds of 20X to 30X representing a phenomenon known as *specsmanship* (which refers to using inflated numbers to give the impression of a better product). Those numbers represent the *potential* top speed of the CD-ROM drive, the speed at the outer track of the CD; the problem is, all CDs are recorded from the *inner* track, so in order to benefit from these high speeds, you have to have a CD that's completely filled with data, *and* the data you want has to be stored in the outer tracks. It's not that these new CD-ROM drives are bad, it's that you shouldn't pay extra money for them unless you're (1) upgrading from a really old drive or (2) it's built into the system you're buying (see Figure 18.8).

Figure 18.8
An external CD-ROM drive.

Mastering Modems

A modem is one of those made-up words from the computer world that stands for *MOdulation-DEModulation*. That's a fancy way of explaining how the transmitting modem takes digital information (your file) and translates it to analog information so that it can transmit the data along telephone lines. The receiving modem takes the analog data and translates it back into digital data.

You'll use your modem to log onto your online service or the Internet, as well as to access your company's Macintosh server over Apple Remote Access (we'll talk more about ARA in Hour 22).

How To Set Up a Modem

The Macintosh makes this easy. Just as the socket for your monitor has an iconic representation of a monitor, the socket for your modem has an iconic representation of a telephone. The same icon is on the plug for your modem (see Figure 18.9). Match the plug to the socket, connect the telephone jack between the modem and the phone line, and you're plugged in.

Figure 18.9

The socket for your modem is clearly marked with a telephone icon, as is the plug for the modem.

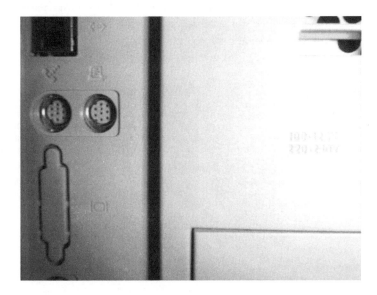

Once you've done that, you'll also have to set up your Macintosh to recognize the modem. To do that, perform the following steps.

1. In the Menu Bar, go to Apple Menu➡Control Panels➡Modem (see Figure 18.10).

2. Click on the modem box. A list of modems will appear, alphabetized by company name. Click on the name of your modem. If the name of your modem does not appear, click on the one marked "generic."

3. Click on your choice of sound (do you want to hear your modem) or dialing (tone means touch-tone, the likely choice). Close the box.

18

Figure 18.10

*The Modem Control
Panel.*

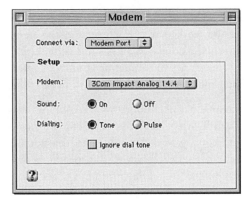

TIME SAVER

As annoying as a modem can sound, leaving the sound on will always make you aware that it's working. If it doesn't screech, you know something's wrong (typically, a cable is unplugged).

What Speed Rating Means

Like CD-ROM drives, modems are categorized by their speeds. You'll find modems labeled with numbers like 28.8, 33.6, and 56. These represent the transfer rate of data in kilobytes per second (Kbps). Like CD-ROM drives, the number represents the highest *potential* speed, the key word here being potential. Tests of 28.8Kbps modems show that you'll probably get data transmission speeds at around 26.3Kbps; not bad, but not 28.8. It's theoretically possible to achieve the highest possible speed, as long as you're transmitting data over a telephone line free of interference and you're talking to the exact same brand of modem at the data's destination.

This is an unlikely scenario, however, if you're calling an online service like America Online. If you're linking to your Internet service provider (ISP), they may have already told you what kind of modems they have so you can get the best data rates. This is great until you switch ISPs.

New Speeds Available

As we go to press, there are new modems coming onto the market that you should know about. They claim to run at 56Kbps, but only when you're downloading information from another server, as you would with data from the World Wide Web. You cannot get these speeds uploading information. And again, this number represents a potential maximum, not what you should expect.

18

Unfortunately, as frequently happens with new, faster products, there are some problems that need to be worked out. For instance, the standards body that ratifies specifications for telecommunications devices has not done so for 56K modems. To further complicate the process, there are two competing groups of companies that are offering these faster modems, and their modems won't necessarily interact with each other.

Eventually kinks like this get worked out. We mention them, though, so you'll be aware of the situation when you buy a modem. At this point, we recommend buying a 33.6Kbps modem. You'll get good speed (again, this number represents the potential maximum), and the standards body has okayed this specification so that any vendor's 33.6Kbps modem will transmit to and accept data from any other vendor's 33.6Kbps modem.

Adding Accessories

Apple and the clone manufacturers couldn't possibly build everything you want into your Macintosh. There are going to be times when you want to add a particular capability. You can do that by adding what's known as internal cards (see Figure 18.11). They fit into your computer in what's known as the *PCI slot* (that stands for peripheral controller interface).

Figure 18.11
A PCI card.

What Internal Cards Do

Internal cards add specific functionality that's not available in the Macintosh. For instance, SCSI is already built into the Macintosh, but if you want faster data transfer to your external hard drives, you can install a faster SCSI card. Similarly, Ethernet is already built into the

18

Macintosh, but if you want to connect to a faster Ethernet network (say, one that runs at 100 megabits per second rather than 10 megabits per second), you'd have to add a PCI-based Ethernet card.

When To Add Cards

The time to add internal cards is when you want to ratchet up the capabilities of your Macintosh. For instance, say you want to punch up the speed of your graphics. Add a video card. If you want to add a television tuner, or 3-D capability, or even virtual reality, you'll need a high-end video card.

The most likely addition you'll make to a new Macintosh in the future is a FireWire card. FireWire is a new standard for plugging in certain peripherals like scanners and digital cameras. We anticipate it to be more prevalent soon, so much so that soon it will be built onto the Macintosh motherboard. Until that happens, you'll need to add a card for FireWire.

If you want to run Microsoft Windows on your Macintosh, one of your options is to add a card with an Intel CPU built right on it. We'll talk about this more in Hour 21, when we discuss PC compatibility.

Summary

In this Hour, we talked about two kinds of peripherals—the kind you add to your Macintosh because you need them (monitors and keyboards) and the kind you want to maximize your productivity (scanners, internal cards). Hopefully you found the process of adding peripherals fairly easy, since that's one of the advantages of the Macintosh—the ease with which you can add to it to make it a tool that suits *you*.

We would only caution you as you consider buying new peripherals that speed is relative. Sometimes what seems like the newest and fastest may only be that way in relation to the previous generation of products. Don't spend extra on the latest technology unless you're well aware of any limitations. If you're new to computing, it may be better to buy a product or technology that's six to nine months old to make sure the kinks have all been worked out.

That'll save you headaches until the day you're so proficient in technology that you anticipate the adventure of playing with new products.

Term Review

Input Device   Any peripheral that can transmit data or commands into your computer, like a keyboard, mouse, scanner, or digital camera.

Internal Cards   Cards that fit into a slot inside your computer to add capabilities that weren't initially built into the computer.

Modem   A device that lets your computer communicate over telephone lines to another modem-equipped computer.

Monitor   The all-important display that lets you see the results of your work.

Output Device   Any peripheral that transmits or displays data, like a monitor or a modem.

Peripheral   Any device that works with your computer, but may not have been sold with it.

Speed Rating   A number relating to peripherals like modems and CD-ROM drives that represents its potential maximum speed, not the speed you're most likely to get.

Q&A

Q **If every peripheral vendor markets its products using the same criteria (highest speed, lowest price, whatever), how do I distinguish between a good one and a bad one?**

A It's important to cut through marketing hype when buying a peripheral. Price may not be the best consideration, although it's frequently high on anyone's list. We recommend talking to friends, other users, checking Internet newsgroups on particular hardware topics (there's one for all of them). When people have problems with something, they sound off about it, and the Internet is a world-wide village square for conversations like this.

Q **Are there other ways to differentiate?**

A Check warranty and return information to see if the company stands by its product. For instance, will they send you a replacement product when you ask to exchange your peripheral, or will they wait until they receive yours? This can cut down the amount of time you're waiting to use the peripheral.

Q **If I upgrade my peripherals, what do I do with the old one?**

A You can donate almost anything to your local school, since they're likely to have equipment that is even older than yours. Be sure to keep manuals and software to donate along with the product. There's nothing more useless than hardware without a manual.

Hour 19

Memory

In Hour 5, "Floppy Disks and Hard Drives," you learned about floppy disks and hard drives, the devices your computer uses to store data permanently. In this hour, you'll learn about your computer's memory, and how it stores data temporarily—that is, where your data is during the time you're using the software. That area of temporary data storage is called random access memory, or *RAM*.

Using Mac OS 8, you can adjust the way your Macintosh uses its RAM in a variety of ways. Depending on your settings, you can boost overall performance, make individual programs run faster, or a combination of both.

Managing your Macintosh's memory can seem like a daunting task, but by tackling a few basic concepts and learning the underlying reasoning behind Mac OS 8's various RAM-management schemes, you can achieve greater performance and efficiency from the Mac OS *and* all of your application programs.

In addition to teaching you how to manage the software side of RAM, this hour will also outline the basics of upgrading your physical RAM, the memory chips inside your computer.

The highlights of this hour include:

☐ Why your System software can use so much RAM, and what to do about it

☐ How the Memory Control Panel helps you maximize your Macintosh's efficiency

☐ How to adjust the size of your Disk Cache to get the best performance

☐ When to use Virtual Memory to boost your available RAM

☐ Why and how to set up a RAM disk

☐ How to adjust your application programs' memory usage for maximum efficiency

☐ How to upgrade your RAM if you don't have enough memory

Memory Essentials

Your Macintosh's memory is distributed among the various application programs you run, as well as the Mac OS. Although Mac OS 8 uses around 8 MB of RAM in its most streamlined mode, few Macintosh users have such lean-and-mean System configurations.

To see how much RAM Mac OS 8 is using on your Macintosh, perform these steps:

1. Quit all currently running programs.

2. From the Finder, click the Apple icon in the tool bar.

3. Drag down to choose About This Computer. The About This Computer box will appear (see Figure 19.1).

4. The dialog box will display the amount of RAM the Mac OS is currently using, and a graphical depiction of its memory use. The number shown is the amount of RAM used by the Mac OS, as well as its various components (including extensions, control panels, fonts, and so on).

Figure 19.1

*The About This Com-
puter box shows how
much memory the Mac
OS uses. Mac OS 8 uses
9.4 MB of RAM on this
Mac.*

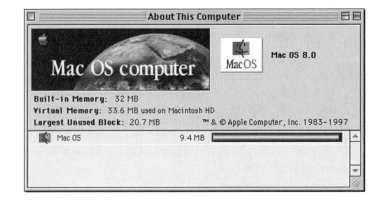

19

The About This Computer box also lists other valuable information, including your System software version, and the total memory available in your Macintosh.

To get a more accurate measurement of how much memory your extensions and control panels eat up, hold down the Shift key as you restart your Macintosh. You should see the "Extensions Off" message under "Welcome to Mac OS" on the splash screen. Repeat steps 1 through 4 earlier in this chapter and compare the two numbers (see Figure 19.2). The difference is the amount of RAM used by your control panels and extensions. Booting with extensions off also sets your disk cache to 96K and disables Virtual Memory (see sections later in this hour for details on disk cache and Virtual Memory). (Extensions will be reenabled the next time you reboot.)

Figure 19.2

Without any extensions or control panels, Mac OS 8 uses 6.5 MB of RAM on this Power Macintosh 7100/80.

By turning off unnecessary extensions and control panels, you can reduce the amount of RAM your System software will use. Turning off necessary extensions, however, can wreak havoc on your system's stability, or cause programs to work improperly (or not at all). Be sure to check the manual for any software whose extensions you plan to disable. Conflict Catcher from Casady & Greene (www.casadyg.com) can help you choose wisely.

The Memory Control Panel

The Memory Control Panel is the part of Mac OS 8 that enables you to balance and tune your system's use of RAM for optimal performance.

After you adjust the Memory Control Panel for the way you use your computer, you probably won't have to return to it on a regular basis. If you find yourself working on special projects that require lots of memory for a single application, adjusting these settings will make your work go faster. Just remember to restart your computer every time you change a setting in the Memory Control Panel.

To access the Memory Control Panel, perform the following steps:

1. Click the Apple icon in the menu bar.
2. Drag down to Control Panels and follow the arrow to the right.
3. Drag the mouse to the Control Panel marked Memory to display the Memory Control Panel (see Figure 19.3).

Figure 19.3

The Memory Control Panel.

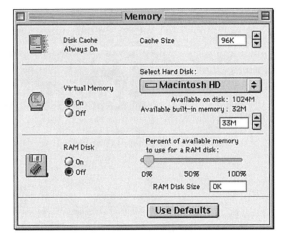

TIME SAVER

When you make adjustments in the Memory Control Panel, you may want to only change one setting at a time and judge how it affects your system performance. If you change more than one setting simultaneously, you'll have a hard time knowing which one did the most good.

19

Disk Cache: An Easy Speed Boost

The first section of the Memory Control Panel controls the Disk Cache. Cache is a French word meaning "hidden storage place"—an apt description of this feature.

The Memory Control Panel enables you to set aside a portion of your RAM to store frequently accessed data from your hard drive, which effectively speeds up your Mac's ability to work. The larger the number you specify here, the more RAM will be devoted to disk cache, and—theoretically—the faster your Macintosh will run. (Most people with reasonably fast Macintosh models can't tell the difference between a large or small disk cache, though.) Of course, the more RAM you allocate to the disk cache, the less you have available for applications.

CAUTION

> Do not confuse disk cache with other forms of cache, such as a cache card (also known as an L2 or Level 2 Cache). These processor caches store frequently made calls to the Macintosh's processor (its central "brain" chip), not information from the hard disk.

If you tend to run a lot of applications, you'll want to keep your cache small so there's more RAM available for opening them. If you tend to run one large application, you may want to make your disk cache larger so that the application can use that extra space to run faster. Try increasing your disk cache and see if you notice an improvement. If the increase isn't perceptible to you, a larger disk cache will be a waste of otherwise-valuable RAM.

To adjust your disk cache, perform the following steps:

1. Open the Memory Control Panel, as described earlier in this hour.
2. From within the Memory Control Panel, click the arrows to the right of cache size to adjust the cache up or down (see Figure 19.4). Remember, the more cache you allocate here, the less total RAM you'll have available for your applications.
3. Restart your Macintosh for the changes to take effect.

19

Figure 19.4

To adjust the size of the disk cache, click the arrows to the right of the current cache size.

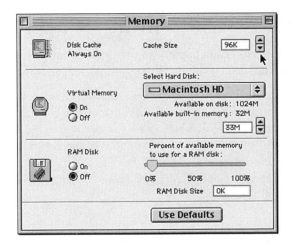

Virtual Memory: Double for Nothing?

Virtual Memory is a way to set aside part of your hard drive for use as RAM. It's something of a last resort for increasing RAM, though, for the simple reason that RAM can transfer data to your Macintosh dramatically faster than your hard drive can.

On the other hand, enabling Virtual Memory does have positive side effects. For reasons known only to Apple's OS engineers, turning on even a tiny amount of Virtual Memory— say, 2 MB—enables most applications to run using less RAM.

To disable or enable Virtual Memory, perform the following steps:

1. Open the Memory Control Panel, as described earlier in this hour.
2. From within the Control Panel, click the "on" toggle button to the right of the Virtual Memory icon.
3. Click the up arrow to increase your Virtual Memory. (You can't go any higher than double the amount of actual RAM you have installed.)
4. Restart your Macintosh for the change to take effect.
5. After restarting, check About This Computer—as described in Memory Essentials, earlier in this hour—to see the effects of your changes (see Figure 19.5).

If you have an external hard drive or you've created partitions on your internal drive, the names of these other volumes will appear in the drop-down menu under Select Hard Disk. By choosing among them, you're selecting which one will lose space to provide Virtual Memory.

19

Figure 19.5.
With Virtual Memory enabled, this 40 MB Power Macintosh appears to have twice as much RAM.

CAUTION

Many games won't operate properly with Virtual Memory turned on.

TIME SAVER

If you can't afford more RAM but you need more memory, another solution is a product from Connectix Corp. called RAM Doubler 2. Unlike Apple's Virtual Memory, it doesn't dramatically affect the speed of your Macintosh, nor does it borrow space on your hard drive.

RAM Disk: A Virtual Hard Drive

As its name implies, a RAM disk enables you to use a portion of your RAM as a temporary storage device, much like a virtual hard disk. In many ways, a RAM disk is the functional opposite of Virtual Memory: you have less memory to launch your applications so certain tasks will probably run faster when you're using it. Like Virtual Memory, though, RAM disks have their drawbacks.

CAUTION

The biggest pitfall of a RAM disk is that it's only temporary. If you crash, lose power, or even shut down your Macintosh on purpose, you lose the contents of the RAM disk.

Many applications run dramatically faster on a RAM disk. The Mac OS is no exception, although you need a very large RAM disk to accommodate an average-sized System folder.

To create a RAM Disk, perform the following steps:

1. Open the Memory Control Panel, as described earlier in this hour.
2. From within the Control Panel, click the "on" toggle button to the right of the RAM Disk icon.
3. Move the slider to the left or right to increase or decrease the size of your RAM disk.
4. Restart your Macintosh for the change to take effect. The RAM disk will appear on your desktop (see Figure 19.6).
5. Copy any files or applications to the RAM disk, and work as you normally would.

Figure 19.6

RAM disks appear on your desktop, just like a hard disk.

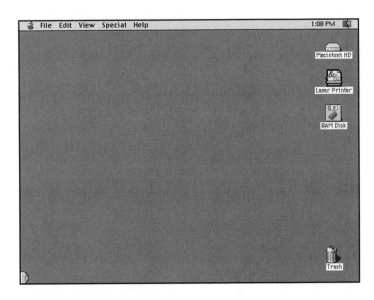

JUST A MINUTE

To set up a RAM disk, you'll need at least 8 MB of RAM that isn't being used by any other application, including your System software.

To resize a RAM Disk, perform the following steps:

1. Open the Memory Control Panel, as described earlier in this hour.
2. Move the slider to the left or right to increase or decrease the size of your RAM disk. Alternately, you can type a number into the box to the right of RAM disk size, and the slider will pop to the respective location.

3. Close the Control Panel for your changes to take effect.

To delete a RAM Disk, perform the following steps:

1. Open the Memory Control Panel, as described earlier in this hour.

2. From within the Control Panel, click the "off" toggle button to the right of the RAM Disk icon.

3. Close the Control Panel for your changes to take effect.

CAUTION

> If you erase or resize a RAM disk, you'll lose the contents. Be sure to move any necessary data back onto your hard drive first.

Applications Use RAM, Too

After you've fully optimized your memory configuration and fine-tuned the Mac OS's use of RAM, you can boost your Mac's efficiency even further by adjusting the amount of RAM used by each application.

Just as with System software, you can see how much RAM each application uses by viewing the About This Computer box while applications are running (see Figure 19.7).

Figure 19.7
The About This Computer box displays the memory used by each application.

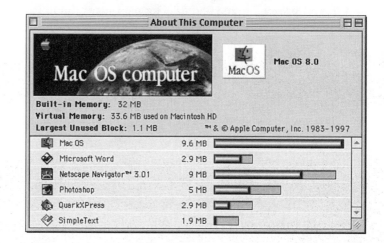

In Figure 19.7 above, Mac OS 8 uses 9.6 MB of RAM; Microsoft Word uses 2.9 MB; Netscape Navigator uses 9 MB; Photoshop uses 5 MB; QuarkXpress uses 2.9 MB; and SimpleText uses 1.9 MB. Even on this 40 MB system, the largest unused block of memory is 1.1 MB—probably not enough to launch another application.

Trying to run an application that uses more than this amount of RAM would result in a message from your Macintosh indicating that you do not have enough memory to launch the application, followed by a suggestion of which application(s) you'd need to quit to make the necessary amount of RAM available (see Figure 19.8).

By using Virtual Memory (or RAM Doubler) as described earlier in this hour, you can gain additional memory for use in other applications.

Figure 19.8

Trying to run an application that uses more than the available amount of RAM results in this message.

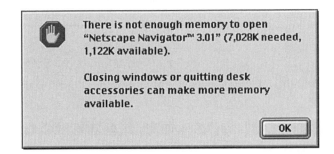

Another way to run another application in this scenario is to adjust the amount of RAM that each (or some, or even one) of the other applications uses.

So how do you determine the right numbers for each application's Minimum size and Preferred size? The Suggested size is the amount of memory the manufacturer recommends for the program to run optimally for most users. But in reality, the Preferred size depends quite a bit on the type of application you're using, and the size of the documents you're using it with.

If you're tweaking SimpleText and you only open single-page documents, you're probably safe with a number closer to the Minimum than the Suggested size. If you're adjusting Photoshop for use with multi-megabyte photographic files, your Preferred size isn't really negotiable—tampering with it will result in dramatically slower performance.

When in doubt, check the documentation that came with each application for any dire warnings about minimum RAM sizes, and experiment. If you have trouble opening a typical-sized file in your favorite application due to low memory, chances are you've gone too low (see Figure 19.9).

Returning to the About This Computer box can help you determine if you're allocating too much memory to one or more of your applications. In Figure 19.10, Microsoft Word is using nearly all of its allocated memory (as shown by the total length of the bar). SimpleText's in-use memory (as shown by the dark area), though, is less than half of its allocation; the unused portion is shown by the light part of bar. In this example, you could probably reduce SimpleText's Preferred size by 40 percent or more.

19

Figure 19.9

This message appears when you haven't allotted enough memory to an application.

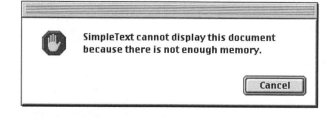

Figure 19.10

SimpleText's memory indicator shows a large portion of its allocated RAM isn't being used.

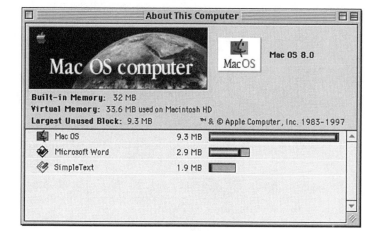

To adjust an application's memory size, perform the following steps:

CAUTION

Approach adjustment of memory allocation with caution. Most programs have been optimized by their manufacturers to work best when the Minimum and Preferred sizes are left untouched. Assigning too low a value—especially in the Preferred size box—can result in unstable performance, including crashes.

19

1. Quit the application, if it's running. (You cannot make changes to a program while it is in use.)

2. Click the application's icon in the Finder to select it.

3. From the menu bar, choose File➡Get Info. The Application's Get Info window appears (see Figure 19.11).

Figure 19.11

Get Info displays each application's memory requirements.

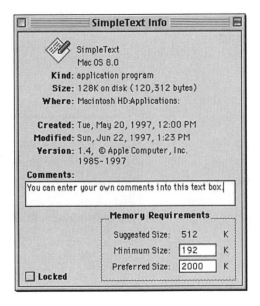

4. Modify the application's Minimum size and/or Preferred size (more below on determining these amounts).

5. Close the Info window. (Changes do not take effect until the Info window is closed, even if you launch the application.)

JUST A MINUTE

Get Info also lists other valuable information, including the version number of your application and its creation and modification date.

TIME SAVER

Get Info isn't just for adjusting applications' memory usage and verifying your version numbers. Every icon in the Finder has an Info box—even the Trash (see Figure 19.12). You can enter your own comments in the provided field and lock your files to prevent modification.

19

Figure 19.12
*Even the Trash has
a Get Info box.*

> **Trash Info**
>
> Trash
>
> **Where:** On the desktop
>
> **Contents:** 4 files and 1 folder are in the Trash for a
> total of 2.5 MB.
>
> **Modified:** Sun, Jun 22, 1997, 1:30 PM
>
> ☐ **Warn before emptying**

Adding More Memory

If you've followed the steps earlier in this chapter and maximized your Macintosh's memory, but yet you still don't have enough RAM to perform your daily work, you'll want to consider upgrading your physical RAM—the memory chips inside your Macintosh.

TIME SAVER

> Adding more RAM to most Macintosh models is easy and relatively inexpensive—around $7 to $15 per megabyte as we went to press, although RAM prices can fluctuate wildly depending on the economy, demand, and various other economic factors. Check around: prices on the same components can vary dramatically from one vendor to the next, and your best buys may come from reputable mail order sources listed in the back of your favorite Macintosh magazine.

19

Individual RAM chips are fastened to small circuit boards called SIMMs (single inline memory modules) or DIMMs (dual inline memory modules), depending on your Macintosh model—SIMMs were used in early Power Macintosh and earlier Macintosh models, and DIMMs are used in later model Power Macintosh systems and clones. These RAM modules are then snapped into sockets on the Macintosh's main logic board. Most Macintosh models have at least two RAM sockets, although some low-end models have a single socket, and most high-end systems have four or more.

All Macintosh models also have a certain amount of RAM soldered onto the main logic board (you can find out how much by referring to your Macintosh's manual, or by calling the manufacturer's tech support line, should you need to know). Note that the amount of RAM soldered onto the main logic board isn't necessarily the same as the amount of RAM you bought it with. Most Macintosh systems have soldered RAM and socketed RAM installed when they ship.

TIME SAVER

Many RAM vendors offer useful guidelines and charts detailing the various installable RAM levels on nearly every Macintosh ever made, the implications of the various speeds (in nanoseconds, or ns) of SIMMs and DIMMs, and the ins and outs of installing RAM yourself. (As you can imagine, this chart could take an entire chapter of its own, so we won't duplicate it here.)

TIME SAVER

Newer Technology (800/678-3726) offers a freeware application called GURU (GUide to RAM Upgrades), which details the amount of RAM your Macintosh can accommodate, how many RAM slots you can fill, and what combinations of SIMMs (or DIMMs) you'll need to attain various configurations. You can download GURU from Newer's web site on the World Wide Web at http://www.newerram.com.

After you've decided how much RAM you need, you have a variety of options. You can buy RAM at your local computer store and have the dealer install it for you. You can also buy your RAM through a local reseller or mail-order house, and then take your Macintosh to any Apple Authorized Service Center for installation (they all work on Macintosh clones, too).

Most service centers charge a flat rate for RAM installation (which varies dramatically depending on your model and location) for which you get the peace of mind of having a professional tampering with the inside of what's probably the third-most-expensive purchase you'll ever make (after your house and your car).

CAUTION

Because Apple and clone vendors use different designs inside their computers, it's not as simple to buy RAM as it is to buy, say, gasoline. Depending on your computer model, you may need 5-volt DIMMs, 3.3-volt DIMMs, or SIMMs. Be sure to ask your RAM vendor if the RAM you're buying will work in your specific model, and verify you can return it if it doesn't.

19

As long as you own a Macintosh that's easy to open, you can probably tackle a RAM upgrade yourself—most Macintosh owners are surprised at how easy it is to install SIMMs and DIMMs. Often the hardest part is getting the case open, although some tower-style Macintosh models (the Quadra 700 and the Power Macintosh 8100 and 9100 come to mind) are notoriously difficult to upgrade, requiring you to remove components—such as the hard drive or the floppy drive, or even the entire main logic board—in order to access the RAM sockets.

Many RAM vendors offer how-to videos with your purchase. If yours doesn't, you may want to ask someone who's done it before to assist you the first time.

Caution

> Installing your own RAM may void the warranty on your Macintosh. Check with the manufacturer; policies vary among Apple and the various Macintosh OS licensees (clone makers).

Summary

This hour demystified the process of managing memory on your Macintosh.

Applications make use of RAM, but the Mac OS is probably one of the most overlooked users of memory—and one of the biggest consumers of available RAM. By carefully tweaking your System software, you can enable the Mac OS to use less RAM, leaving more for your applications.

Within the Memory Control Panel, you can give your Macintosh the ability to open more applications, use hard disk space in place of RAM, enable faster application performance and disk access times, and tune your memory usage to suit your individual needs.

As you learn how to adjust the RAM settings of various applications, you'll enable your programs to run more effectively, too. By modifying the settings under each application's Get Info window, you can enable more programs to run in the same amount of RAM, and optimize each application's memory allocation based on your use.

Term Review

Disk Cache   A portion of your RAM used to store frequently accessed data from your hard drive, which effectively speeds up your Macintosh's ability to work.

RAM Disk   A portion of your RAM as a temporary storage device, much like a virtual hard disk.

19

Random Access Memory (RAM)   The memory in your computer that holds the data you're currently working on, as opposed to the data that's stored on your hard drive.

SIMM (or DIMM)   Single (or dual) inline memory module; the RAM components you add to your Macintosh to increase memory.

Virtual Memory   A way to increase RAM by using unused hard drive space.

Q&A

Q What can I do to minimize the amount of RAM that Mac OS 8 uses?

A Disabling unneeded control panels and extensions enables you to make more RAM available for your applications. Also, reducing the size of your Disk Cache can have an effect on the amount of RAM used by your System software.

Q Is it okay to use the default options on the Memory Control Panel?

A Sure. They're preset based on the configuration of your computer. If you add more RAM or swap out your hard drive for a bigger one, then think about adjusting the parameters in the Control Panel.

Q My Macintosh tells me that there is not enough memory to launch another application. What can I do?

A Try closing down other applications to free up memory. If you've already closed all the applications you don't absolutely need to use, you can enable Virtual Memory (use a third-party utility such as RAM Doubler) to increase the available RAM for applications. If that still doesn't buy you enough space, you may need to consider upgrading your physical RAM.

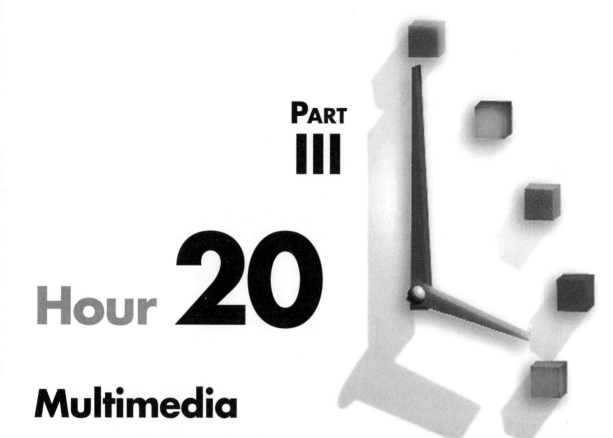

Hour 20

Multimedia

Multimedia is all the rage these days—sound, music, video. Everyone wants it. Lucky for you, multimedia is easy to learn and use on the Macintosh. No, don't think you're going to turn into Steven Spielberg by the end of this hour, but we will show you how to make your Macintosh talk, sing, and play movies.

Some advanced lessons in video editing and video effects software will be necessary before your work starts becoming all-talking, all-singing, all-dancing, as they used to say, but in this hour, we'll cover the basics.

The highlights of this hour include:

- [ ] How to use the microphone and add your own sounds
- [ ] How to play audio CDs in your Macintosh
- [ ] How to play video clips (and where to find some good ones)
- [ ] How to use a camera to add your own pictures

Audio Actions

Although the speaker built into your Macintosh is tiny, you can make a lot come out of it, including your own voice or your favorite CD. We'll show you how to do this and make the proper adjustments to your system. By the way, if you're a real audiophile, we recommend adding external speakers.

Monitors & Sound Control Panel

To get sounds out of your Macintosh, you'll have to configure the Monitors & Sound Control Panel.

To do this, perform the following steps:

1. In the menu bar, click on Apple Menu➡Control Panels➡Monitors & Sound (remember that we also used this same Control Panel in Hour 18, "Hardware," when we were looking at monitors).

2. Click on the Sound icon (see Figure 20.1).

Figure 20.1

The Sound Control Panel.

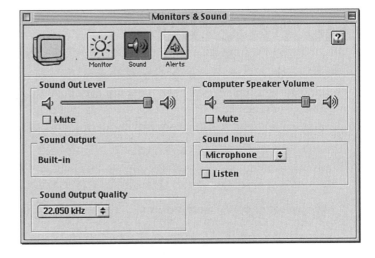

3. Adjust the sliders for your preferred volume level. The Sound Out Level option relates to the jack itself (you would use this if you were working with video applications), while the Computer Speaker Volume relates to the internal speaker.

4. In the Sound Input panel, click on the disclosure triangles. Your choices for input are Microphone, Internal CD, and AV Connector. For the moment, leave it set to Microphone and leave the box next to "Listen" unchecked. Unless you have attached external speakers, the Sound Output panel will only indicate the built-in speaker.

20

5. In the Sound Output Quality panel, you have two choices: 44.100 kHz (kilohertz) and 22.050 Khz. These relate to the frequency of sound waves. 44.100 is the standard for CDs, while 22.050 is the standard for other sound files. If you're going to be playing a lot of CDs, click on the option for 44.100.

Now, let's look at the Alerts Control Panel (see Figure 20.2). You can move the slider to adjust the volume of system alerts (those noises that indicate you've clicked on the mouse erroneously).

Figure 20.2

The Alerts Control Panel.

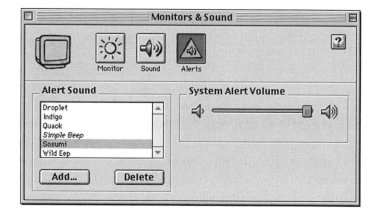

You can also add your own alerts, as long as you have a PlainTalk microphone. To do so, perform the following steps:

1. Plug the PlainTalk microphone into the jack in the back of your Macintosh labeled with a microphone icon. You can place the microphone anywhere you want, but it is built with a tiny lip so that it can rest on the top of your monitor.

2. In the Alerts Control Panel, click on "Add..." A dialog box that resembles the interface to a tape deck will appear.

3. Determine what you're going to say, and click on Record. When you're finished, click on Stop (see Figure 20.3).

Figure 20.3

Recording an alert.

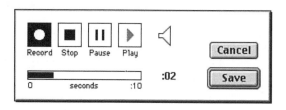

20

4. You'll be asked to give the sound a name (we called this one "Ouch!," so that whenever you click on something incorrectly, the Macintosh will respond accordingly). Do so, and click on OK. The named sound will be added to the list under Alert Sound (see Figure 20.4). Click the Close box.

Figure 20.4

Ouch! now appears in the Alert Sound list.

Speech Control Panel

You can also make your Macintosh talk, using the Speech Control Panel. You'll have many settings to choose from, depending on the voice you want. You can also add phrases of your own.

First, you'll need to familiarize yourself with the Speech Control Panel. To do this, perform the following steps:

1. In the menu bar, click on the Apple Menu➡Control Panels➡Speech (see Figure 20.5).

Figure 20.5

The Speech control panel.

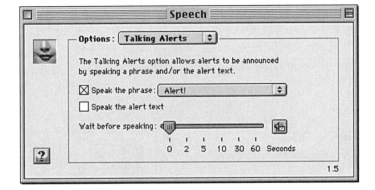

2. Click on the Options box and select Talking Alerts.

3. Select the box next to "Speak the phrase:" and click on the panel to reveal the phrase options. Select "Excuse me!"

20

4. Select the box next to "Speak the alert text" and then click on the speaker icon. The Macintosh will say, "Excuse me. This is a demonstration of your Talking Alerts settings."

5. To change the voice in which it speaks, go back to the Options box and click on the "Talking Alerts" panel. Choose the "Voice" option (see Figure 20.6).

Figure 20.6

You can change the voices in the Speech Control Panel.

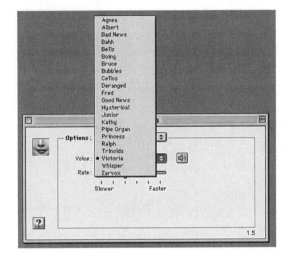

6. Click on the "Voice:" panel, and choose any of the voices listed in the menu. Then click on the speaker icon.

7. If you prefer to hear the voices speaking the alerts, return to the Talking Alerts option and click on the speaker icon. The phrase you've highlighted in this window will be spoken by the voice you've chosen in the previous window. Now, whenever an alert comes up on screen, it will be read aloud.

You can also create your own talking-alert phrases in the Speech Control Panel, just as you did in the Alerts Control Panel. To do this, perform the following steps:

1. Open the Speech Control Panel.

2. Click on the "Speak the phrase:" panel and select the last option, "Edit phrase list" (see Figure 20.7).

3. Click on the "Add" button. In the dialog box that appears, type a phrase. Click OK.

4. Click OK again to return to the Speech Control Panel. Open the "Speak the phrase:" panel. Your phrase will automatically be highlighted.

5. Click on the speaker icon to hear your phrase. Again, you can change the voice to hear how it will sound with other voices. When an alert comes on the screen, the computer will speak your phrase prior to what appears on the screen.

20

Figure 20.7

You can add phrases for the Macintosh to speak.

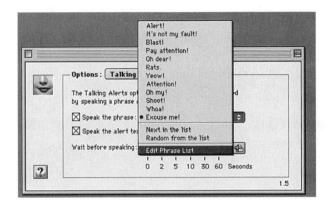

Playing Speech-to-Text

You can also set your Macintosh to read text from documents using SimpleText's Sound capability. For people who have poor eyesight, or those who are just learning English, this is a big help.

To create a document in SimpleText that your Macintosh will read to you, perform the following steps:

1. Open the SimpleText application.
2. Click on File➡New.
3. Type "Four score and seven years ago."
4. Select Sound➡Speak All (or press ⌘-J). The computer will speak the phrase.
5. If you want to change the voice, select Sound➡Voices. Change the voice and press ⌘-J again.

You can also record your own voice in a SimpleText document. It won't sound like your voice, of course, simply because while the Macintosh may be a great computer, it's not necessarily a great recording device. Besides, your voice never sounds the way you think it does.

To record your voice, perform the following steps:

1. Open a new SimpleText document.
2. Select Sound➡Record.
3. Click on the Record icon and say any phrase you like, up to 25 seconds long.
4. When you're done, click on the Stop icon.

20

5. Save the document. To hear it again, open the document and click on Sound➡Play.

You'll note that the dialog box that you've done your recording in is the same one that you used to record the "Ouch!" alert. That's just another example of how learning one facet of the Macintosh helps you learn another.

Setting Up a Shut-Down Sound

A friend of ours once set up his Macintosh to express his excitement at going home for the day. He created a sound file of Fred Flintstone yelling "Yabba-dabba-do!" and stored it in his Shutdown Items folder (which we previously discussed in Hour 6). Now we're going to show you how to do that yourself (although you're going to have to say "Yabba-dabba-do!" yourself, or we may get in trouble with Hanna-Barbera).

To place a sound file in your shutdown folder, perform the following steps:

1. First, as a safety precaution, close any applications that you have open.
2. Just as you've done previously, create a sound using the Speech Control Panel; let's call it "signoff." Close the Control Panel.
3. Double-click on your hard drive. Double-click on your System Folder.
4. Within the System Folder, there's a folder named "System." Double-click on System, and within it you'll see a sound file named "Signoff." Drag that file into the Shutdown Items folder (see Figure 20.9).

Now, whenever you turn off your computer, your signoff will play. If you really want to get fancy, you could record the "parting is such sweet sorrow" speech from Romeo and Juliet or find an old recording of Jimmy Durante saying, "Good night, Mrs. Calabash, wherever you are." (Uh-oh, my age is showing.)

Adjusting the Apple CD Audio Player

Did you know that you can play audio CDs in your Macintosh? Because digital CDs are based on the same principles as audio CDs, all you have to do is put your favorite in the CD tray and play it, just as you would in your stereo system.

To play a CD, perform the following steps:

1. Open the Monitors & Sound Control Panel as you did previously. Click on the Sound Input option and select Internal CD. Click the Close box.
2. Load your favorite audio CD into the CD-ROM drive. The traditional CD icon will appear on the desktop, but unlike a digital CD, it will not display its name (see Figure 20.8).

20

Figure 20.8

Unlike a digital CD, an audio CD icon will not reveal what it is.

3. Double-click on the CD icon to open a window of all its tracks (see Figure 20.9).

Figure 20.9

Each of the audio CD's tracks appear in a window.

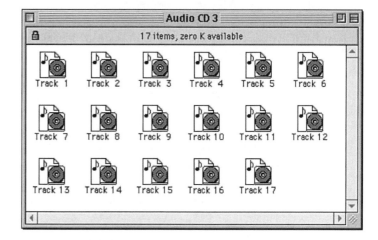

4. Click on Track 1 and the Apple CD Audio Player appears (see Figure 20.10). You can also open the Audio Player by selecting it in the Apple menu or by going into the Apple Extras folder on your hard drive.

Figure 20.10

The Apple CD Audio Player.

5. Notice that the interface resembles that of your stereo. Click on the "Play" button (the right-facing triangle), and the music begins.

20

JUST A MINUTE

The other buttons work the same way as your stereo (the top three correspond to stop, pause, and eject, while the bottom four correspond to reverse by track, advance by track, rewind, and advance).

The Apple CD Audio Player has many more options, however, and it's probably easier to program than your home stereo system.

To personalize your Audio CD, perform the following steps:

1. Click on the upper panel reading "Audio CD" and you'll see a list of numbered tracks. Now click on the downward triangle in the lower-left corner of the interface. This brings up a similar list of the tracks (see Figure 20.11).

Figure 20.11

The Track List for the Apple CD Audio Player.

2. Select the lower panel that reads Audio CD: type the name of the CD, and press either Return or Tab.

3. This advances you to Track 1. Reading from the CD's case, type in the name of Track 1, Track 2, and so on. We've done it with the Eagles' *Hell Freezes Over* CD (see Figure 20.12).

4. Now let's look at the four buttons on the left, starting with the one labeled "Normal." This is the default button. Click on the one next to it, labeled "Shuffle." Note that your Macintosh will automatically shuffle the order of the tracks.

20

Figure 20.12

The track list from the Eagles' Hell Freezes Over *CD.*

5. Click on the label marked "Prog," which stands for *program.* Now you can play any tracks from the CD that you want, choosing your favorites and ignoring the ones you don't like.

6. To do this, click on the tracks you like in the left column and drag them to the right column. In the right column, you can drag the tracks up or down to change the order.

7. Click on the disclosure triangle (now pointing upward) to hide the track list.

8. Click on the upper panel reading Hell Freezes Over, and now, where the track numbers were previously listed, all of the selected track titles appear (see Figure 20.13).

Figure 20.13

You can access the track list even when you've hidden the window.

TIME SAVER

You don't have to keep the Audio CD Player onscreen if you don't want to. Just click the Close box, and it will disappear (the CD will continue to play). To bring it back onscreen, click on the Apple Menu➡Apple CD Audio Player.

20

Video Ventures

Besides helping you play sounds, your Macintosh also lets you play video too. This capability works in two different ways, and we're going to show you both of them. First, we're going to show you how to play a movie on the Macintosh, and then, with the help of a peripheral device, we're going to show you how to capture your own picture.

Playing with QuickTime

Your Macintosh comes with a system extension called QuickTime. This system extension lets your Macintosh display video files and play audio files. If an application supports QuickTime, you can also use it to play or record movies (we'll discuss recording movies in the next section). An application that supports QuickTime and comes with your Macintosh is called MoviePlayer.

In order to see how MoviePlayer works, you'll need to download a movie first. To do this, perform the following steps:

1. In the menu bar, click on Apple Menu➡Connect To...

2. In the dialog box that appears, type this URL: `http://www2.apple.com/whymac/ads.html`. This takes you to a page listing some of Apple's most famous commercials.

3. Click on the hyperlink marked "1984 Commercial" to download this famous television advertisement. (Note: this is a 5.3 MB file, and it may take a long time to download if you have a slow (14.4 or slower) modem.)

4. To save the file, click on File➡Save as... and place 1984.mov in the directory of your choice. Open your hard drive and drag the commercial's icon into the folder marked Apple Extras➡Movie Player. Drop the icon on the MoviePlayer application.

5. The commercial will appear on your screen (see Figure 20.14). To play the movie, click the "play" icon. When it's done, store the commercial wherever you like for playing another time.

JUST A MINUTE

At first, a 5 MB movie file won't cause too much of a space problem if you have at least a gigabyte of capacity on your hard drive. But if you keep finding video clips that you like, and want to keep, you may develop a storage problem. Consider offloading video clips to an external drive.

20

Figure 20.14

Apple's famous 1984 commercial.

Using Cameras

To take still pictures or make videos, you'll need to use a peripheral called a digital camera. Whether it's a handheld digital camera like an Apple QuickTake or one that plugs into the back of your Macintosh like a Connectix QuickCam (415-571-5100; www.connectix.com) doesn't matter. To demonstrate this, we used the QuickCam (see Figure 20.15). It comes with QuickTime-enabled software that enables you to take still pictures (in its QuickPICT format) or movies (with its QuickMovie format).

Figure 20.15

The Connectix QuickCam camera.

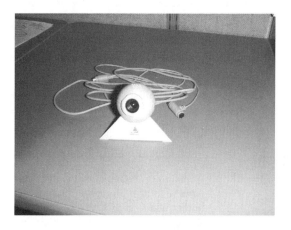

What can you do with the camera? You can snap pictures of yourself to post on your web page. Or you could record videos of you and your friends singing Happy Birthday, compress it, and send it to a friend of yours across the country. Howard used it to take a picture of his cat, Fluffy

20

(see Figure 20.16). Depending on the camera you buy and the software it has, the steps you take to capture pictures or video will differ.

Figure 20.16
Fluffy the cat.

Videophone and Videoconferencing

Other ways you can use a camera like the QuickCam is with Internet videophone or videoconferencing applications. You can download a demo version of Vocaltec's Internet video applications from its web site (www.vocaltec.com), and make calls to other people who have the same application (and have it running on their machine when you call). With your QuickCam turned on, they'll be able to see your face (but you won't see theirs unless they have a camera as well). Videoconferencing applications, such as CU-SeeMe from White Pine Software and Meet-Me from Sat-Sagem, work the same way.

To use these applications, you'll need to know your TCP/IP address. To get the address, refer back to Hour 12.

Summary

The Macintosh makes many multimedia applications relating to audio and video easy. As we've shown, you can also use the Apple CD Audio Player to play your favorite musical CDs while you work.

We've only scratched the surface of what your Macintosh can do with audio and video effects, however. As long as you have enough hard drive capacity and the appropriate third-party software, you can create amazing films with sound and special effects on your Macintosh. To learn more about these kinds of applications, visit the web sites of companies that specialize in video software for Macintosh—Adobe (www.adobe.com), Macromedia (www.macromedia.com), and MetaCreations (www.metacreations.com).

20

Term Review

Camera   A device that plugs into the back of your Macintosh that enables you to take or broadcast pictures, depending on the application.

PlainTalk   A microphone that plugs into a special socket in the back of your Macintosh that enables you to record your own voice and sounds.

QuickTime   A technology that, when built into applications, enables you to play movies on your Macintosh.

Q&A

Q **I put my audio CD in the tray, but I can't hear the music. The volume sliders are set at maximum. What's wrong?**

A Make sure that in the Sound area of the Monitors & Sound Control Panel, your Sound Input is set on "Internal CD." If you've been using your PlainTalk microphone to record something, you'll have to reset this.

Q **Can I take movies with a video camera and download them into my Macintosh?**

A Yes. There are now handheld cameras that record digital movies. You can download the images you shoot in the same way that you download images from a digital camera that takes snapshots.

Q **Once I get digital pictures into my Macintosh, how can I crop them or make them sharper?**

A You'll need a photo-editing application, such as Adobe Photoshop. A limited version of Photoshop or another application may come with your digital camera. You can use this to improve the pictures you take.

20

Hour 21

Security and Safety

We're fairly confident that the last time you bought a car, it wasn't the safety belts that fascinated you most. Similarly, the security and safety features of a Macintosh probably weren't high on your list of what to buy in a computer. That's understandable, but it's also important to remember that you probably spent as much on your Macintosh as you have on an appliance or a sofa. However, no one is going to break into your house and cart away your refrigerator. Your Macintosh, maybe.

In this hour, we're going to show you some common-sense ways to both avoid that scenario and to protect yourself should something go wrong. We'll show you not just how to protect your Macintosh from burglars and natural disasters, but from your child accidentally deleting the presentation you're creating for your biggest client, or from crashing. We'll also show you how you can take simple precautions to ensure people don't go peeking into files you don't want them to.

The highlights of this hour include:

- ☐ How to avoid losing your data
- ☐ What to do before a natural disaster strikes
- ☐ When to back up your data and where to store it
- ☐ What to buy to protect both your Macintosh and your data

Physical Security

Wondering what physical and digital security are? Simple—physical security relates to the safety of real objects, like your computer, your floppy disks, and your Zip cartridges. Digital security, which we'll discuss below, relates to the safety of your data while it's still in your Macintosh.

Backing Up Your Files

It's easy to laugh and compare file-backup to flossing and life insurance. But when the day comes that your hard drive malfunctions, or your PowerBook disappears, you'll be darn glad you did it. There are several ways to back up your files. You can simply slip a floppy disk into your floppy drive and copy an important file or two on to it (for larger files, consider using larger removable storage devices from Iomega, Syquest, or any number of magneto-optical vendors).

A more comprehensive method is to use backup software. The backup software that runs on more Macintoshes than any other is Retrospect (see Figure 21.1) from Dantz Software (510-253-3000; www.dantz.com). We recommend this $249 application for business situations, because you can configure the software to copy your entire hard drive one day, and then only copy the files that have changed for the rest of the week. This way, you're not recopying every file, but you have updated versions of everything you've worked on. Retrospect will also work if you have multiple computers, including PowerBooks.

Figure 21.1

You can configure Dantz Software's Retrospect backup software to do incremental backups.

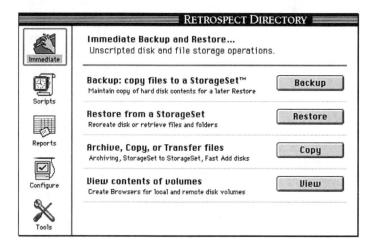

TIME SAVER

21

Check the Preferences file of your applications. There's likely to be an option that, when checked, will create an automatic backup file of the document. This won't help you if your hard drive crashes, but it will if you accidentally delete a large portion of the document. Open the backup file and retrieve the data you deleted.

There may also be an option for a feature called "fast-saves." Consider selecting this option as well, especially if you're using a PowerBook. It will save the file at regular intervals (but will not create a backup file). If your battery runs low or your computer crashes, you will only have lost the work you've done since the last fast save (depending on your work style, every five or ten minutes is a good interval).

Storing Backup Files

Consider this scenario: you keep important documents—word processing files, spreadsheets—on your Macintosh. You've set up your applications to automatically create backups whenever you save a document; if you accidentally delete something you shouldn't, you're protected. Then your hard drive crashes and needs to be reformatted before it will work again. Now what?

Removable Media

Obviously, this is where backup files on removable media come in handy. Your backup media should be kept in a locked cabinet (to prevent anyone from walking away with it), clearly labeled, and easily accessible. That way, you can restore the files quickly and easily.

TIME SAVER

If you are your own boss, you have to think like the people in a big company who are responsible for maintaining the computer system. One trick these folks have: create a copy of Mac OS 8 and put it on a portable drive (whether it's an external hard drive or a Zip drive doesn't matter). You can plug it into the back of a malfunctioning Macintosh and boot it up again.

Offsite Storage

Now consider this scenario: you diligently back up your Macintosh's files every Friday. You take the removable media and place it in a locked cabinet as we've recommended. You go home and on Saturday morning your office building burns to the ground. Then what?

This is the time to consider what's known as offsite storage. Depending on how frequently you work on your most important files, consider making a second full backup of your files and keeping it somewhere far away from your computer. If you work in an office, take a copy home. If you work at home, ask your spouse to take it to work. You can even send a copy to siblings by electronic mail and ask them to keep it safe.

21

You may never need an offsite copy of your files, but you also never know when it'll come in handy.

TIME SAVER

Several companies specialize in retrieving data from hard drives that have malfunctioned, been dropped in rivers, run over, or otherwise mistreated. You send them the malfunctioning hard drive, and they'll resurrect whatever they can from it. Contact DriveSavers (800-440-1904), Lazarus Data Recovery (800-341-3282), Ontrack Data Recovery (800-872-2599), or Total Recall (800-734-0594).

Protecting Your Mac from Theft

We're sure you're excited about your new computer, but it's important that in your excitement, you don't let your guard down. Here are three important tips about making sure it's safe from theft.

1. Never put your Macintosh where it can be easily seen from outside. That's an invitation for a burglar. It also signifies that if you can afford a computer, you can probably afford other neat stuff.

2. Always write down the serial number of your computer or any other peripheral. You'll find the serial number on the back of your Macintosh, probably near a bar code. This is a unique number, which the police will use to trace your computer if it's stolen. A company called the American Computer Exchange, which sells used computers, now maintains a stolen computer database on its web site (www.amcoex.com). If your computer is stolen, input its serial number into the database. If it's recovered, the local law enforcement agency can access the database to find you.

3. Consider locking devices.

   This is especially important if you have a PowerBook. On the side of your PowerBook is a vertical notch. Several companies, including Kensington (800-535-4242; www.kensington.com) build cables with locks that attach to this notch. You can use epoxy to attach a similar device to your desktop machine or other peripheral so they can be essentially chained to your work surface.

JUST A MINUTE

It's also a good idea to have your computer covered by your homeowner's insurance policy. Talk to your insurance agent about a special item called a "rider" that sets aside money specifically for your computer in case of theft or damage.

21

Protecting Your Mac from Disaster

We live in California, where the price we pay for spectacular beauty and weather is the chance that at any given moment, the ground beneath us may start to shake. If you live in the South, you face hurricanes and electrical storms. Almost every part of the country has some sort of built-in reminder of Mother Nature's superiority.

Here are some tips for protecting your Macintosh from a natural disaster:

1. Restraining straps.

   Even though *Macworld*'s San Francisco office is built on bedrock, one of the safest places to be in an earthquake, we've invested in adjustable straps that are attached to our work surfaces. In a strong earthquake, these will keep the computers from toppling off the desktops.

2. Uninterruptible power systems (UPS).

   This is a fancy name for what we call a battery-in-a-box. It plugs into the electrical socket and you plug the Macintosh into it. If there's a blackout—or even a brown-out—a UPS will provide power to your computer. It won't let you go forever, but it will give you enough time to close your files and shut down your computer. If where you live is susceptible to lightning and electrical storms, such as the South and Southwest, most UPSs can also protect you from power surges.

3. Surge protectors.

   You can pick these up for about $10 in a computer store. Essentially a row of sockets in which to plug your computer devices, a surge protector is designed to protect your equipment in the case of an electrical surge.

Digital Security

We've already talked a little about protecting your data from prying eyes in Hour 12. Now we're going to elaborate on that, along with some tips for keeping accidents from happening.

Folder Locking

For instance, say that you always want to access the same folder from across the network. You don't want this folder to be renamed or moved from where it's supposed to be on your computer. For that, there's a locking mechanism.

To lock a folder, perform the following steps:

1. On your hard drive, highlight the folder.

2. In the menu bar, click on File➥Sharing.

3. Click on the first box, labeled "Can't move, rename, or delete this item" (see Figure 21.2).

21

Figure 21.2

Click on the first box to lock the folder.

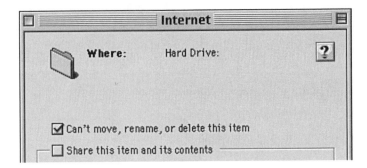

4. Now the folder will always stay in place, and it'll be apparent because a lock will appear next to it in the Finder (see Figure 21.3). (The folder can be accessed, but nothing else.) This lock, however, will only appear if you're in List View, not if you're viewing icons or buttons.

Figure 21.3

In List View, a lock indicates an unmovable folder.

File Locking

You can lock folders to keep prying eyes out, but frequently you can also lock files to do the same, depending on the application. Check the applications you use the most to see how they handle this feature.

To protect a file in Microsoft Excel for Mac, perform the following steps:

1. Open a new sheet by selecting File➡New.
2. In the Command menu, select Tools➡Protection. Choose whether you want to protect the worksheet or the entire workbook.
3. Click on any of the three choices and then create a password (see Figure 21.4).
4. Remember the password rules from Hour 12 and pick something that won't easily be guessed. Now, whenever you open the file, you must type in the password.

Password security is especially important if you have documents on a shared file server, or if your computer is used by a number of people. The danger may not be that someone might maliciously change your document. It's also easy to open a file by mistake and accidentally make changes.

21

Figure 21.4

*Protecting a document in
Microsoft Excel.*

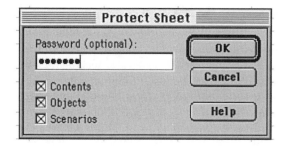

Utilities

While we're focusing this book on the Mac OS 8 operating system, it's important to note another class of products called *utilities*. They work closely with Mac OS 8 in order to add features and make you more efficient and better protected. We always say that utilities are like angels: they should be invisible but omnipresent. Here are some suggestions for utilities that will enhance Mac OS 8 when it comes to safety and security.

Disk Drive Utilities

Norton Utilities for Macintosh, from Symantec (541-984-2490, www.symantec.com), consolidates six important features (see Figure 21.5). It can be a big help when you need to deal with a disk that's damaged or crashed, as well as when an application crashes. You can determine whether your system is performing at optimum speed, and tune it if necessary. Best of all, Norton Utilities can even resurrect files that you've accidentally deleted—even after you've executed the Empty Trash command.

Figure 21.5

*Symantec's Norton
Utilities for Macintosh.*

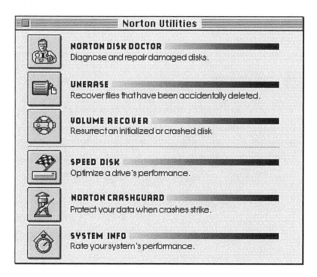

Security Software

It may sound like some utilities do the same thing as Mac OS 8, but frequently they do it better, with more options. Several disk-protection utilities are available, which give you more extensive choices when it comes to locking files, folders, applications, and your hard drive. Some of these products also enable you to restrict the times your computer can actually be used (this is a real benefit if you're afraid your kids are waking up in the middle of the night to play computer games or surf the Internet).

In this category, consider contacting the following companies: ASD Software (909-624-2594) for DiskGuard and FileGuard; Claris (408-987-7000) for At Ease; Smartstuff Software (503-231-4300) for FoolProof; Power On Software (216-735-3116) for On Guard; and usrEZ Software (714-756-5140) for ultraSecure.

Anti-Virus Software

If nothing else, you've heard of viruses. They're nasty little applications that latch onto legitimate files and snake into your system, corrupting and destroying your work so that it's unreadable and unusable. If this happens, you'll have to go back to your backup files (this is another reason that they're important).

There are anti-social programmers around the world who actually take pleasure in creating viruses, and you can actually find instructions for writing viruses on the World Wide Web.

You never know how you're going to get one—from a neighbor's disk, or downloading from a bulletin board that hasn't scanned its files—but it's important to be careful.

Consider VirusScan from McAfee Associates (408-988-3832) or AntiVirus for Macintosh from Symantec (541-984-2490). These utilities will scan new files as they arrive on your computer, either by disk or from the Internet, to intercept any viruses before they can infect your system.

Summary

We really don't want to unduly alarm you about the possibilities of disaster, either natural or man-made. Howard has used computers for ten years, owning four and using many more in a variety of workplaces. Not once has he ever experienced a hard disk crash. On the other hand, *Macworld's* lab director recently experienced one on a Macintosh that was only a few months old. You just never know, and it never hurts to be prepared.

The same thing goes for viruses. If you were to go out looking for them, you could probably find them (believe it or not, there are electronic bulletin boards where virus-writers post their handiwork for friends), but with some precaution, you can avoid them. Forewarned is forearmed.

Term Review

File Locking   A method found within many applications that requires a password to open a file.

Folder Locking   A method within Mac OS 8 that stops anyone from moving, renaming, or deleting a folder.

Offsite Backup   A copy of your files kept away from your primary place of business in order to protect yourself against catastrophe.

UPS   An uninterruptible power system, basically a battery for your computer in case of blackout or brownout.

Utilities   A category of software that includes security and anti-virus applications.

Virus   A computer application written specifically to corrupt or destroy data.

Q&A

Q All this makes me feel paranoid—was that your intent?

A Yes. An ounce of paranoia is worth a pound of cure. You may never lose your data, but if you do, and you can re-create what you need quickly, you'll be a hero.

Q My part of the country is not affected by any of the potential disasters you mentioned. Am I safe?

A Granted, if you eliminate earthquakes, floods, lightning, hurricanes, volcanoes, tornadoes, and blackouts, you're probably safe in certain parts of Montana (unless snow is a problem). However, given that a broken water main can flood your home, it's probably a good idea to be prepared.

Q Should I really worry about viruses?

A If you never share disks and never download files from the Internet or the World Wide Web, no. But do your kids swap games with their friends? Do you borrow disks from clients or coworkers? Then you're susceptible. Viruses are like bad drivers. You know they're out there. You could go through your whole life without encountering one, but when you do meet one, the damage can be worse than you ever expected.

21

Hour 22

Compatibility with DOS and Windows

Let's face it—there are times when you are going to want to get information from friends or colleagues who are running Microsoft Windows applications on PCs. There may even be times when you want to run Windows applications yourself. We understand (we've been known to use a PC ourselves on occasion).

Fortunately, Apple makes it easy for you to work with files and applications that normally run on the PC. In addition, a number of third-party vendors also build products that help you as well.

☐ Software utilities enable you to *transfer* files back and forth between similar applications (for instance, between Microsoft's Word for Mac and Word for Windows).

☐ Conversion software enables you to *convert* files written in a word processing application on one platform into files for another word processing application on another platform.

☐ Emulation software enables you to run Windows applications on your Macintosh through a process whereby software impersonates hardware, or *emulates* it, in this case the hardware being the Intel CPU. You can buy internal cards equipped with a Pentium CPU that enable you to run Windows using that processor.

We've tested all of these, and will recommend the ones we feel perform the best.

The highlights of this hour include:

- ☐ How to use PC floppy disks in your Macintosh
- ☐ How to use Macintosh floppy disks in a PC
- ☐ How to convert Macintosh documents for use on a PC
- ☐ What you need to share external storage media between a Macintosh and a PC
- ☐ What you can install on your Macintosh to run Windows

Moving Files Back and Forth

When we said we've been known to use PCs on occasion, we were fibbing. Howard uses a PC laptop all the time, because he has some applications from his days of writing for a PC magazine that aren't available on the Macintosh. So he's constantly putting floppy disks in his PC's floppy drive, copying files onto them, and moving them to his Macintosh (he has the same word processing and spreadsheet applications on both machines). If you have the right tools, it's easy.

Using PC Exchange

When you go to the store to get floppies, you'll probably notice that most, if not all, of them say they're "preformatted for IBM PCs" (we talked about this back in Hour 4). When you insert one of these floppy disks into your floppy drive, its icon is emblazoned with a large DOS (see Figure 22.1).

Figure 22.1

Most floppies are preformatted for PCs.

If you want, you can reformat it for your Macintosh (refer back to Hour 4 to refresh your memory on how to do this), or you can just use it the way it is, thanks to a Control Panel in Mac OS 8 called PC Exchange (see Figure 22.2). It lets you insert floppy disks from PCs into your Macintosh.

Every DOS or Windows application has a suffix—for Microsoft Word, it's ".doc" and for Microsoft Excel it's ".xls." It relates to the application that created the file. Even Windows

22

95 files, which can have long filenames, have DOS suffixes when they appear on Macintosh computers. Using the PC Exchange Control Panel, you can make sure that PC files are opened by the Macintosh application you prefer.

Figure 22.2

The PC Exchange Control Panel.

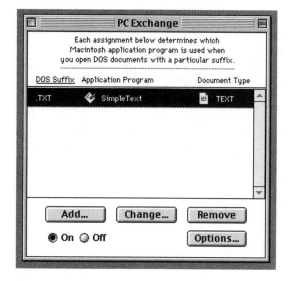

To use PC Exchange, perform the following steps:

1. In the menu bar, click on the Apple Menu➡Control Panels➡PC Exchange.
2. Click on the "Add..." button.
3. In the DOS suffix box, type in .doc.
4. Under the Hard Drive button, scroll down to the folder where your word processing application is installed. Highlight it.
5. Now type in the corresponding document type for the Macintosh. Click OK.

Now, whenever you get a file on a floppy that has the ".doc" suffix, your word processing application will open it.

JUST A MINUTE

If you click on the DOS suffix box, you'll see a range of choices. These are called "file types" and they indicate the range of files that an application can open. These may include earlier versions of applications (that is Excel 4.0) or other similar applications (that is, another spreadsheet). Stick with the default, as you'll only need the other file types in very specialized situations.

Using Rich Text Format

Word processing is a common enough application that we wanted to show you a simple way to transfer files back and forth.

In most word processing applications, there's a format called Rich Text Format (RTF). If you save a document in this file format on your PC prior to moving it to the Macintosh, it will preserve most of the formatting you have already done (such as making text bold or italic). If you don't save a document in RTF, you'll end up with a lot of gibberish characters before and after the part of your file you really want to save.

To save a file in RTF format, perform the following steps:

1. In your word processing application, save a file in RTF. Each word processing application differs, but in this example, we use Microsoft Word (see Figure 22.3).

Figure 22.3

Saving an RTF file in Microsoft Word.

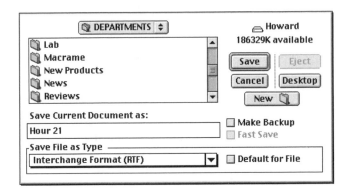

2. After the file is saved on the floppy disk, transfer the floppy disk to your Macintosh's floppy drive.

3. Double-click on the floppy disk icon, and double-click on the file. A dialog box will appear explaining that the Macintosh is translating it and the document will automatically appear in an untitled file.

4. The file will open with the original formatting. Rename the new file as you wish.

Understanding File Formats

Every application has a file format (also known as file type or creator code on the Macintosh). If one company makes both applications, the file format and creator code will be the same (for instance, the format for Microsoft's Excel spreadsheet is ".xls" no matter which platform it's on). You'll need to know an application's file format if you want to transfer files from one company's application to another company's application.

To determine an application's creator code, perform the following steps:

1. In the menu bar, click on File➡Find....

22

2. Double-click on "More Choices."

3. In the option box marked "kind," click on the arrows and select the "file type" option.

4. Return to the desktop. Strangely enough, the Find File dialog box is now grayed out, but it will still perform the action you want. Drag the icon of the file you're interested in onto the panel at the right. Its type will appear in the box.

If you do the above action with a screen capture made with SimpleText, for instance, it will show that its file type is .pict. If you do it with a text document made with SimpleText, it will show the file type as .text.

Exchanging Files Between Macs and PCs

Bundled with Mac OS 8 is a tool for document conversion called MacLinkPlus, developed by DataViz (800-733-0030; www.dataviz.com). It works with a multitude of text, spreadsheet, graphics, and database formats to let you convert documents from one file format to another (see Figure 22.4).

Figure 22.4

MacLinkPlus enables you to convert a wide variety of file formats.

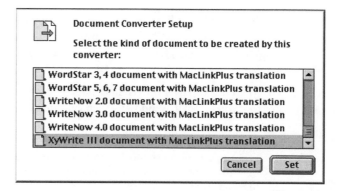

This conversion process is more complicated, and it's something you'd probably use more as a one-way, one-time mechanism for each file. For instance, consider the scenario where a coworker gives you a screen capture that was created in Paintbrush on a PC. You can use MacLinkPlus to open it on your Macintosh and translate it into the Macintosh's .pict format. To do this, perform the following steps:

1. Create a screen capture on a PC using Windows' Paintbrush by bringing up a window and hitting the Print Screen command.

2. Open the Windows Paintbrush application and press Ctrl-V to paste the screen capture.

3. Click on File➡Save As... and save the file to a floppy disk, naming it "PCFile.bmp" (.bmp is the suffix for a bitmap file).

4. Insert the floppy into your Macintosh and drag the icon for the file to your desktop (see Figure 22.5). This will speed up the translation process.

Figure 22.5

Your Paintbrush file looks like this on your Macintosh desktop.

5. Warning: Do not double-click on the file icon. This will only give you gibberish characters. Instead, go to the folder on your hard drive called MacLinkPlus➡ Document Converter. Click on it.

6. Go to File➡Duplicate (or type ⌘-D). Drag the Document Converter copy to the desktop.

7. Double-click on the Document Converter copy icon and find the file named "Windows Bitmap BMP graphic with MacLinkPlus translation" (yes, it's really that long). Click on Set. The Document Converter will be renamed the equally long-winded "to Windows Bitmap BMP graphic."

8. Drag PCFile.bmp over the renamed Document Converter and it will open. Presto—you've got a Windows screen capture on your Macintosh (see Figure 22.6).

TIME SAVER

You can also use MacLinkPlus to convert documents created in a Macintosh application that you don't have to documents that can be read by a Macintosh application that you do have.

Figure 22.6

Using Document Converter, you can have a Windows screen capture on your Macintosh.

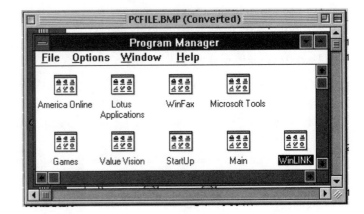

22

JUST A MINUTE

For PC users, DataViz's counterpart to MacLinkPlus is called Conversions Plus, which as its name implies, converts documents for the PC into documents for the Macintosh.

Investing in Other Hardware and Software

If you're one of those people who uses both a Macintosh and a PC, you're not alone. Apple estimates that almost 40 percent of Macintosh users also use a PC on a regular basis. Given this healthy statistic, there are several developers who have come up with ways to make sure the two computer platforms can coexist.

DOS Mounting Utilities

PC Exchange only works with floppy disks. If you want to use other storage media from a PC—such as Zip cartridges—with your Macintosh, you'll need another file-transfer utility such as DOS Mounter 95 from Software Architects (206-487-0122; www.softarch.com). It enables you to read PC-based media from other removable storage devices on your Macintosh.

DOS Mounter also lets you open documents with a wider variety of file formats than PC Exchange, as you can see from its Control Panel (Figure 22.7).

Figure 22.7
Software Architects' DOS Mounter Control Panel.

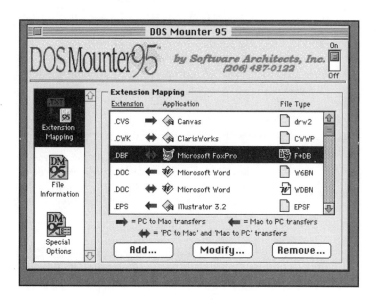

Windows 95 File-Transfer Utilities

If you want to take your Macintosh files and use them on a PC running Windows 95, you'll need a third-party file transfer utility. We prefer either Software Architects' Here & Now (see Figure 22.8) or DataViz's MacOpener. Be aware that these applications only handle *file-transfer*, not file conversion. In other words, if you're running Microsoft Word for Mac on your Macintosh, you'll need to have Microsoft Word for Windows running on your PC.

Figure 22.8

Software Architects' Here & Now extension mapping editor.

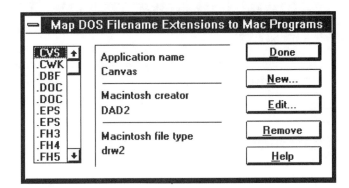

Watch out for long filenames. As you may know, DOS was limited to 11 characters in its filenames, eight on the left side of the period (or dot) and three on the right side of the period. One of the Macintosh advantages has been longer filenames—up to 31 characters. Windows 95 allows up to 225 characters in a filename. So if you take a Macintosh file and move it to Windows 95, you'll see the whole name. But if you take a Windows 95 file with a name longer than 31 characters and move the file to the Macintosh, you'll experience an effect known as truncation—the name will be shortened.

Some of these products also work with Windows 3.1, but because Windows 95 allows longer filenames than both Windows 3.1 and Macintosh, you'll frequently encounter some obstacles with truncated names (just as you do when you go back from Windows 95 to the Macintosh).

JUST A MINUTE

Filename truncation is only a problem if you begin a lot of file names with the same characters, such as "Macworld Reviews for [month]." If you're going to be doing a lot of exchanging, it's better to create filenames whose differentiation will be clear even if they get truncated.

If you're going to be exchanging files frequently between a Macintosh and a PC, it's important to have full-featured file-transfer or file-conversion utilities on both platforms.

22

CAUTION

Transferring files between the Macintosh and the PC isn't foolproof, even with the best file-transfer utilities or conversion methods. Always be sure to proofread documents that you've transferred.

Other Third-Party Products

Other products help you run Windows on your Macintosh or let you network your Macintosh to your PC in what's known as a peer-to-peer network (we'll discuss advanced networking in Hour 23). These cross-platform products come in three varieties: software, hardware, and a combination of both. We'll discuss each in sequence.

CAUTION

Third-party products may require you to add more RAM or install a PCI card in your Macintosh. Seriously consider how much you really need to run Windows applications before you invest in these products. Be sure to calculate the price of not only the product, but also of installation if you choose to have someone do it for you. Depending on your needs, it may actually be cheaper or more convenient to simply buy a used PC.

Software Solutions

Occasionally you might need to run a Windows application. You might not want to do it often enough to actually buy a PC, but you need it nonetheless. (Howard came to *Macworld* with a DOS-based personal information manager with 2,500 contact names in it; that's a perfect scenario for running emulation software.)

Two examples of emulation software are SoftWindows 95 from Insignia Solutions (408-327-6000; www.insignia.com) and Virtual PC from Connectix (415-571-5100; www.connectix.com). When you run these products, they use software to *emulate* Microsoft Windows (see Figure 22.9). That means it looks and feels like Windows, running just as Windows runs on a PC. However, the emulation process is tough on a CPU, so it won't run as fast as you would expect it to on a PC. Why? Because the CPU is not only doing what you're telling it to, but it's also working hard running Windows as well. Because Macintosh doesn't use the same CPUs that PCs do, you're essentially asking the Macintosh CPU to complete tasks it wasn't initially designed to carry out. It works harder, and thus, slower. These products also take a lot of RAM, so you'll have to add more (at least 24 MB just for the emulation software) before you can use them properly.

If your Macintosh is on a network, and you'd like to access a server running Windows NT, consider Dave (that's really the product's name) from Thursby Software Systems (817-478-5070; www.thursby.com). With this software loaded on your Macintosh and on the server, you can access files on the latter through the Chooser, the same as you would if you were accessing a Macintosh server.

Figure 22.9

*Insignia Solutions'
SoftWindows looks like
Microsoft Windows, but
it runs on a Macintosh.*

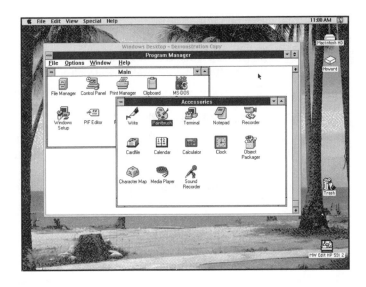

Hardware Solutions

Apple Computer (800-538-9696; www.apple.com), Orange Micro (714-779-2772; www.orangemicro.com), and Radius (800-227-2795; www.radius.com) offer Pentium CPUs affixed to internal PCI cards (see Figure 22.10). Once installed in your Macintosh, they let you run Windows on the same CPU that PCs use. Although they're costly (more than $2,000), these cards are especially valuable if you're short on workspace.

Figure 22.10

*These PCI cards have
Pentium CPUs so you
can run Windows on
your Macintosh.*

The alternative is buying an actual PC to run Windows—a tempting one given the card's cost—but if you did, you would also have to pay for associated peripherals, such as printers.

After you've installed one of these PC Compatibility cards (or purchased a Macintosh with one already built-in), you'll need to set it up. To do this, perform the following steps:

1. In the menu bar, select the Apple Menu➡Control Panels➡PC Setup.

2. In the dialog box that comes up, configure each mapping option according to your available hardware (see Figure 22.11).

22

Figure 22.11

*If you install a PC
Compatibility card in
your Macintosh, you'll
use this Control Panel to
configure it.*

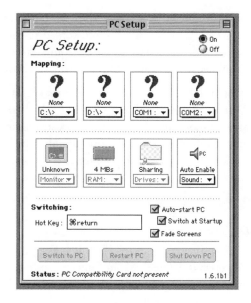

3. Select a hotkey to enable switching between the Macintosh and the PC (or use the default).

4. After you've configured the PC Compatibility card, click on the Close box.

Now you're ready to load and run Windows and its applications.

Hardware/Software Solutions

Timbuktu from Farallon Communications (510-814-5000; www.farallon.com) is a combination hardware/software product that uses Ethernet to link your PC and your Macintosh into what's known as a peer-to-peer network—that is, one that does not require a server as a central repository of files (you'll probably need to add an Ethernet card to the PC, while it's already built into the Macintosh).

From the PC, you can access files, printers, and peripherals on the Macintosh, and vice versa. By networking the two machines together, you can share peripherals just as you would on any network. Although it's relatively inexpensive, at just $139 per user, Timbuktu is not necessarily a breeze to install and configure.

Summary

Just because you've chosen a computer that's not on the majority of desktops doesn't mean you've exiled yourself to some technological Siberia. As you can see, there are many tools available for helping you use PC files on your Macintosh and vice versa.

Speaking for those who use both kinds of computers every single day, we can confidently say that it's fairly easy to become accustomed to the command differences between the two platforms. Only once have we tried to quit a frozen application on the PC by pressing Ctrl, Alt, Shift, and Esc at the same time (which is how you do it on the Macintosh).

We would only caution you to take extra special care when translating files between like applications, as file-transfer applications, while useful, are not 100 percent foolproof. When it comes to more complicated solutions, such as those from Thursby Software Systems and Farallon Communications, be sure to enlist the help of someone who's knowledgeable in networking to help you set these up.

Term Review

DOS suffix   Every DOS file has a three-character designation after its filename, which identifies the application that created it.

File format   The three- or four-character extension that appears after a file to indicate its origin (such as .doc or .html).

MacLinkPlus   A third-party application bundled with Mac OS 8 that enables you to convert documents from PCs (or from Macintosh applications that you don't have).

PC Compatibility Cards   Internal PCI cards from Apple and other vendors equipped with a Pentium CPU that enables you to run Windows on your Macintosh.

PC Exchange   A control panel built into every Macintosh that enables the floppy drive to read floppy disks from PCs.

Q&A

Q I'm not sure I understand the difference between file-transfer and file-conversion utilities.

A Think of it as the difference between a one-way street and a two-way street. Use file-transfer utilities to swap files back and forth in both directions. Use file-conversion utilities when a file originates on a PC and ends up on a Macintosh.

Q If I buy a PC Compatibility card, will it use my Macintosh software?

A No. You'll have to buy PC-compatible software to use with it. As a result, you're most likely to use the card with PC software that's not available on the Macintosh. There's no reason to buy two versions of Microsoft Word or Excel.

Q What's the hardest thing about cross-platform computing?

A Discovering the application that you love on one platform doesn't exist on the other platform.

22

Hour 23

Advanced Networking

In this hour, we'll go beyond the basics of networking as covered in Hour 12. You'll learn how to use file servers, including working with file restrictions and passwords, and discover some quick ways to make your life on the network easier. We'll also briefly discuss Personal Web Sharing (and point you in the right direction for more details) and teach you how to set up Apple Remote Access to move files over an ordinary phone line.

Please note, this hour assumes that your Macintosh is already set up for networking, and that you know how to use the Chooser to access shared files; we won't go back over the basics covered in Hour 12 and Hour 14.

The highlights of this hour include:

- [ ] How to access files on servers
- [ ] What to do when you encounter file access restrictions
- [ ] How to change your server password
- [ ] How to automate your server activities
- [ ] Where to find more information on Personal Web Sharing
- [ ] How to use Apple Remote Access (ARA) to log-on to your network over a phone line

Accessing Files on Servers

Back in Hour 14, we taught you how to set up your Macintosh for File Sharing. When you enabled others to view and use files off of your Macintosh, you were using your system as a *server*, a computer set up to share files over a network. When you retrieved files from other computers, you were a *client* connected to a File Sharing server.

Any Macintosh can share up to ten folders or drives using Mac OS 8's built-in File Sharing. Dedicated file servers, though, that need to serve more than File Sharing's limit, must use Apple's AppleShare server software. Unless you need to set up a dedicated server, you don't need to know anything about AppleShare; the process for accessing server volumes is identical to the one you use for accessing shared folders and servers on shared Macintosh systems. (If you *do* need to set up a dedicated server, you can get more information on AppleShare at `http://www.servers.apple.com`.)

Network file servers—just like other computers—can have more than one hard drive. Each accessible drive on a networked server is known as a *volume*. (Networking gurus may tell you we're oversimplifying a bit, but if you're expert enough to know better, you don't need this tutorial.)

Just as with personal File Sharing, you use the Chooser to access servers. To do so, perform the following steps:

1. Select the Chooser from the Apple menu.

2. Click on the AppleShare icon. A list of networked computers and servers will appear in the box on the right.

3. Select the appropriate Zone, if necessary (your network administrator can fill in the gaps here, if you're unsure).

4. Select the server you want to access from the scrolling list by highlighting its name and clicking on the OK button (you may also double-click on the server's name in the list, if you prefer). A dialog box will appear.

JUST A MINUTE

> If your preferred server is set up to share files via the World Wide Web, and you're either directly connected to the Internet or currently using a dial-up connection, you can press the Server IP Address... button and type the address in the text entry box provided (see Figure 23.1).

5. If the server allows Guest access—access by people not previously designated as users in the Users & Groups Control Panel—you can click on the radio button and proceed to log on to the server. Your access may be limited, however. If the server does not allow Guest access, the Guest radio button will be dimmed; you'll need to

23

log on as a Registered User. Enter your predefined user name and password in the text entry fields to access the server (see Figure 23.2).

Figure 23.1

Clicking on the Server IP Address button in the Chooser enables you to manually connect to a server set up to share files over the Internet.

Figure 23.2

Some file servers (top) enable you to log on as a Guest; others (bottom) require a user name and password.

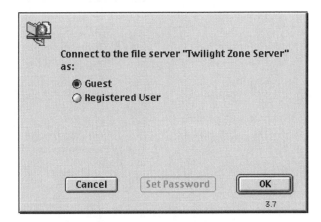

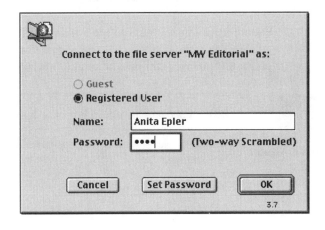

6. After you log on either as a Guest or a Registered User—a second dialog box appears showing the available shared volumes (see Figure 23.3).

Figure 23.3

The first server has two shared volumes available; the second has three total volumes, but two are restricted.

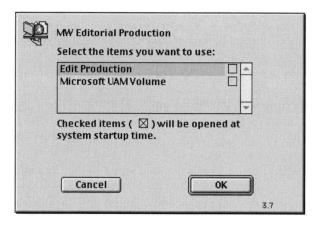

7. Select the volume you want to use by selecting its name and clicking on the OK button. You may double-click on the volume's name in the list instead, if you prefer, and you can shift-click to mount multiple volumes simultaneously.

JUST A MINUTE

> At the bottom of the dialog box, you'll see a message that reads: Checked items will be opened at system startup time. By clicking the check box beside a volume's name, you can automatically mount that drive (or server volume) each time you reboot your Macintosh—a helpful time-saver if you use the same server every day. We'll take you through this process step by step later in the hour.

8. Close the Chooser. The server volume's icon will appear on your desktop, below your hard drive(s) and desktop printer(s), or any other icons you have on your desktop (see Figure 23.4).

23

Figure 23.4

The server volume appears on the desktop.

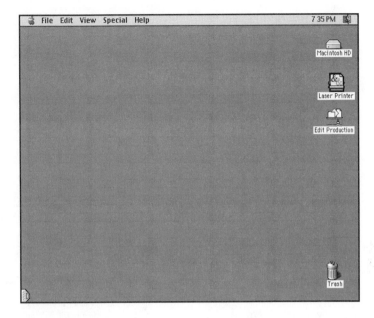

9. Double-click on the server's icon to access its files, just as you would a folder or hard drive on your own system. Because you're accessing files across a network, performance will be noticeably slower.

Encountering Restricted Access

Actually, accessing server volumes differ from using local volumes in one major way: the server's owner may have set up limitations on what you can and cannot do or see on the server.

To view your access limitations for a given folder, perform the following steps:

1. Click on the folder or volume you want to investigate.

2. From the File menu, select Sharing…. A dialog box will appear (see Figure 23.5).

In the figure shown, the user Anita has full access to the volume Ether Bunny, including the right to see folders and files, and make changes to the drive's contents. No other users or groups have access.

You can also rely on Mac OS 8's visual cues to determine your access privileges. When viewing the contents of a server, folders with buckles around them are not accessible to you. If you try to access them, you'll receive an error alert (see Figure 23.6).

Similarly, windows with write-modification restrictions display a crossed-out pencil icon in the upper-left corner. If you try to write files to them, you'll receive an error alert (see Figure 23.7).

Figure 23.5

To view your access privileges, use File➡ Sharing… with the volume selected.

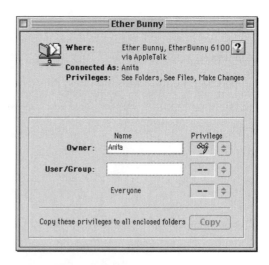

Figure 23.6

Attempting to open restricted folders results in an error.

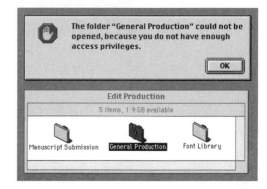

Figure 23.7

Attempting to move files to a write-protected folder results in an error.

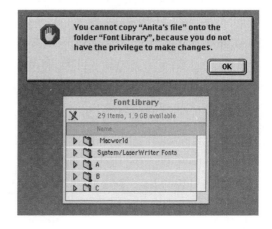

23

Likewise, windows with reading restrictions will display a crossed-out file icon in the upper left corner. If you try to write files to them, you'll receive a warning alert (see Figure 23.8). After you move files to a read-protected folder, they become invisible to you, just like all the other files in that folder.

Figure 23.8

Attempting to move files to read-protected results in a warning.

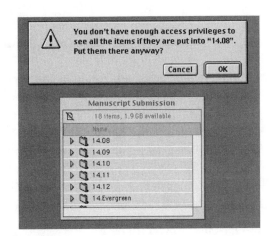

Changing Your Server Password

If your network administrator or the person who defined the server's Users & Groups has allowed it, you may be able to change your password from the one you were given. This enables you to protect server access so that even the server's owner won't know your password. You can ask the administrator to provide you a temporary "dummy" password—like your name—and arrange to change your password when you log on to the server.

To modify your password on a server, perform the following steps:

1. Open the Chooser (Apple Menu➡Chooser).

2. Click on the AppleShare icon, and select the server from the list.

3. At the user name and password dialog box, click on the Set Password button. A new dialog box appears (see Figure 23.9).

4. Type your old password into the Old Password text entry field (bullets will appear rather than the letters or numbers you type).

5. Type your new password in the New Password text entry field (your new password must be different from your old one, or you'll get an error later in the process).

6. An alert dialog box will appear, asking you to reenter your new password for confirmation (this protects you in case you made a typo the first time you entered your new password).

7. Click OK, and reenter your new password in the text entry field.

Figure 23.9

The Set Password dialog box.

8. When you get to the next dialog box, your new password has been accepted. Continue with the log-on process as described earlier in this hour.

Automating Your Log-on Process

When you use a file server frequently, there are various ways to simplify your activities. If you know you'll always want to use a server volume at the beginning of each work session, you can set the server to mount automatically at startup.

To set up a volume for automatic mounting, perform the following steps:

1. Open the Chooser (Apple Menu➡Chooser).
2. Click on the Apple Share icon, and select the server from the list (select the appropriate zone first, if necessary).
3. Select the server you want to access from the scrolling list by clicking on its name and clicking on the OK button.
4. Log on as Guest, or as a Registered User, as described earlier in this hour.
5. In the dialog box that displays the server's volumes, click on the check box of the volume you want to mount automatically at startup (see Figure 23.10). With the check box selected, you can ask Mac OS 8 to save your user name, or your user name and password, to save time on future log-ins.

Figure 23.10

Click on a server volume's check box to mount it at startup.

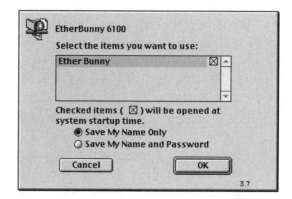

23

6. The selected server's volume will be automatically mounted on the desktop each time you start your Macintosh.

If you don't need constant access to a volume, you can make aliases to your commonly-used servers, just as you can for files and folders. You can leave the alias on your desktop, or combine them in a folder. (You could even create a pop-up server launcher as we did for "Applications" in Hour 11.)

TIME SAVER

> If all this sounds too complicated, the simplest way to access a server you use a lot is actually built in to the Mac OS; there's a shortcut to your most recently used servers in the Apple menu (Apple Menu➡Recent Servers).

Using Personal Web Sharing

Personal Web Sharing enables you to create your own Internet-based server to share files over the Internet if you computer is connected to a TCP/IP network. Earlier in this hour we encountered the Server IP Address button in the Chooser; this button enables you to access other people's Personal Web Sharing volumes.

Personal Web Sharing software is installed on your hard drive, but it is inactive by default. To turn it on, open the Web Sharing Control Panel (Apple Menu➡Control Panels➡Web Sharing) (see Figure 23.11).

Figure 23.11

The Web Sharing Control Panel enables you to turn Personal Web Sharing on or off.

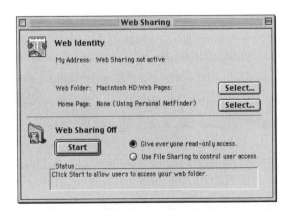

Because most home and small office users aren't directly connected to a TCP/IP network, we won't discuss Personal Web Sharing in detail. If you *are* properly connected, and want to use Personal Web Sharing, the Mac OS Info Center icon on the desktop offers detailed, step-by-step information on its use.

Additional technical setup instructions can be found in the Web Pages folder (Internet→Web Pages→About Personal Web Sharing).

Accessing Files Via Modem: ARA

Apple Remote Access (ARA) enables you to dial in over a phone line to access files on shared Macintosh systems and servers on your network. Many predominantly-Macintosh offices offer an ARA dial-in server, allowing their employees to access files from home.

To enable your system to use ARA, perform the following steps:

1. Open the Remote Access Setup Control Panel (Apple Menu→Control Panels→Remote Access Setup). A dialog box will appear (see Figure 23.12).

2. Choose your modem's name from the pop-up menu.

Figure 23.12

The ARA Setup Control Panel.

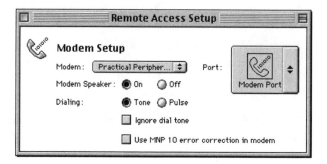

3. You can enable or disable your modem's speaker using the radio buttons. Leave the remaining radio buttons and check boxes at the defaults, unless you're sure you need to change them.

4. Close the control panel for your changes to take effect.

In order to configure a Macintosh as an ARA client, perform the following steps:

1. Launch the Remote Access Client program in the Applications folder (System folder→Remote Access Client). A dialog box appears (see Figure 23.13).

2. Fill in the fields for your user name, password, and the number of the ARA server you'll be calling.

Caution

If you select "Save My Password," you don't have to type your password in every time you log on. If you're the only person using your Macintosh, this can be a time-saver, although it poses a security risk—anyone who clicks on Connect can log in as you.

23

Figure 23.13

The Remote Access Client's main screen.

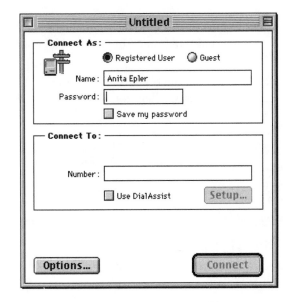

3. Click on the Options button. A new dialog box will appear (see Figure 23.14).

4. In this window, you can set your redialing preferences, define an alternate number to use if you have trouble connecting, and ask ARA to flash an icon or warn you periodically that you're connected (it's very easy to forget). Click OK to save your options.

Figure 23.14

The Remote Access Client's options screen.

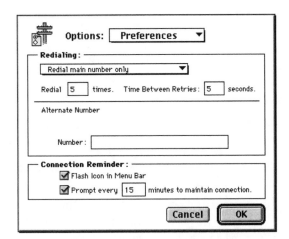

5. Close the window. A dialog box will prompt you to pick a name for this configuration. Save the file into the Remote Access Client folder (Applications➡Remote Access➡your file).

To log into a remote network, perform the following steps:

1. Locate your saved configuration file, and double-click on it. Its window will appear.

2. Click on the Connect button. ARA begins the dial-up process. A new status message appears, telling you that ARA is dialing your predefined number (see Figure 23.15).

Figure 23.15

The Remote Access Client's status screen tells you that ARA is dialing your present number.

3. If your modem's speaker is turned on, you'll hear it dial the number. After the modem connects, a new status message appears, showing your connection speed. A second window displays the name of the ARA server, your time limit, and the amount of time you've been connected (see Figure 23.16).

Figure 23.16

The Remote Access Client's status screen provides additional information about your connection.

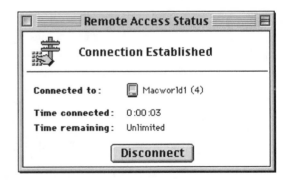

4. Open the Chooser, and click on AppleShare. Slowly, a list of the remote network's servers will be displayed on the right side of the Chooser. You can select them and use them just as you would a server on a local network, although your access and response times will be dramatically slower.

23

To disconnect from ARA, perform the following steps:

1. Bring the Remote Access Client to the front (Applications menu➡Remote Access Client).

2. From the Window menu, select Status. The Remote Access Status window appears.

3. Click on the Disconnect button. The Status window will tell you it is disconnecting.

4. When the Status window reads Idle…, your connection has been terminated. If you had any server volumes mounted, you'll get an error message (see Figure 23.17).

Figure 23.17

If you disconnect from ARA with server volumes mounted, you'll get an error.

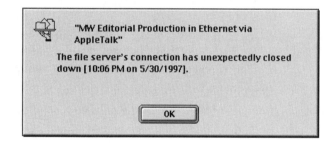

"MW Editorial Production in Ethernet via AppleTalk"

The file server's connection has unexpectedly closed down [10:06 PM on 5/30/1997].

OK

Summary

In this hour, we've taught you how to access servers over a network. You've learned to log on to a server as a Guest or as a Registered User, change your password, and specify volumes to mount automatically at start-up.

You've learned what Personal Web Sharing does, and how to find more information about installing and using it. You've also learned to set up and use Apple Remote Access to retrieve and send files to your office network from another location using a phone connection.

Term Review

Apple Remote Access (ARA) Software that enables you to dial in over a phone line to access files on a remote network.

Client A computer logging in to use files on a server.

Guest A person *not* previously designated in the Users & Groups Control Panel.

Personal Web Sharing Mac OS 8's built-in capability that enables you to share files over the Internet.

Registered User A person designated in the Users & Groups Control Panel.

Server   A computer set up to share files over a network.

Volume   A single hard drive (of many possible) on a file server.

Q&A

Q Why would I want to put a file on a read-restricted volume if I won't be able to see it once it's there?

A Think of it like a drop box. Your colleague can let you (and other people) deposit files into this folder, but you can't see anything that's been left there.

Q Whenever I use ARA, I keep getting taken offline when a second call comes in. How can I avoid this?

A You can cancel your telephone's Call Waiting feature in most areas. In the ARA Setup screen, type "*70," (asterisk, 7, 0, comma) before your ARA server's access number. You may want to check with your local phone company for the Cancel Call Waiting code in your area.

23

Hour **24**

Automation

Traditionally, you tell your computer to do one thing at a time. You point and click and drag and open and save in a logical sequence of events. It may have occurred to you, as you were going through a sequence that you'd already been through before, that it would be great to automate the process, or at least use some sort of shortcut, to get to the same conclusion. We agree.

In this hour, we'll look at some of the options Mac OS 8 gives you for saving time and trouble, including its built-in shortcuts, AppleScript, and third-party automation tools.

Shortcuts

We previously discussed shortcuts in the Mac OS Info Center in Hour 9. Some of the shortcuts there you'd already learned, but time and space limitations prevented us from going into detail about them. Now you're about to learn some of the Macintosh's best shortcuts. Try each one of these individually (see Figure 24.1).

Figure 24.1

The Shortcuts window.

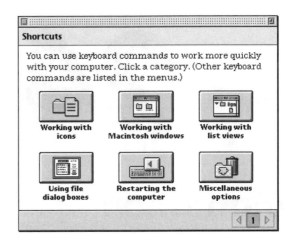

Icon Shortcuts

There are several ways to simplify your work when you rearrange the icons in windows.

Selecting Multiple Icons

If you want to select a number of icons for moving or deleting, you can take one of two actions. If they're in a group, you can drag the mouse around the icons to highlight them all. If they're not in a group, you can hold down the Shift key and click on the icons you want to select.

Cancel Dragging

Say you're dragging an icon from the desktop into a deeply nested folder, and you change your mind. You can't just let go of the icon because that will drop it in whichever folder you're in at the moment. Drag it to the menu bar at the top of the screen and let go. It will appear back on the desktop.

Windows Shortcuts

If you're working with a lot of windows, it's easy to clutter up your desktop quickly. Here are some shortcuts that can help you avoid disarray.

Closing Windows

By holding down the Option key and opening a folder, its parent folder will close automatically. This keeps your desktop free from unneeded folders.

24

Turning Windows into Windowshades

If you want to use the Windowshade command to close all open windows simultaneously, hold down the Option key and click on any open window's title bar. If you want to reopen them all, hold down the Option key and click on any Windowshade.

List Shortcuts

If you prefer to view your folders as lists rather than as icons, you have several options for viewing them via keyboard shortcuts.

Sorting Lists

To sort your list by column heading, click on the heading (unfortunately, you can't yet resize the columns, which would be a real space-saver).

Opening and Closing Lists

Here are some shortcuts for dealing with an entire folder.

- ☐ To expand the contents of a folder, press ⌘ and the right arrow.
- ☐ To collapse the contents, press ⌘ and the left arrow.
- ☐ To expand the contents of a folder and all the folders within it, press ⌘ and Option and the right arrow.
- ☐ To collapse the contents of a folder and all the folders within it, press ⌘ and Option and the left arrow. As an alternative, you can press Option and the disclosure triangle to perform this task.
- ☐ If you want to collapse the contents of multiple folders, press ⌘-A (or Edit➡Select All) and perform the expansion commands.

Moving Items Within Lists

To bring a file or folder to the top-most level of the folder, drag it to the toolbar and let go.

Dialog Box Shortcuts

As you work with your Macintosh, you'll see a lot of dialog boxes (as you remember from Hour 10, a dialog box is distinguished from a window because it has no scroll arrows, close box, or grow box).

Navigating within Dialog Boxes

When you want to open or save a new file in a particular folder, you can navigate through the folders by pressing ⌘ and the up or down arrow. To go up one level, you can click on the hard drive icon, or to get back to the desktop, press ⌘-D (for desktop).

In Open dialog boxes, you can open an item by pressing ⌘-O or ⌘ and the down arrow.

In Save dialog boxes, you can create a new folder by pressing ⌘-N.

24

Restarting Shortcuts

Here are some shortcuts to try when your computer freezes.

☐ To quit a frozen application, press ⌘ and Option and Esc; unsaved work will be lost.

☐ To restart your computer (depending on the model), press ⌘ and Option and shift and the power key (upper right on your keyboard); unsaved work will be lost.

☐ If your cursor freezes (depending on the model), press ⌘ and Control and the power key; unsaved work will be lost.

TIME SAVER

If you do have to restart your computer, you want to lose as little work as possible. Check the applications you use most frequently for an option called "auto-save" or "quick-save." This lets you set an interval of time after which the computer will automatically save the application. This is an especially good idea if you're using a battery-powered PowerBook.

Reviewing Other Shortcuts

There are other shortcuts in Mac OS 8 that can save you time and trouble. The same goes for the applications you'll use. Sometimes they're not even documented, and you'll trip over them accidentally. We'll review a few here.

Learning a Few Shortcuts

Every time you select Special➡Empty Trash, you'll get a dialog box asking you to confirm the action. This gives you one more chance to change your mind. If you're positive you want to empty the trash, hold down the Option key when you select the Empty Trash command.

To erase a disk automatically when you insert it in the floppy drive, hold down the ⌘, Option, and Tab keys while you insert the floppy disk (you may have to contort your fingers somewhat, but it is possible).

To hide an application's windows when you want to switch to another application, press the Option key while you select another application in the Application menu.

When you're connecting to another computer, press ⌘-G to sign on as a guest. Press ⌘-R to sign on as a registered user.

Learning About AppleScript

AppleScript couldn't be better named—it's an application used to build *scripts*; that is, automatic sequences of events that would be tiresome if you had to go through them with the mouse.

24

What It Is

A script is similar to a macro, a term you may have heard of if you use spreadsheets a lot (a macro will do calculations automatically) or if you've used Microsoft Windows. There's a fine difference between a Mac OS 8 script and a Windows macro, and it's important to understand if you're a beginner.

A Windows macro is *recordable*, which means that you can go through a sequence of events and the computer will record it for playback, just as if you were speaking commands into a tape. A Mac OS 8 script is *scriptable*, which means you have to *write* the commands for it to execute in the proper order *and* with the proper terminology (see Figure 24.2).

Figure 24.2

The contents of an AppleScript for file sharing.

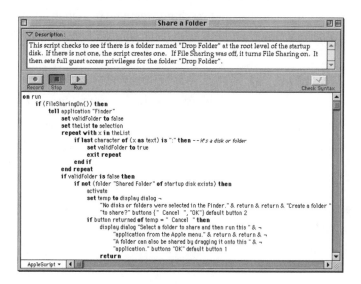

24

It's not as easy to pick up as most Mac OS 8 activities. Trust us—we're fairly savvy about the Macintosh, and we find it a little daunting, to say the least. That's not to be discouraging—it's just an explanation as to why we're not going into detail about building AppleScripts.

Who Uses It, and Where

Who does use AppleScripts? Mostly, it's people with programming experience. At *Macworld*, the Information Systems (IS) department has written an AppleScript to backup our Macintoshes to a central server every time we invoke the Special➥Shut Down command.

It can be used to script activities that involve multiple applications. For instance, the backup script that *Macworld's* IS department uses not only uses the backup software, but the Chooser and various network commands as well. However, it's not necessary to do so. There are scripts built into your Macintosh that are built with commands solely within Mac OS 8. We'll discuss those below.

Other applications may also include their own languages for building scripts. Among the most common are the Microsoft Excel spreadsheet and the Claris FileMaker Pro database. You may wonder why a Claris product has its own scripting language when Apple owns Claris, but the answer is simple—Claris built a scripting language into its database before Apple developed AppleScript.

Using AppleScript Automated Tasks

Having said all that, there are ways you can take advantage of AppleScripts *now*. There are ten AppleScripts that come with Mac OS 8, covering activities such as file sharing, changing monitor settings, and synchronizing folders, among others. When you or someone within your company builds more AppleScripts, you can store them with these pre-built scripts for easy access.

Where To Find Automated Tasks

To locate these prebuilt AppleScripts, perform the following steps:

1. On your hard drive, double-click on Apple Extras. Double-click on the AppleScript folder.

2. Double-click on either the Automated Tasks or the More Automated Tasks folder (see Figure 24.3).

Figure 24.3

The Automated Tasks folders are in the AppleScript folder.

3. If you want a description of each of the tasks, double-click on the "About Automated Tasks" or "About More Automated Tasks" documents. Double-click on any one of these automated tasks to perform them.

24

Time Saver

If you want to tackle AppleScripts, there is a two-part tutorial in your AppleScript folder.

How to Take Advantage of Automated Tasks

To show you how they work, let's go through an automated task:

1. To take advantage of the first automated task, "Add Alias To Apple Menu," first select a document on your hard drive (we suggest highlighting the "More Automated Tasks" folder, for reasons that will become obvious).

2. In the menu bar, select the Apple Menu➡Automated Tasks➡Add Alias to Apple Menu.

3. The computer will perform the script, and you will get a dialog box confirming the action (see Figure 24.4).

Figure 24.4

When you run an automated task, a dialog box confirms that it has been completed.

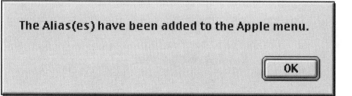

The Alias(es) have been added to the Apple menu.

OK

4. Now you can access the other set of automated tasks from the Apple menu as well by repeating the steps.

Caution

Not all of the AppleScripts are automatic. For instance, if you run the "Change Monitor to 256" script, it will ask you to find the Monitors & Sound Control Panel. It can't do it by itself.

Time Saver

If you'd like the computer to perform one of these AppleScript tasks automatically when you turn your computer on or off, drag the icon representing the script to the Startup Items or Shutdown Items folder in your System Folder. They will launch automatically at the beginning or ending of your day.

Other Automation Tools and Tips

You'll find other automation tools in your Macintosh or from other developers. Among such automation utilities are QuicKeys from CE Software (515-221-1801; www.cesoftware.com) and Keyquencer from Binary Software (310-449-1481; www.binarysoft.com). We're going to set up a sequence in QuicKeys to show you how the process works.

QuicKeys

QuicKeys lets you automate typing, so that if you have sentences, company names, signatures, or other groups of words that you type frequently, you can simply create a shortcut for them. Type the shortcut, and the entire section will appear. All of the actions within QuicKeys are created through its QuicKeys Editor. Under its "Define" menu, you can choose a variety of ways to create a sequence, but we're going to do just a short one.

If you've ever gotten electronic mail, you'll notice that a lot of people sign their messages with their name, address, and a statement of their philosophy. But it would be a drag to type this every single time you sent an email message. That's where software like QuicKeys comes in.

To create a signature in QuicKeys, perform the following steps:

1. In the menu bar, you'll find the QuicKeys icon to the right of the data. Select the QuicKeys icon➡QuicKeys.

2. The QuicKeys Editor appears (see Figure 24.5) with 15 preconfigured sequences, or shortcuts. Select Define➡Text.

Figure 24.5

The QuicKeys Editor.

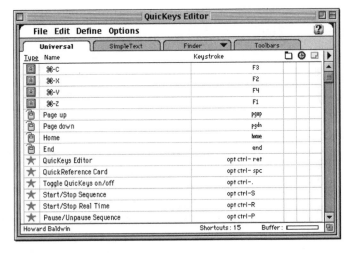

3. In the "Name:" panel, type what you want to name your sequence (we chose Signature).

24

4. In the "Keystroke" panel, type the shortcut you want to use (we chose Ctrl-S, for Signature).

5. In the "Text to type:" panel, type the text you want (we chose to do one for President Clinton) (see Figure 24.6).

Figure 24.6

How we imagine President Clinton signs email messages.

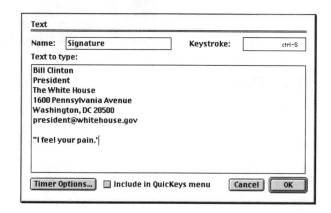

6. Now in the QuicKeys Editor, there are 16 sequences, including the Signature (see Figure 24.7). The T icon indicates that it's text. Now, when you press Ctrl-S in any application that accepts type, this signature will appear.

Figure 24.7

The new shortcut appears in the QuicKeys Editor.

Other Tips

If you have an Apple keyboard, you may notice the words printed underneath your first four function keys (the ones marked F1 through F4). These are four important shortcuts

☐ To Undo, press F1 (also handled by ⌘-Z)

☐ To Cut, press F2 (also handled by ⌘-X)

☐ To Copy, press F3 (also handled by ⌘-C)

☐ To Paste, press F4 (also handled by ⌘-V).

If you're wondering why they're in this particular order, notice that on your keyboard, these four keys are next to each other (see Figure 24.8).

Figure 24.8

The four most common commands are handled by the four typewriter keys in the lower-left corner of the keyboard.

Summary

In this hour, we've given you an overview of ways you can automate your Macintosh. Some of them require third-party applications or more depth than we can provide here, but others are included within your Macintosh for easy and immediate use.

If you find yourself performing a lot of repetitive tasks, we recommend you delve into the more sophisticated applications available for the Macintosh. The time you spend learning applications like AppleScript or QuicKeys can be quickly recouped by the time you save running scripts and sequences.

Term Review

AppleScript   An application that enables you to run an automatic sequence of events using multiple applications.

Automated Task   A prebuilt AppleScript application that comes with Mac OS 8.

Macro   Another word for script.

Script   An automatic sequence of events that can be built using multiple applications (with AppleScript) or within one application (using that application's own scripting capability).

Shortcut   A time-saving way to navigate the keyboard quickly and easily without using the mouse.

Q&A

Q Keyboard shortcuts are great! How can I find out more?

A Other books are devoted solely to teaching you about these secret shortcuts, including *Mac OS 8 Unleashed,* also from Hayden Books.

24

Q Is it my imagination, or does AppleScript look more complicated than real English?

A It does. Although it's simpler than most programming languages, it's still not something that you should tackle without some basic classes and indoctrination into the concepts of things like *compilers* and *run-time applications*. I've heard professional programmers admit they sometimes have trouble with AppleScript, but that doesn't mean you can't tackle it. You just have to have a logical, organized mind (which excludes some of us immediately).

Q But you said that some Macintosh applications don't use AppleScript. Which scripting language is the most important to learn?

A The most important one to learn is the one you'll use most. The basic concepts of scripting and programming are similar: you have to tell the computer what to do in the proper sequence of events so that it doesn't get confused. Just as knowing one foreign language will give you a boost in another foreign language, the fundamentals you learn from one scripting language will probably be applicable in another.

Q Say I excel at scripting—should I consider it as a career?

A As information becomes more digitally driven, we'll always need great programmers. As a career path, it can't be beat. How do you think Bill Gates got started?

24

Appendix A

What's New in Mac OS 8

If you're already familiar with Apple's System 7.X operating system, Table A.1 shows the significant additions to Mac OS 8.

Table A.1. New Features in Mac OS 8

Feature	Description
Appearance Control Panel	This new control panel lets you choose accent and highlight colors for windows and set the default system font.
Automatic Browsing	The Browse the Internet icon appears on the desktop to automatically launch your web browser (Netscape Navigator is installed with Mac OS 8, while Microsoft Internet Explorer is included on the CD).
Automatic e-mail	The Mail icon appears on your desktop to launch your mail application (ClarisEmailer Lite is installed with the Mac OS).

continues

Table A.1. continued

Feature	Description
Button views	You can select View➡as Buttons to display files as buttons that open with just one click. You can move a button by dragging its name, and select a button by dragging the cursor across it.
Connect To...	After you've set up Internet access, the Connect To command under the Apple menu lets you quickly access your favorite web page.
Contextual menus	Hold down the Control key when you click on an item (icon, window, or text) and a menu appears displaying relevant commands.
Desktop Pictures	An update of the Desktop Patterns Control Panel, this lets you use your own pictures (in GIF, JPEG, Photoshop, and Macintosh Pictures format) as your desktop. Other pictures are also provided.
File Menu Options	The file menu now includes options for moving a highlighted file to the Trash (with a keyboard shortcut of ⌘–Del) and for finding the original of a highlighted alias.
Finder Preferences	Now under the Edit menu, this preferences list combines options that were previously in the Labels and Views Control Panels. There's now an option for a simplified Finder, which limits the number of choices the user can see (designed for new users).
Grow Box	The grow box in the lower-right corner of a window has been replaced by diagonal lines. You can resize a window by dragging these lines.
Help Menu	Usability studies indicated that few people understood what the question mark in the menu bar meant, so Help menus are now accessed through the word *Help*, displayed on the menu bar to the immediate right of other options.

A

Feature	Description
Internet Dialer	If you're connecting to the Internet with a modem and you have more than one ISP, the Internet Dialer lets you choose which one.
Internet Sign-Up	An Internet Setup Assistant walks you through the configuration steps necessary to access the Internet, whether you're connecting through a modem or a local area network. You can also create a new account with an Internet service provider (ISP) or link to your existing ISP account.
Live scrolling	Dragging the scroll box will update the window's contents as you scroll, not when you stop.
Mac OS Runtime for Java	You can now run applications written in Java on your Macintosh.
Multiprocessor speed	Although you're probably several years away from having a multiprocessing Macintosh on your desktop, applications that take advantage of multiprocessing will run faster under Mac OS 8.
Multithreaded Finder	That's a fancy way of saying you can perform simultaneous operations, such as copying files while you're emptying the Trash or opening other documents. In addition, for the first time, the code for the Finder has been rewritten to take advantage of the PowerPC CPU's speed.
Personal Web Sharing	You can set up your own web page on your Macintosh, effectively turning it into your personal web server. Think of this as file sharing over the web.
Pop-up windows	You can select View➡as Pop-up Window to turn a window into a pop-up window. Its name will appear on a tab, and you can drag the tab to the bottom of the desktop for easy access. Click on the title to display the window. Select View➡as Window to return it to a traditional window.

A

continues

Table A.1. continued

Feature	Description
QuickDraw 3D	This extension lets you display, move, and rotate three-dimensional objects.
QuickTime MPEG	This extension lets you display full-screen video files.
QuickTime VR	This extension lets you display "virtual reality" applications.
Sharing Setup	You can now access the Users & Groups Control Panel through the Sharing Setup dialog box.
Spring-loaded folders	One of our favorite new features. Dragging an icon over a folder opens the folder. You can do this for multiple levels to make sure you're putting the icon in the proper folder. Once you let go of the icon, it appears in the last window, and all the intervening windows close. You can similarly navigate through folders using the new "click-and-a-half"— click the mouse and then hold it down. The cursor will turn into a magnifying glass for navigating through folders.
Sticky Menus	A steal from Windows: click on the menu name to make it "stick" open.
View Options	You can set up the View menu to show files as icons, as buttons, or as a list. You can also arrange these icons, buttons or sort lists by a variety of criteria. For instance, with list views you can include relative dating (such as *today* or *yesterday*), and now have *date created* and *date modified* options. With icon views, you can determine the size of icons, how they're ordered, and whether they snap to the window's grid.
Window Collapsing	You can collapse a window down to the title bar by clicking the new collapse box at the upper-right corner of a window (previously a Control Panel named WindowShade allowed

A

Feature	Description
	this). To reopen the window, click the box again. To collapse all open windows, press the option key and clicking on any window's collapse box.
Window Dragging	You can move a window by dragging on any of its borders, not just its title bar.

Appendix B

Contact Information

Table B.1. Sources for Macintosh Buying Information

Company	Telephone	URL
Graphics & Publishing		
Adobe	408-536-6000	www.adobe.com
Extensis	503-274-2020	www.extensis.com
Macromedia	415-252-4096	www.macromedia.com
MetaCreations	805-566-6200	www.metatools.com
Quark	303-894-8888	www.quark.com
Networking		
AG Group	510-937-7900	www.aggroup.com
Asante Technologies	408-435-8401	www.asante.com
Dayna Communications	801-269-7200	www.dayna.com
Farallon Communications	510-814-5000	www.farallon.com

continues

Table B.1. continued

Company	Telephone	URL
Miramar Systems	805-966-2432	www.miramarsys.com
Sonic Systems	408-736-1900	www.sonicsys.com
Thursby Software Systems	817-478-5070	www.thursby.com
Peripherals		
Adaptec	408-945-8600	www.adaptec.com
ATI Technologies	905-882-2600	www.atitech.com
Atto Technology	716-691-1999	www.attotech.com
Global Village	408-523-1000	www.globalvillage.com
Iomega	801-778-1000	www.iomega.com
La Cie	503-520-9000	www.lacie.com
Radius	408-541-6100	www.radius.com
Streamlogic	818-701-8400	www.streamlogic.com
Productivity Software		
CE Software	515-221-1801	www.cesoftware.com
Claris	408-987-7000	www.claris.com
Corel	613-728-0826	www.corel.com
Microsoft	206-882-8080	www.microsoft.com
Nisus	619-481-1477	www.nisus-soft.com
Utilities		
Aladdin Systems	408-761-6200	www.aladdinsys.com
Casady & Greene	408-484-9228	www.casadyg.com
Connectix	415-571-5100	www.connectix.com
Dantz Development	510-253-3000	www.dantz.com
DataViz	203-268-0030	www.dataviz.com
Software Architects	206-487-0122	www.softarch.com
Symantec	408-253-9600	www.symantec.com

B

Company	Telephone	URL
System Vendors		
Apple	408-996-1010	www.apple.com
APS Technologies	816-483-1600	www.apstech.com
Daystar Digital	770-967-2077	www.daystar.com
Motorola	800-759-1107	www.mot.com/starmax
Power Computing	512-388-6868	www.powercc.com
Power Tools	512-891-0646	www.pwrtools.com
Umax	510-226-6886	www.supermac.com

Table B.2. Catalog/Direct Retailers

Company	Telephone	URL
Big Mac Computers	800-761-1999	www.wcn.com
Bottom Line Distribution	800-990-5698	www.blol.com
Club Mac	800-260-8549	www.club-mac.com
Computer Discount Warehouse	800-509-4239	www.cdw.com
CRA Systems	800-375-9000	n/a
DigiCore	800-858-4622	www.digicore.com
Mac Bargains	800-619-9091	n/a
Mac Zone	800-436-0606	www.maczone.com
MacConnection	800-800-4396	www.macconnection.com
MacMall	800-217-9498	n/a
MacMarket	800-905-3034	www.macmarket.com
MacWarehouse	800-434-3035	www.warehouse.com

Table B.3. Publications

Name	Telephone	URL
Mac Home Journal	415-957-1911	www.machome.com
MacAddict	415-468-4684	www.zd.macuser.com
MacUser	415-547-8600	www.macuser.com
MacWeek	415-547-8000	www.macweek.com
Macworld	415-243-0505	www.macworld.com

B

Macintosh Web Sites

Based on round-ups we've done for *Macworld* in the past two years, the following represent the very best in what we call "compendium" sites for Macintosh users. They link to all the pertinent Macintosh information on the World Wide Web. Go to your web browser and create bookmarks for these sites, and you'll never be more than a few clicks away from everything you'll need to know about the Macintosh.

Table B.4. Web Sites

Web Site	URL
Everything Macintosh	www.acm.cps.msu.edu/~flaminio/apple.html
The Well-Connected Mac	www.macfaq.com
Macintosh for the Rest of Us	www.ralentz.com/old/mac/net/net-rest-of-us.html
Ultimate Macintosh	www.freepress.com/~myee/umac.html

B

INDEX

Symbols

(") double-hash symbol, 146-148
(') single-hash symbol, 146-148
(…) ellipses, 146-148
3-D icons, 17
1984 Macintosh commercial, downloading, 311

A

About This Computer command (Apple menu), 74
About This Computer dialog box, 286
accent colors (Appearance Control Panel), 254-257

access privileges
groups, file sharing, 208
monitoring for groups, 211
server restrictions
on files, 341-343
on folders, 341-343
accessing
applications, online help, 120
balloon help, 121-122
Chooser, 181-182
Extensions Manager, 95-96
files on servers, 338-341
Memory Control Panel, 288
other computers on network, 212-213
Scrapbook, 83-84
Usenet newsgroups, 243-247
web, 235-242
activating
AppleTalk, 178-179
balloon help, 121-122

Personal Web Sharing, 345-346
pop-up windows, 24
Activity Monitor tab, 211
Adaptec web site, 370
Add Bookmark command (Bookmarks menu), 240
Add Newsgroup command (File menu), 246
Add Newsgroup dialog box, 246
adding
devices to LANs, 172
group members, 210
hard drives, external, 67-68
internal cards, 282-283
sounds to shutdown folders, 307
Adobe Illustrator, 154-155
Adobe Persuasion, 157-158

Adobe Photoshop, 155
Adobe Systems web site, 136, 369
Adobe Type Manager, 138-142
Adobe Type Reunion, 142
AfterDark screen savers, 158
AG Group web site, 369
Aladdin Systems web site, 370
Aldus PageMaker, 153-154
alerts
    customizing with PlainTalk microphone, 303-304
    voice type, creating, 304-305
aliases (files), creating, 111
American Computer Exchange, stolen computers database, 318-319
Anti-Virus for Macintosh, 322
aperture grille monitors, 274
Appearance Control Panel
    Color screen choices, 254-257
    Crayon Picker, 255-257
    modifying, 254-257
    windows, collapse preferences, 256-257
Apple CD Audio Player, 265
    playing, 307-310
    personalizing, 309-310
    stereo controls, 78
Apple command (Bookmarks menu), 237
Apple Guide, 115-116
Apple Internet Connection Kit, 223
Apple Menu
    Apple CD Audio Player, 78
    Calculator, 79
    Chooser, 75-76
    commands
        About This Computer, 74
        Automated Tasks, 357
        Chooser, 181, 212-213
        Connect To…, 35
        Control Panels, 179
        Find File, 77
        Graphing Calculator, 79
        Key Caps, 77
        Recent Servers, 345

    Scrapbook, 83
    Startup Disk, 69
    Stickies, 84
    Web Sharing, 345
    Connect To shortcut, 82
    Control Panels, 75
    Find File, 76-77
    Graphing Calculator, 79-80
    Jigsaw Puzzle, 84
    Key Caps, 77
    multicolored Apple logo, 48
    Note Pad, 85
    Recent Applications, 80-81
    Recent Servers, 80-81
    Scrapbook, 83-84
    shortcut options, 112
    Stickies, 84-85
    System Profiler, 75
Apple QuickTake, digital cameras, 312-313
Apple Remote Access (ARA)
    configurations, 346-349
    disconnecting, 349
    enabling, 346
    remote networks, logging on, 348-349
Apple Software Archive web site, 126
Apple SOS Line, Macintosh technical support, 128-129
Apple System Profiler
    hardware statistics, 75
    launching, 75
Apple web site, 371
    Macintosh technical support, 128
Apple's Education site, 127
AppleScripts
    applications, 355-356
    automated tasking, 82
    automated tasks, 355
        implementing, 357
        locating, 356-357
    uses, 355-356
    versus macros, 355
AppleShare, server access, 338-341
AppleTalk, enabling, 178-179

Application menu
    functions, 56-57
    options, 56-57
applications
    balloon help, activating, 122-123
    Custom Install option, 163-166
    Easy Install option, 163-166
    files, format overview, 328-329
    icons
        appearance, 18-19
        name, changing, 18-19
    installer utilities, 163-166
    installing, 163-166
        source destination, 166
    launcher customization, 265
    launching, 10
        in custom launcher, 265
    memory allocation, 295-296
    modifying RAM, 293-296
    online help, accessing, 120
    RAM requirements, 293-296
    Startup Folder, placing, 96-97
    System Folder, Preference settings, 97-100
    troubleshooting (Extensions Manager), 95-96
    Undo command (Edit menu), 53-54
APS Technologies web site, 371
ARPAnet, Internet precursor, 232
Arrange menu commands, By Name, 265
arrows in nested menus, 30-32
articles, reading from Usenet newsgroups, 243-247
As Buttons command (View menu), 19, 108
As Icons command (View menu), 106
As List command (View menu), 107

As Pop-up Window command (View menu), 24, 110
Asante Technologies web site, 369
assistants
    Internet Editor, 160-163
    Internet Setup, 160-163
    ISP Registration, 160-163
    Mac OS 8 Setup, 160-163
    PowerBook File, 160-163
AtEase security software, 322
ATI Technologies web site, 370
Atto Technology web site, 370
audio CDs (Apple CD Audio Player)
    play options, 309-310
    playing, 307-310
automated settings for Internet connections, 227-229
automated tasks (Apple Scripts)
    implementing, 357
    locating, 356-357
    preconfigured scripts, 82
Automated Tasks command (Apple menu), 357
automatic browsing, 363
automatic email, 363
automating server log-ons, 344-345

B

background printing
    disabling serial type printers, 187
    enabling serial type printers, 187
    Print dialog box, 193
backing up files, 316-317
    offsite storage, 317-318
    removable media, 317
backup software, Retrospect, 316-317

balloon help
    accessing, 121-122
    disabling, 122
    within applications, 122-123
Big Mac Computers web site, 371
bitmapped fonts, 136-137
    limited by printer resolution, 136-137
bookmarking web pages, 240-241
bookmarks, pre-loaded, 240
Bookmarks menu commands
    Add Bookmark, 240
    Apple, 237
Bottom Line Distribution web site, 371
building
    Ethernet connections, 173
    LocalTalk connections, 170-172
bundled software, 159-160
    assistants, 159-160
    utilities, 159-160
buttons
    New Group, 209-210
    New Users, 209-210
    Printer Info, 184
    viewing folders, 108
By Name command (Arrange menu), 265
By Name command (View menu), 19

C

Calculator
    keyboard operation, 79
    mouse operation, 79
CanOpener, 158
capacities, monitoring hard drives, 67
Casady & Greene web site, 370
catalog retailers, web resources, 371

CD-ROMs (Compact Disk Read Only Memory)
    audio (Apple CD Audio Player), 307-310
    data transfer rates, 278-279
    speed measurement controversy, inner track versus outer track, 279
CE Software web site, 370
Chooser
    accessing, 181-182
        modems, 75-76
        networks, 75-76
        printers, 75-76
    AppleShare, server access, 338-341
    files, server access, 338-341
    functions, 75-76
    laser printers, configuring, 182-184
    networks, device connections, 212-213
    servers, selecting, 338-341
Chooser command (Apple menu), 181, 212-213
ClarisDraw, 154-155
ClarisEmailer Lite
    features, 232
    launching, 242-243
Claris web site, 243, 370
ClarisWorks, 157
Clean Up command (View menu), 265
cleaning up desktop, 109-110
Clear command (Edit menu), 55
clicking mouse, 6-7
Clipboard
    Clear command (Edit menu), 55
    Cut command (Edit menu), 54
    Edit menu options, 53
    Select All command (Edit menu), 53
    Show Clipboard command (Edit menu), 53, 56
clock, setting, 260-261

Close box on windows, 20
Close command (File
  menu), 49
closing
    lists, shortcuts, 353
    Mac OS Setup Assistant, 177
    Macintosh, 10-12
    windows, 20-21
        shortcuts, 352
Club Mac web site, 371
collapse box
    on windows, 20
    resizing windows, 22
collapsing
    folder contents, 107
    window preferences, 256-257
color depth
    modifying
        monitors, 273-274
color matching on
  printers, 194
Color screen (Appearance
  Control Panel), 254-257
Color wheel (Appearance
  Control Panel), creating
  colors, 255-258
colors
    Appearance Control Panel
        accent, 254-257
        highlight, 254-257
    Crayon Picker, 255-257
    creating (Appearance Control
        Panel), 255-269
    Labels feature, 264
    web page hypertext
        links, 239
Command-C (Copy) keyboard
  shortcut, 55
Command-M (Make Alias)
  keyboard shortcut, 111
Command-N (New) keyboard
  shortcut, 29-30
Command-O (Open) keyboard
  shortcut, 39
Command-P (Print) keyboard
  shortcut, 29-30, 49
Command-Q (Quit) keyboard
  shortcut, 49

Command-S (Save) keyboard
  shortcut, 41
Command-V (Paste) keyboard
  shortcut, 55
Command-W (Close) keyboard
  shortcut, 49
Command-X (Cut) keyboard
  shortcut, 54
Command-Z (Undo) keyboard
  shortcut, 54
commands
    Apple menu
        About This Computer, 74
        Automated Tasks, 357
        Chooser, 181, 212-213
        Connect To..., 35
        Control Panels, 179
        Find File, 77
        Graphing Calculator, 79
        Key Caps, 77
        Recent Servers, 345
        Scrapbook, 83
        Startup Disk, 69
        Stickies, 84
        Web Sharing, 345
    Arrange menu, By Name,
        265-266
    Bookmarks menu
        Add Bookmark, 240
        Apple, 237
    Edit menu
        Clear, 55
        Copy, 55
        Cut, 54-55
        Paste, 55
        Preferences, 35
        Select All, 53-56
        Show Clipboard, 53-56
        Undo, 53-54
    File menu
        Add Newsgroup, 246
        Close, 49
        Duplicate, 52, 104
        Find File, 50
        Get Info, 51, 67
        Label, 52
        Make Alias, 52, 111

        New Folder, 29, 50
        Open, 39
        Open Location, 239
        Page Setup, 51, 187
        Print, 49
        Print Desktop, 33, 191
        Print One Copy, 191
        Put Away, 52, 110
        Quit, 49
        Save, 41
        Save As..., 43
        Sharing, 52, 206
    Help menu
        Hide Balloons, 122
        Show Balloons, 121
        SimpleText Guide, 120
    keyboard shortcuts, 29-30
    Options menu
        General Preferences, 236
        Show All Newsgroups,
            245-246
    Sound menu
        Play, 307
        Record, 306
        Speak All, 306
        Voices, 306
    Special menu
        Eject Disk, 58, 64
        Empty Trash, 18
        Erase Disk, 58, 62
        Restart, 70
        Shut Down, 12
        Sleep, 58
    Tools menu, Protection, 320
    View menu
        As Buttons, 19, 108
        As Icons, 106
        As List, 107
        As Pop-up Window,
            24, 110
        By Name, 19
        Clean Up, 265
        Icon View Options, 108
        Labels, 264
        View Options, 105, 262
commercial fonts versus
  shareware fonts, 136

commercial software
database applications,
Claris FileMaker Pro,
157-158
desktop publishing
Aldus PageMaker,
153-154
Quark XPress, 153-154
graphics applications
Adobe Illustrator,
154-155
ClarisDraw, 154-155
image editors
Adobe Photoshop, 155
PhotoDeluxe, 155
presentation programs
Adobe Persuasion,
157-158
Microsoft PowerPoint,
157-158
selecting, 152-158
software suites
ClarisWorks, 157
Microsoft Office, 157
spreadsheets, Microsoft Excel,
155-156
utilities
CanOpener, 158
Connectix Desktop
Utilities, 158
DiskCopy, 158
Norton Utilities, 158
QuicKeys, 158
Retrospect, 158
word processing
Corel WordPerfect,
152-153
Macromedia FreeHand,
154-155
MarinerWrite, 152-153
Microsoft Word, 152-153
**Computer Discount Ware-
house web site, 371**
computers
file sharing, naming, 205
restarting, 354
configuring
file sharing, 204-205
folder hierarchies, 104-106

groups for file sharing, 207
LANs manually, 177-179
laser printers (Chooser),
182-184
modems, 280-281
Monitors & Sound Control
Panel settings, 302-304
networks (Mac OS Setup
Assistant), 174-177
printers
serial type, 185-187
StyleWriter, 189-190
**Connect To… command
(Apple menu), 35**
**Connect To shortcut,
launching, 82**
connecting
monitors, 273
to Internet (Internet Dialer
utility), 234-235
**Connectix Desktop
Utilities, 158**
**Connectix QuickCam, digital
cameras, 312-313**
Connectix web site, 370
contextual menus, 364
control panels
Appearance, 254-257
Date and Time, 266-268
Desktop Pictures, 257-259
File Sharing, 204-205
functions, 75
General Controls, 259-261
Keyboard, 266-268
Memory, 288
Monitors & Sound, 302-304
Numbers, 266-268
Personal Web Sharing,
345-346
Speech settings, 304-305
Text, 266-268
Users & Groups, 208-211
**Control Panels command
(Apple menu), 179**
Control Strip
appearance, 93-95
modifying, 93-95
original PowerBook feature,
93-95

converting
file formats, PC to
Macintosh, 329-331
windows to window-
shades, 353
**Copy command (Edit
menu), 55**
Corel web site, 370
Corel WordPerfect, 152-153
**cover pages for printed
documents, 193**
CRA Systems web site, 371
**Crayon Picker (Appearance
Control Panel), 255-257**
creating
(") double-hash symbol,
146-148
(') single-hash symbol,
146-148
(…) ellipsis, 147-149
alerts, voice type, 304-305
colors (Appearance Control
Panel), 255-269
customized launcher, 265
em dashes, 147-148
en dashes, 147-148
folders, 104
aliases, 111
menu bar, 28-29
groups for file sharing,
208-210
LANs, 171-172
RAM disk, 291-293
signatures (QuicKeys),
358-359
**CU-SeeMe, videoconferencing
software, 313**
customizing
alerts (PlainTalk micro-
phone), 303-304
launcher, 265
views (View menu), 262-263
**Cut command (Edit menu),
54-55**

D

daisy chains in LANs, 172
Dantz Software web site, 316-317
dashes
    em, 146-148
    en, 146-148
data recovery services
    DriveSavers, 318
    Lazarus Data Recovery, 318
    Ontrack Data Recovery, 318
    Total Recall, 318
database applications, FileMaker Pro, 157-158
DataViz web site, 370
Date & Time Control Panel
    clock options, 90-91
    date options, 90-91
    multilingual options, 267-268
    set time zone, 90-91
Dayna Communications web site, 369
Daystar Digital web site, 371
deleting
    group members, 210
    RAM disk, 293
Deneba Canvas, 154-155
desktop
    aliases, 111
    cleaning up, 109-110
    icons, 16-17
        dragging, 17
    image backdrops, selecting, 258
    menu bar, at system start-up, 5-6
    navigating, 110-112
    patterns, selecting, 257
    printers
        drag-and-drop printing, 198-200
        files, printing, 81
        print jobs, 198-200
    publishing software
        Aldus PageMaker, 153-154

        Quark XPress, 153-154
    scanned photos, placing, 259
Desktop Pictures Control Panel, 257-259
    launching, 257-259
    Pattern screen, 257
    patterns, 92-93
    pictures, 92-93
    scanned images, 92-93
devices
    adding to LANs, 172
    daisy chaining, 172
dialog boxes
    About This Computer, 286
    Add Newsgroup, 246
    File Sharing, 206
    Find File, 50
    Finder Preferences, 261
    functions, 35
    navigating shortcuts, 353
    Open, 38-39
    Open Location, 239
    Page Setup, 187
    Preferences, 35
    Print, 191-193
    Sample Desktop Pictures Open, 259
    Save, 38-43
    universal, 38-39
    View Options, 262
    Warning, 38-39
DigiCore web site, 371
digital cameras
    Apple QuickTake, 312-313
    Connectix QuickCam, 312-313
    costs, 277-278
    picture space requirements, 277-278
dimmed selections in menus, 32-34
DIMMs (dual inline memory modules), 297
disabling
    automated settings for Internet connections, 227

background printing in serial type printers, 187
balloon help, 122
OS 8 appearance preferences, 257
virtual memory, 290-291
disconnecting
    Apple Remote Access (ARA), 349
    Internet, 248-249
disk cache, 289
    modifying, 289
disk drive utilities, 321
disk space
    hard drives, checking, 67
    monitoring, 74
DiskCopy, 158
DiskGuard security software, 322
display fonts usage, 144
display size, modifying monitors, 273-274
documents
    printer layout options, 195
    rich text format (RTF), saving, 328
    selecting fonts, 145
    SimpleText sound capabilities, 306-307
DOS (Disk Operating System), software
    conversion, 325-326
    emulation, 325-326
    file transfer, 325-326
DOS Mounter 95, 331
double-clicking mouse, 8-9
double-hash symbol ("), 146-148
downloading
    freeware, 163
    Internet Relay Chat programs, 233
    movies
        file storage, 311
        file transfer, 311
    shareware, 163

drag-and-drop printing for desktop printers, 198-200
dragging
  files
    desktop printer icons, 81
    to Trash icon, 17-18
  icons on desktop, 17
  menus, 28-29
  mouse, 8-9
  multiple icons, 352
drives
  applications, installing, 166
  disk utilities, 321
DriveSavers, 318
dropping mouse, 8-9
Duplicate command (File menu), 52, 104
duplicating files, 52

E

email (electronic mail)
  ClarisEmailer Lite, 232, 242-243
  Internet usage categories, 232
  Netiquette, basic rules, 233-234
Edit menu commands
  Clear, 55
  Copy, 55
  Cut, 54-55
  Paste, 55
  Preferences, 35
  Select All, 53-56
  Show Clipboard, 53-56
  Undo, 53-54
Eject Disk command (Special menu), 58, 64
ejecting floppy disks, 64-65
electronic mail, *see* **email**
ellipses (…), 146-148
  in menus, 30-32
em dashes, 146-148
Empty Trash command (Special menu), 18
emptying
  Trash, shortcuts, 354
  Trash icon, 18

emulation software
  SoftWindows 95, 333
  Virtual PC, 333
en dashes, 146-148
enabling
  Apple Remote Access (ARA), 346
  AppleTalk, 178-179
  background printing in serial type printers, 187
  virtual memory, 290-291
Erase Disk command (Special menu), 58, 62
erasing floppy disks, 62-63, 354
error handling for printing, 195
establishing group folder access, 210-211
Ethernet
  connections, building, 173
  connectors, 173
  RJ-45 cables, 173
Everything Macintosh web site, 372
exchanging files between Macintosh and PCs, 329-331
Excite web site, 236
exiting Macintosh, 10-12
expanding folder contents, 107
Extensions Manager
  accessing, 95-96
  system checks, 95-96
Extensis web site, 369
external hard drives
  adding, 67-68
  initializing, 68

F

FAQs (Frequently Asked Questions) site, accessing, 233-234
Farallon Communications web site, 369
file icons
  appearance, 18
  Trash, dragging, 18

File menu commands
  Add Newsgroup, 246
  Close, 49
  Duplicate, 52, 104
  Find File, 50
  Get Info, 51, 67
  Label, 52
  Make Alias, 52, 111
  New Folder, 29, 50
  Open, 39
  Open Location, 239
  Page Setup, 51, 187
  Print Desktop, 33, 191
  Print One Copy, 191
  Put Away, 52, 110
  Quit, 49
  Save, 41
  Save As…, 43
  Sharing, 52, 206
File Sharing dialog box, 206
FileGuard security software, 322
FileMaker Pro, 157-158
files
  access privileges in groups, 210-211
  backing up, 316-317
    offsite storage, 317-318
    removable media, 317
  dragging to Trash icon, 17
  duplicating, 52
  format overview, 328-329
  formats, converting PC to Macintosh, 329-331
  Labels feature, 264
  locking, 320
  Open dialog box, 40-41
  ownership, 205
  Personal Web Sharing, activating, 345-346
  printing to desktop printers, 81
  read-only access, 205
  renaming, Save As… command, 43
  rich text format (RTF), saving, 328
  Save dialog box, 41-43
  saving to floppy disks, 65

servers
    accessing, 338-341
    restricted access, 341-343
sharing
    Activity Monitor tab, 211
    computer names, 205
    configuring, 204-205
    group access privileges,
        208-209
    group creation, 208-210
    group membership, 207
    group monitoring,
        211-212
    multi-user licenses, 206
    password modifications,
        206-207
    password settings, 205
    program links, 205-206
financial software
    Intuit MacInTax, 157
    Intuit Quicken, 157
Find File
    executing, 76-77
    search parameters, setting,
        76-77
**Find File command (Apple
    menu), 77**
Find File dialog box, 50
**Finder Preferences dialog
    box, 261**
    file labels, 261-262
    font selection, 261-262
    grid spacing, 261-262
    SimpleFinder, 261-262
    spring-loaded folders,
        261-262
FireWire card, 283
floppy disks
    character naming limits, 64
    ejecting, 64-65
    erasing, 62-63, 354
    formatted status, 63
    icon, 17
    initializing, 62
    naming, 64
    PC to Macintosh, 326-327
    saving to, 65
    versus Zip drives, 66

folders
    access privileges for groups,
        210-211
    aliases, creating, 111
    as buttons, viewing, 108
    as icons, viewing, 106-107
    as list, viewing, 107
    contents
        collapsing, 107
        expanding, 107
    creating, 104
    dragging to Trash icon, 17
    duplicating, 52
    hierarchies, configuring,
        104-106
    icon appearance, 18
    Labels feature, 264
    locking, 319-320
    magnifying glass, implement-
        ing, 111
    menu bar, creating, 28-29
    naming, 104
    Open dialog box, 40-41
    Save dialog box, 41-43
    servers, restricted access,
        341-343
    spring-open, viewing,
        110-111
    view options, 104-106
fonts, 135-136
    Adobe Type Manager,
        138-139
    bitmapped, 136-137
    commercial versus share-
        ware, 136
    display type, 144
    documents
        Ransom Note Syn-
            drome, 145
        selecting, 145
    installing, 140-141
    monospaced, 146
    OS 8 version, 136
    PostScript, 136-137
    reference resources, 147-148
    removing, 141
    sans serif, 144
    serif, 144

    suitcases, 137-139
        opening, 139
    symbol type, 144
    TrueType versus PostScript,
        140-141
    utilities
        Adobe Type Mana-
            ger, 142
        desired features, 142
        MasterJuggler, 142
        Symantec Suitcase, 142
        TypeBook, 142
    versus typefaces, 135-136
**FoolProof security
    software, 322**
formatting floppy disks, 63
**free software, selecting,
    159-163**
freeware
    downloading, 163
    user responsibilties, 163
FTP (File Transfer Protocol)
    Internet usage categories, 233
    shareware, downloading, 233
    software, downloading, 233

G

**Gamma Color (Monitor
    Control Panel), 274**
General Controls
    desktop start items, 88-89
    folder protection, 88-89
    insert point blinking, 88-89
    menu blinking, 88-89
    shut down warnings, 88-89
**General Preferences command
    (Options menu), 236**
**Get Info command (File
    menu), 51, 67**
gigabytes, 66
Global Village web site, 370
graphics
    software
        Adobe Illustrator,
            154-155
        ClarisDraw, 154-155

Macromedia FreeHand, 154-155
web resources for Macintosh, 369
Graphing Calculator
window display, 79-80
x values, 79-80
y values, 79-80
Graphing Calculator command (Apple menu), 79
groups
access privileges, monitoring, 210-211
file sharing
access privileges, 208
configuring, 207
creating, 208-210
folder access, establishing, 210-211
members
adding, 210
deleting, 210
New Group button, 209-210
New User button, 209-210
on networks, configurations, 207-211
grow box, resizing windows, 22-24
GUide to RAM Upgrades (GURU) software, 298

H

Happy Macintosh icon, 5
hard drives
capacities, monitoring, 67
external
adding, 67-68
initializing, 68
gigabytes, 66
icon, 17
megabytes, 66
partitioning, 68-69
hardware
Apple System Profiler
statistics, 75
monitors
connecting, 273
costs, 272-273

pixel resolution, 272-273
sizes, 272-273
types, 272-273
help
Internet resources, 126
Macintosh technical support, 126-127
Help menu
commands
Hide Balloons, 122
Show Balloons, 121
SimpleText Guide, 120
Index option, 116-118
Look For option, 119-120
options, 58
Topics option, 118-119
Here & Now, Windows 95 file transfer utilites, 332-333
Hide Balloons command (Help menu), 122
highlight colors (Appearance Control Panel), 254-257
home pages, 236
Netscape Navigator, setting, 236-240
horizontal scroll bars in windows, 20
hypertext links, color indication, 239

I

Icon View Options command (View menu), 108
icons, 16-17
active indication, 17
applications, 18-19
launching, 10
dragging on desktop, 17
files, 18
floppy drive, 17
folders, 18
Happy Macintosh, 5
hard drive, 17
Mac OS Info Center, 124
multiple
dragging, 352
selecting, 352

OS 8 version, three dimensional appearance, 17
renaming, 18-19
system start-up, 5-6
Trash, 17
viewing folders, 106-107
image backdrops, selecting, 258
image editors
Adobe Photoshop, 155
PhotoDeluxe, 155
implementing
AppleScript automated tasks, 357
web search engines, 240
Index option (Help menu)
launching, 117-118
task tips, 116-118
topical definitions, 116-118
initializing
floppy disks, 62
hard drives, external, 68
inkjet printers, selecting, 185-187
input devices
digital cameras
costs, 277-278
picture space requirements, 277-278
keyboards, country settings, 274
mouse
double-click speeds, 275
track speeds, 275
scanners
costs, 277
proliferation, 277
tablets, 276
installing
applications, 163-166
fonts, 140-141
modems, 216, 280-281
internal cards
adding, 282-283
FireWire, 283
internationalizing system appearance, 266-268

Internet
Apple Internet Connection
Kit, 223
ARPAnet roots, 232
automated settings
log-offs, 227-229
log-ons, 227-229
FAQs, 233-234
help resources, 126
logging off, 248-249
logging on, 234-235
Mac OS 8 shortcuts, 247
modems
installing, 216
transmission speeds, 216
Netiquette
basic rules, 233-234
concept, 233-234
new users, registering,
216-222
remote accesses (Telnet), 233
site exploration, 127
usage categories
email, 232
FTP downloads, 233
Internet Relay Chat, 233
Usenet newsgroups, 232
World Wide Web
(WWW), 232
videoconferencing, 313
videophone technology, 313
Internet Dialer utility, 222
logging off, 248-249
logging on, 234-235
Internet Editor Assistant,
160-163
Internet Relay Chat
Netiquette basic rules,
233-234
programs, downloading, 233
Internet Search web site, 127
Internet Service Providers,
see ISPs
Internet Setup Assistant,
160-163
Conclusion screen, 226-227
configurations
modifying, 222-227
saving, 226-227

email settings, 225-227
host computers, 225-227
ISP selection advice, 218-219
Netscape Navigator,
launching, 218-219
new users
modem configurations,
217-222
registeration, 216-222
settings, updating, 222-227
interruptible power supply
(UPS) protection, 319
Intuit MacInTax, 157
Intuit Quicken, 157
Iomega web site, 370
ISP Registration Assistant,
160-163
ISPs (Internet Service
Providers)
billing, 221-222
information on costs
(Netscape Internet Account
Server), 219-222
license agreements, 221-222
location (Netscape Internet
Account Server), 219-222
rated by *Macworld* magazine,
219-222
selecting (Internet Setup
Assistant), 218-219
settings, updating, 222-227
technical support, 221-222

J - K

Jigsaw Puzzle, piece sizes, 84
Key Caps
features, 77
launching, 77
Key Caps command (Apple
menu), 77
Keyboard Control Panel,
multilingual options
alphabets, 266-268
board layout, 266-268
country settings, 274

keyboard shortcuts, 29-30
Command-C (Copy), 55
Command-M (Make
Alias), 111
Command-N (New), 29-30
Command-O (Open), 39
Command-P (Print),
29-30, 49
Command-Q (Quit), 49
Command-S (Save), 41
Command-V (Paste), 55
Command-W (Close), 49
Command-X (Cut), 54
Command-Z (Undo), 54
Mac OS 8 Info Center, 125
Keyquencer automation
tool, 358

L

La Cie web site, 370
Label command (File
menu), 52
Labels command (View
menu), 264
Labels feature, color applica-
tion
to files, 264
to folders, 264
LANs (Local Area Networks)
AppleTalk, enabling,
178-179
configuration review (Mac
OS Setup Assistant), 176
creating, 171-172
daisy chains, 172
devices, adding, 172
Mac OS Setup Assistant,
configuring, 174-177
manual configurations,
177-179
physical connections
Ethernet connections, 173
LocalTalk connections,
170-172
ports, 170
printer connections (Mac OS
Setup Assistant), 176

laser printers
  configuring, 182-184
  selecting, 183-184
launching
  Apple System Profiler, 75
  AppleTalk, 178-179
  applications
    from icons, 10
    in custom launcher, 265
  ClarisEmailer Lite, 242-243
  Connect To shortcut, 82
  Desktop Pictures Control
    Panel, 257-259
  Key Caps, 77
  Look For option (Help
    menu), 119-121
  Mac OS Info Center, 124
  Mac OS Setup Assistant,
    174-177
  Macintosh, 4-6
  Netscape Navigator, 235
    Internet Setup Assistant,
    218-219
  online help (Index option),
    117-118
  PC Exchange, 326-327
  pop-up windows, 24
  SimpleText, 10
  Speech Control Panel,
    304-305
  Topics option (Help menu),
    118-119
Lazarus Data Recovery, 318
linking programs
  for file sharing, 205-206
  multi-user licenses, 206
listing Usenet newsgroups, 245
lists (shortcuts)
  closing, 353
  moving, 353
  opening, 353
  sorting, 353
  viewing folders, 107
Live Home Page web site, 127
live scrolling, 365
Local Area Networks, *see* **LANs**
local user groups, Macintosh
  technical support, 129

LocalTalk
  connectors, 170-172
  PhoneNet connectors,
    170-172
locating AppleScripts for
  automated tasks, 356-357
locking
  files, 320
  folders, 319-320
logging off Internet, 248-249
logging on
  automating for servers,
    344-345
  Internet, 234-235
  remote networks, Apple
    Remote Access (ARA),
    348-349
Look For option (Help menu),
  119-120

M

Mac Bargains web site, 371
***Mac Home Journal* web**
  site, 371
Mac OS 8 Setup Assistant,
  160-163
Mac OS Info Center
  help
    basics, 125
    compatibility, 125
    multimedia, 125
    networking, 125
    power, 125
  icon, 124
  keyboard shortcuts, 125
  launching, 124
  new features, 124
Mac OS Late-Breaking News
  web site, 126
Mac OS Setup Assistant
  closing, 177
  launching, 174-177
  networks
    configuration review, 176
    configuring, 174-177
    file sharing, 175

    naming, 174
    passwords, 174
    printer connections, 176
Mac OS Troubleshooting web
  site, 126
Mac OS web Site, 126
Mac Zone web site, 371
MacAddict web site, 371
MacConnection web site, 371
Macintosh
  Apple Remote Access (ARA)
    configurations, 346-349
  automation tools
    Keyquencer, 358
    QuicKeys, 358-359
  DOS mounting utilities,
    DOS Mounter 95, 331
  emulation software
    SoftWindows 95, 333
    Virtual PC, 333
  memory usage, 286-287
  multilingual options,
    266-268
  PC compatibility cards
    brands, 334-335
    configuring, 334-335
    costs, 334-335
  PCI slots, card additions,
    282-283
  RAM, upgrading, 297-299
  restarting, 354
  shutting down, 10-12
  technical support, 126-127
    Apple SOS Line, 128-129
    Apple web site, 128
    local user groups, 129
  turning on, 4-6
  web resources
    catalog retailers, 371
    graphics and publish-
     ing, 369
    networking, 369-370
    peripherals, 370
    productivity software, 370
    publications, 371
    utilities, 370-371
  web sites, 372

Windows 95 file transfer
utilites
Here & Now, 332-333
MacOpener, 332-333
**Macintosh for the Rest of Us
web site, 372**
**MacLinkPlus, file format
conversion, 329-331**
MacMall web site, 371
MacMarket web site, 371
**Macromedia FreeHand,
154-155**
Macromedia web site, 369
MacUser **web site, 371**
MacWarehouse web site, 371
MacWeek **web site, 371**
Macworld **Online web
site, 136**
shareware libraries, 163
magnifying glass, 111
**Make Alias command (File
menu), 52, 111**
**manual configurations for
LANs, 177-179**
MarinerWrite, 152-153
**MasterJuggler, font
utilities, 142**
maximizing windows, 21-22
**Meet-Me, videoconferencing
software, 313**
megabytes, 66
members (groups)
adding, 210
deleting, 210
memory
disk cache, 289
minimum for applications,
295-296
monitoring, 74
preferred for applications,
295-296
Memory Control Panel
accessing, 288
disk cache settings, 289
settings, modifying, 288
menu bar
Apple menu, 48
Application menu, 56-57
at system start-up, 5-6

components, 48-58
Edit menu, 53-56
File menu, 48-52
Help menu, 58, 116-120
Special menu, 58
View menu, 57, 106-108
menus
creating folders, 28-29
dimmed selections, 32-34
dragging, 28-29
ellipses (…), 30-32
nested, 30-32
**MetaCreations Expression and
Painter, 154-155**
MetaCreations web site, 369
Microsoft Excel, 155-156
**Microsoft Internet Explorer,
235-242**
Microsoft Office, 157
**Microsoft PowerPoint,
157-158**
Microsoft web site, 370
Microsoft Word, 152-153
minimizing windows, 21-22
**Miramar Systems web
site, 370**
**modems (MOdulation-
DEModulation), 279**
Apple Remote Access (ARA),
346-349
configurations (Internet
Setup Assistant), 217
configuring, 280-281
data destination, 281
data transmission sounds,
280-281
data transmission speeds, 281
future, 281-282
Internet requisites, 216
purchasing advice,
281-282
installing, 216, 280-281
phone line interference, 281
modifying
Appearance Control Panel,
254-257
application icon names,
18-19

Control Strip, 93-95
disk cache, 289
Internet settings (PPP Control Panel), 227-229
Memory Control Panel
settings, 288
monitors
color depth, 273-274
display size, 273-274
pixel resolution, 273-274
passwords
for file sharing, 206
on servers, 343-344
RAM in applications,
293-296
startup drives, 69-70
monitoring
disk space, 74
group accesses, 211
memory, 74
RAM, 286-287
space availability on hard
drives, 67
monitors
aperture grille, 274
color depth, modifying,
273-274
connecting, 273
costs, 272-273
display size, modifying,
273-274
Gamma Color versus Mac
Standard Color, 274
pixel resolution, 272-273
modifying, 273-274
screen savers, 158
shadowmask, 274
sizes, 272-273
types, 272-273
**Monitors & Sound Control
Panel**
alerts, 302-304
settings, configuring,
302-304
Sound Input option, 302-304
Sound Out Level option,
302-304
Sound Output Quality
option, 302-304

monospaced fonts, 146-149
Motorola web site, 371
mouse
    clicking, 6-7
    double-clicking, 8-9, 275
    dragging, 8-9
        multiple icons, 352
    dropping, 8-9
    pointing, 6-7
    selecting multiple icons, 352
    track speeds, 275
MoviePlayer, 311
movies (QuickTime), down-
  loading, 311
multilingual options (OS 8),
  266-268
multimedia
    digital cameras, 312-313
    Internet videoconfe-
      rencing, 313
    Internet videophones, 313
    Macintosh 1984 commer-
      cial, 311
    playing speech-to-text
      documents, 306-307
    QuickTime extension, 311
    sound options (Monitors &
      Sound Control Panel),
      302-304
multiple drives, installing, 166

N

naming
    application icons, 18-19
    computers, file sharing, 205
    floppy disks, 64
    folders, 104
natural disaster protection
    restraining straps, 319
    surge protectors, 319
    uniterruptible power supplies
      (UPS), 319
navigating
    desktop, 110-112
    dialog box shortcuts, 353
    text boxes, 38

nested menus, arrow indica-
  tors, 30-32
Netiquette, 233-234
Netscape Internet Account
  Server
    credit card information,
      221-222
    ISPs
      cost information, 219-222
      license agreements,
        221-222
      location, 219-222
    technical support, 221-222
Netscape Navigator, 235-242
    browser features, 235-242
    launching, 235
      Internet Setup Assistant,
        218-219
    pre-loaded bookmarks, 240
    secure document
      warning, 219
    setting home pages, 236-250
    tutorials, 242
networks
    accessing other computers,
      212-213
    Apple Remote Access
      (ARA), 346
    configuration review (Mac
      OS Setup Assistant), 176
    configuring (Mac OS Setup
      Assistant), 174-177
    file sharing, 203-204
      Mac OS Setup Assis-
        tant, 175
    group configurations,
      207-211
    Mac OS Setup Assistant,
      configuring, 174-177
    physical connections
      Ethernet connections, 173
      LocalTalk connections,
        170-172
      ports, 170
    printer connections (Mac OS
      Setup Assistant), 176
    remote access, 213
    web resources for Macintosh,
      369-370

New Folder command (File
  menu), 29, 50
New Group button, 209-210
new users, Internet registra-
  tion, 216-222
New Users button, 209-210
NewsWatcher, dedicated
  newsreader program, 246-247
Nisus web site, 370
Norton Utilities, 158
Note Pad
    Stickies similarity to, 85
    uses, 85

O

offsite storage of files, 317-318
OnGuard security
  software, 322
online help
    accessing through applica-
      tions, 120
    Apple Guide, 115-116
    Index option, 117-118
Ontrack Data Recovery, 318
Open command (File
  menu), 39
Open dialog box, 38-41
Open Location command (File
  menu), 239
Open Location dialog box, 239
opening
    font suitcases, 139
    list shortcuts, 353
    windows, 20-21
Operating System 8, see **OS 8**
Options menu commands
    General Preferences, 236
    Show All Newsgroups, 245
OS 7 (Operating System 7),
  reverting from OS 8 appear-
  ance preferences, 257
OS 8 (Operating System 8)
    appearance preferences,
      disabling, 257
    assistant programs
      Internet Editor, 160-163
      Internet Setup, 160-163

ISP Registration, 160-163
Mac OS Setup, 160-163
PowerBook File, 160-163
automated tasks, locating,
356-357
built-in fonts, 136
bundled software, 159-160
Chooser features, 181-182
ClarisEmailer Lite, 242-243
features, 4
fonts
installing, 140-141
removing, 141
icons, three dimensional
appearance, 17
Internet shortcuts, 247
logo, on system start-up, 5
multilingual options,
266-268
PC Exchange, 326-327
RAM requirements, 286-287
system shutdown procedure,
10-12
outline fonts, *see* **PostScript
fonts, 137**

P

**Page Setup command (File
menu), 51, 187**
Page Setup dialog box, 187
image size ranges, 187-188
page size, 187-188
paper orientation, 187-188
PostScript options
bitmapped fonts, 188-189
built in fonts, 188-189
downloadable fonts,
188-189
precision bitmap
alignment, 188-189
smooth text features,
188-189
visual effects, 188-189
partitioning hard drives, 68-69
passwords
changing, 343-344
file sharing, setting, 205

modifying for file
sharing, 206
selection guidelines, 205
**Paste command (Edit
menu), 55**
**Pattern screen (Desktop
Pictures Control Panel), 257**
**patterns, selecting for desk-
top, 257**
PC Exchange
.doc file format, 326-327
floppy disks, PC to
Macintosh, 326-327
launching, 326-327
**PCI (peripheral component
interconnect) slots, card
additions, 282-283**
PCs (personal computers)
compatibility cards
brands, 334-335
configuring, 334-335
costs, 334-335
conversion software, 325-326
emulation software, 325-326
file transfer software, 325-326
**peer-to-peer networking,
333-336**
peripherals
FireWire card, 283
web resources, 370
**Personal Web Sharing,
activating, 345-346**
**personalizing Apple CD Audio
Player, 309-310**
**PhoneNet connectors on
LocalTalk networks, 170-172**
PhotoDeluxe, 155
**pixel resolution, modifying in
monitors, 273-274**
placing
applications (Startup Folder),
96-97
desktop, scanned photos, 259
sounds in shutdown folder,
97, 307
**PlainTalk microphone, alerts,
customizing, 303-304**
**Play command (Sound
menu), 307**

playing
audio CDs (Apple CD Audio
Player), 307-310
speech-to-text documents,
306-307
Point-to-Point Protocol,
see **PPP**
pointing mouse, 6-7
pop-up windows
activating, 24
appearance, 24
transforming to windows, 24
viewing, 110
ports
Ethernet, 173
LocalTalk, 170-172
serial, 170
PostScript fonts, 137
components
printer font, 137-139
screen font, 137-139
invented by Adobe
Systems, 137
outline fonts, also known as,
137
scalability, 137
versus TrueType fonts, 140
**PostScript Printer Descriptions
(PPDs), 182-184**
**Power Computing web
site, 371**
power key, 4-6
Power Tools web site, 371
PowerBook trackpads
double-click speed, 275-276
tracking speed, 275-276
**PowerBook File Assistant,
160-163**
**PPP (Point-to-Point Protocol)
Control Panel, Internet
settings, modifying, 227-229**
**Preferences command (Edit
menu), 35**
Preferences dialog box, 35
Check box option, 35-43
Fonts for view option, 35-43
Grid Spacing Preferences
option, 35-43

Labels categories option, 35-43
Simple Finder, 35-43
spring loaded folders, 35-43
presentation programs
Adobe Persuasion, 157-158
Microsoft PowerPoint, 157-158
Print command (File menu), 49
Print Desktop command (File menu), 33, 191
Print dialog box, 191-193
background printing, 193
color matching, 194
cover page options, 193
error handling options, 195
layout options, 195
number of copies, 192
page destination, 192
page ranges, 192
paper source, 192
printer selection, 191
save settings option, 193
Print One Copy command (File menu), 191
print queues, viewing, 198-200
printer font (PostScript), 137-139
Printer Info button, 184
printers
background printing option, 193
bitmapped font resolutions, 136-137
color matching, 194
cover page options, 193
error handling options, 195
inkjet, selecting, 185-187
laser, selecting, 183-184
layout options for documents, 195
number of copies, 192
page ranges, 192
Page Setup dialog box options, 187-188
paper sources, 192
PostScript Printer Descriptions (PPDs), 182-184

Printer Info button, 184
serial type, configuring, 185-187
StyleWriter, configuring, 189-190
printing files to desktop printer icons, 81
program links
files, sharing, 205-206
multi-user licenses, 206
Protection command (Tools menu), 320
Put Away command (File menu), 52, 110

Q

Quark web site, 369
QuarkXPress, 153-154
QuickDraw 3D, 366
QuicKeys, 158
automated typing features, 358-359
signatures, creating, 358-359
QuickTime
features, 311
MoviePlayer application, 311
MPEG format, 366
VR format, 366
Quit command (File menu), 49

R

Radius web site, 370
RAM (random access memory)
and virtual memory, 290-291
consumption, reducing, 287
cost per megabyte, 297
DIMMs (dual inline memory modules), 297
disks
creating, 291-293
deleting, 293
effect on virtual memory, 291-293
resizing, 292-293

temporary status, 291-293
uses, 291-293
GUide to RAM Upgrades (GURU) software, 298
modules, 297-300
monitoring, 286-287
OS 8 requirements, 286-287
SIMMs (single inline memory modules), 297
upgrades, 297-299
installation rates, 298-299
model specific, 298-299
self-installation, 298-299
warranty voids, 299
RAM Doubler 2, 291
Ransom Note Syndrome, 145
read-only access files, 205
reading articles in Usenet newsgroups, 243-247
Recent Applications option, 80-81
Recent Servers command (Apple menu), 345
Recent Servers option, 80-81
Record command (Sound menu), 306
recording voices (SimpleText), 306-307
reducing RAM consumption, 287
registering new users for Internet, 216-222
remote accesses (Telnet), 213, 233
remote networks, logging on, Apple Remote Access (ARA), 348-349
removable media, file backups, 317
removing fonts, 141
renaming
files, 43
icons, 18-19
resizing
RAM disk, 292-293
windows
collapse box, 22
grow box, 22-24
zoom box, 22

Restart command (Special menu), 70
restarting computer, 354
Retrospect, back-up software, 316-317
reverting to OS 7 appearance preferences, 257
review questions
    Chapter 1 summary, 13-14
    Chapter 2 summary, 25
    Chapter 3 summary, 44-45
    Chapter 4 summary, 58-59
    Chapter 5 summary, 70-71
    Chapter 6 summary, 85-86
    Chapter 7 summary, 101-102
    Chapter 8 summary, 112-113
    Chapter 9 summary, 130-131
    Chapter 10 summary, 148-149
    Chapter 11 summary, 166-167
    Chapter 12 summary, 179-180
    Chapter 13 summary, 200-201
    Chapter 14 summary, 213-214
    Chapter 15 summary, 229-230
    Chapter 16 summary, 249-250
    Chapter 17 summary, 268
    Chapter 18 summary, 282-284
    Chapter 19 summary, 299-300
    Chapter 20 summary, 313
    Chapter 21 summary, 322-323
    Chapter 22 summary, 335-336
    Chapter 23 summary, 349-350
    Chapter 24 summary, 360-361
rich text format (RTF), saving, 328
RJ-45 cables, Ethernet networks, 173

S

Sample Desktop Pictures Open dialog box, 259
sans serif fonts, 144
Save As... command (File menu), 43
Save command (File menu), 41
Save dialog box, 38-41
saving
    documents in rich text format (RTF), 328
    to floppy disks, 65
scanned photos, placing on desktop, 259
scanners
    costs, 277
    proliferation, 277
Scrapbook
    accessing, 83-84
    uses, 83-84
    versus Clipboard, 83-84
Scrapbook command (Apple menu), 83
screen font (PostScript), 137-139
    suitcases, 138-139
screen savers (AfterDark), 158
scrolling windows, 22-24
SCSI (Small Computer System Interface), 67-68
search engines
    Excite, 236
    implementing, 240
    Yahoo!, 240
searching web without URLs, 242
secure document warning (Netscape Navigator), 219
security
    American Computer Exchange, stolen computers database, 318
    files, locking, 320
    folders, locking, 319-320
    natural disaster protection
        restraining straps, 319
        surge protectors, 319
        uninterruptible power supplies (UPSs), 319
    software
        AtEase, 322
        DiskGuard, 322
        FileGuard, 322
        FoolProof, 322
        OnGuard, 322
        ultraSecure, 322
    theft protection
        insurance riders, 318
        locking devices, 318
        serial numbers, 318
Select All command (Edit menu), 53-56
selecting
    colors (Appearance Control Panel), 254-257
    commercial software, 152-158
    database applications, 157-158
    desktop
        image backdrops, 258
        patterns, 257
    desktop publishing software, 153-154
    fonts for documents, 145
    free software, 159-163
    graphics applications, 154-155
    image editors, 155
    ISPs, 218-219
    multiple icons, 352
    passwords, 205
    presentation programs, 157-158
    printers
        inkjet, 185-187
        laser, 183-184
    servers (Chooser), 338-341
    software suites, 157
    spreadsheet software, 155-156

utilities, 158
View menu options, 108
word processing software,
    152-153
**serial ports in LAN configura-
tions, 170**
serial type printers
background printing
    disabling, 187
    enabling, 187
configuring, 185-187
serif fonts, 144
servers
accessing files, 338-341
Apple Remote Access
    (ARA), 346
Guest, 338-341
log-ons, automating, 344-345
passwords, changing,
    343-344
Registered User, 338-341
restricted access, 341-343
selecting (Chooser), 338-341
volumes, automatic mount-
    ing, 344-345
setting
clock, 260-261
Find File search parameters,
    76-77
home pages (Netscape
    Navigator), 236-250
passwords for file
    sharing, 205
Preferences, 97-100
shadowmask monitors, 274
shareware
downloading, 163
    via FTP, 233
fonts versus commercial
    fonts, 136
licensing fees, 163
Macworld Online web site
    libraries, 163
Shareware web site, 159
sharing files
configurations, 204-205
group
    access privileges, 208
    group creation, 208-210

membership, 207
monitoring, 211-212
multi-user licenses, 206
password modifications, 206
program links, 205-206
**Sharing command (File menu),
52, 206**
shortcuts
Apple menu functions, 112
dialog boxes, navigating, 353
floppy disks, erasing, 354
lists
    closing, 353
    moving, 353
    opening, 353
    sorting, 353
multiple icons
    cancelling selection, 352
    selecting, 352
Trash, emptying, 354
windows, closing, 352
**Show All Newsgroups com-
mand (Options menu), 245**
**Show Balloons command
(Help menu), 121**
**Show Clipboard command
(Edit menu), 53-56**
**Shut Down command (Special
menu), 12**
**Shutdown Items Folder,
placing sounds, 97, 307**
**signatures, creating
(QuicKeys), 358-359**
**SIMMs (single inline memory
modules), 297**
SimpleText
features, 159-160
launching, 10
sound capabilities, 306-307
voices, recording, 306-307
**SimpleText Guide command
(Help menu), 120**
single-hash symbol ('), 146-148
sites, *see* web sites
situation dependent menus, 32
**Sleep command (Special
menu), 58**

software
bundled, 159-160
commercial, selecting,
    152-158
downloading via FTP, 233
free, selecting, 159-163
multi-user licenses, 206
suites
    ClarisWorks, 157
    Microsoft Office, 157
web resources, 370
**Software Architects web
site, 370**
SoftWindows 95, 333
Sonic Systems web site, 370
sorting lists with shortcuts, 353
Sound menu commands
Play, 307
Record, 306
Speak All, 306
Voices, 306
sounds
adding to shutdown folders,
    97, 307
multimedia options (Moni-
    tors & Sound Control
    Panel), 302-304
**Speak All command (Sound
menu), 306**
Special menu commands
Eject Disk, 58, 64
Empty Trash, 18
Erase Disk, 58, 62
Restart, 70
Shut Down, 12
Sleep, 58
Speech Control Panel
launching, 304-305
Talking Alerts option,
    304-305
**speech-to-text documents,
playing, 306-307**
**spreadsheets (Microsoft Excel),
155-156**
**spring-open folders, viewing,
110-111**
start-up icons, 5-6
starting Macintosh, 4-6

Startup Disk command (Apple menu), 69
startup drives, changing, 69-70
Startup Folder, placing applications, 96-97
Stickies
 as phone message pad, 84-85
 colors, 84-85
 default version, 84-85
 text styles, 84-85
Stickies command (Apple menu), 84
Streamlogic web site, 370
StyleWriter
 configuring, 189-190
 image scalability, 189-190
 multiple documents on single sheet, 189-190
 print options, 197
 watermarks, 189-190
subscribing to Usenet newsgroups, 245
suitcases
 font storage, 137-139
 opening fonts, 139
surge protectors (uninterruptible power supplies), 319
switching startup drives, 69-70
Symantec Suitcase, 142
Symantec web site, 370
symbol fonts, 144
System Folder
 Control Strip, 93-95
 date and time controls
  clock options, 90-91
  date formats, 90-91
  set time zone, 90-91
 Desktop Pictures
  patterns, 92-93
  pictures, 92-93
 fonts, installing, 140-141
 general controls
  desktop start items, 88-89
  folder protection, 88-89
  insert point blinking, 88-89

 menu blinking, 88-89
 shut down warnings, 88-89
 Preferences, setting, 97-100

T

tablets
 as substitute for mouse, 276
 styluses, 276
 uses, 276
technical support
 Apple SOS Line, 128-129
 Apple web site, 128
 local user groups, 129
Telnet, Internet remote access, 233
text boxes, navigating, 38
Text Control Panel, multilingual options
 currency, 266-268
 numbers, 266-268
 presets, 267-268
The Well-Connected Mac web site, 372
theft protection
 American Computer Exchange, stolen computers database, 318
 insurance riders, 318
 locking devices, 318
third party software, peer-to-peer networking, 333
Thursby Software Systems web site, 370
Timbuktu, 335
Tools menu commands, Protection, 320
Total Recall, 318
trackpads
 double-click speed, 275-276
 tracking speed, 275-276
transforming pop-up windows to windows, 24
transmission speeds for modems, 216

Trash icon, 17
 bulging appearance, 17
 dragging file icons, 18
 emptying, 18, 354
 files, dragging, 17
troubleshooting
 applications (Extensions Manager), 95-96
 computer freeze, 354
 RAM consumption, 287
TrueType fonts, 140
 inclusion in OS 8 version, 140
 versus PostScript fonts, 140
turning on Macintosh, 4-6
TypeBook, font utility, 142
typefaces versus fonts, terminology, 135-136
typesetting
 design guidelines, 146-148
 reference resources, 147-148
 tools, 146-148

U

U.S. Department of Defense, ARPAnet development, 232
Ultimate Macintosh web site, 372
ultraSecure security software, 322
Umax web site, 371
Undo command (Edit menu), 53-54
universal dialog boxes
 alerts and warnings, 38-39
 file options
  opening, 38-39
  saving, 38-39
upgrading RAM, 297-299
URLs (Uniform Resource Locators)
 Connect To shortcut, 82
 field content, 237
Usenet newsgroups
 accessing, 243-247
 articles, 243-247
  reading, 243-247

dedicated newsreader programs (NewsWatcher), 246-247
Internet usage categories, 232
listing, 245
local user groups, 129
messages
browsers, 232
news reader programs, 232-233
Netiquette, basic rules, 233-234
number of topics, 232
subscribing, 245
utilities
anti-virus software, 322
CanOpener, 158
Connectix Utilities, 158
disk drive, 321
DiskCopy, 158
Norton Utilities, 158
QuicKeys, 158
Retrospect, 158
security software, 322
web resources, 370-371

V

vertical scroll bars in windows, 20
videoconferencing
CU-SeeMe, 313
Meet-Me, 313
videos, QuickTime extension, 311
View menu
commands
As Buttons, 19, 108
As Icons, 106
As List, 107
As Pop-up Window, 24, 110
By Name, 19
Clean Up, 265
Labels, 264
View Options, 105, 262

functions, 57
options, 57, 106-108
views, customizing, 262-263
View Options command (View menu), 105, 262
View Options dialog box, 262
viewing
access limitations for server files, 341-343
folders
as buttons, 108
as icons, 106-107
as list, 107
memory statistics, 74
pop-up windows, 110
PostScript Printer Descriptions (PPDs) list, 182-184
print jobs, 198-200
spring-open folders, 110-111
virtual memory, 290-291
and RAM, 290-291
disabling, 290-291
enabling, 290-291
Virtual PC, 333
VirusScan, 322
Vocaltec, Internet videophone technology, 313
voices
alerts, creating, 304-305
recording (SimpleText), 306-307
Voices command (Sound menu), 306
volumes, automatic server mounting, 344-345

W

Warning dialog box, 38-39
web (World Wide Web)
accessing, 235-242
bookmarks, pre-loaded, 240
browsers
Microsoft Internet Explorer, 232
Netscape Navigator, 232

Connect To shortcut, 82
home pages, 236
hypertext links, 232
Internet usage categories, 232
Netiquette basic rules, 233-234
search engines, implementing, 240
searching without URLs, 242
URLs, 237
web browsers
Microsoft Internet Explorer, 235-242
Netscape Navigator, 235-242
web pages
bookmarking, 240-241
graphical elements, 235-236
hypertext links, color indication, 239
text elements, 235-236
web resources
catalog retailers, 371
graphics and publishing, 369
networking, 369-370
peripherals, 370
productivity software, 370
publications, 371
utilities, 370-371
Web Sharing command (Apple menu), 345
web sites
Adaptec, 370
Adobe, 369
Adobe Systems, 136
AG Group, 369
Aladdin Systems, 370
Apple, 371
Apple Software Archive, 126
Apple's Education site, 127
APS Technologies, 371
Asante Technologies, 369
ATI Technologies, 370
Atto Technology, 370
Big Mac Computers, 371
Bottom Line Distribution, 371
Casady & Greene, 370
CE Software, 370
Claris, 243, 370

Club Mac, 371
Computer Discount
  Warehouse, 371
Connectix, 370
Corel, 370
CRA Systems, 371
Dantz Software, 316-317
DataViz, 370
Dayna Communications, 369
Daystar Digital, 371
DigiCore, 371
Everything Macintosh, 372
Excite, 236
Extensis, 369
Farallon Communica-
  tions, 369
Global Village, 370
Internet Search, 127
Iomega, 370
La Cie, 370
Live Home Page, 127
Mac Bargains, 371
Mac Home Journal, 371
Mac OS, 126
Mac OS Late-Breaking
  News, 126
Mac OS Troubleshoot-
  ing, 126
Mac Zone, 371
MacAddict, 371
MacConnection, 371
Macintosh for the Rest
  of Us, 372
MacMall, 371
MacMarket, 371
Macromedia, 369
MacUser, 371
MacWarehouse, 371
MacWeek, 371
Macworld Online, 136
MetaCreations, 369
Microsoft, 370
Miramar Systems, 370
Motorola, 371
Nisus, 370
Power Computing, 371
Power Tools, 371

Quark, 369
Radius, 370
Shareware, 159
Software Architects, 370
Sonic Systems, 370
Streamlogic, 370
Symantec, 370
The Well-Connected
  Mac, 372
Thursby Software
  Systems, 370
Ultimate Macintosh, 372
Umax, 371
Yahoo!, 240
windows
  Close box, 20
  closing, 20-21, 352
  collapse box, 20
  collapse preferences, 256-257
  converting to window-
    shades, 353
  horizontal scroll bar, 20
  maximizing, 21-22
  minimizing, 21-22
  opening, 20-21
  pop-up, 24
  resizing, 22-24
  scrolling, 22-24
  transforming to pop-up
    windows, 24
  vertical scroll bar, 20
  zoom box, 20
**Windows 95, file transfer
utilities**
  Here & Now, 332-333
  MacOpener, 332-333
**windowshades, converting to
windows, 353**
word processing
  rich text format (RTF), 328
  software
    Corel WordPerfect,
      152-153
    MarinerWrite, 152-153
    Microsoft Word, 152-153

X - Y - Z

Yahoo! web site, 240
Zip drives
  disk costs, 66
  storage capacities, 66
  uses, 66
  versus floppy drives, 66
zoom box
  on windows, 20
  resizing windows, 22